Military Medicine and the Hidden Costs of War

BRIDGING THE GAP

Series Editors
James Goldgeier
Bruce Jentleson
Steven Weber

The Logic of American Nuclear Strategy: Why Strategic Superiority Matters
Matthew Kroenig

Planning to Fail: The US Wars in Vietnam, Iraq, and Afghanistan
James H. Lebovic

War and Chance: Assessing Uncertainty in International Politics
Jeffrey A. Friedman

Delaying Doomsday: The Politics of Nuclear Reversal
Rupal N. Mehta

Delta Democracy: Pathways to Incremental Civic Revolution in Egypt and Beyond
Catherine E. Herrold

Adaptation Under Fire: How Militaries Change in Wartime
David Barno and Nora Bensahel

The Long Game: China's Grand Strategy to Displace American Order
Rush Doshi

A Small State's Guide to Influence in World Politics
Tom Long

Cyber Persistence Theory: Redefining National Security in Cyberspace
Michael P. Fischerkeller, Emily O. Goldman, and Richard J. Harknett

Beyond the Wire: US Military Deployments and Host Country Public Opinion
Michael A. Allen, Michael E. Flynn, Carla Martinez Machain, and Andrew Stravers

Deploying Feminism: The Role of Gender in NATO Military Operations
Stéfanie von Hlatky

Dangerous Instrument: Political Polarization and US Civil-Military Relations
Michael A. Robinson

Escalation Dynamics in Cyberspace
Erica D. Borghard and Shawn W. Lonergan

Thanks for Your Service: The Causes and Consequences of Public Confidence in the US Military
Peter D. Feaver

Military Medicine and the Hidden Costs of War
Tanisha M. Fazal

Military Medicine and the Hidden Costs of War

TANISHA M. FAZAL

Oxford University Press is a department of the University of Oxford. It furthers
the University's objective of excellence in research, scholarship, and education
by publishing worldwide. Oxford is a registered trade mark of Oxford University
Press in the UK and certain other countries.

Published in the United States of America by Oxford University Press
198 Madison Avenue, New York, NY 10016, United States of America.

© Oxford University Press 2024

All rights reserved. No part of this publication may be reproduced, stored in
a retrieval system, or transmitted, in any form or by any means, without the
prior permission in writing of Oxford University Press, or as expressly permitted
by law, by license, or under terms agreed with the appropriate reproduction
rights organization. Inquiries concerning reproduction outside the scope of the
above should be sent to the Rights Department, Oxford University Press, at the
address above.

You must not circulate this work in any other form
and you must impose this same condition on any acquirer.

CIP data is on file at the Library of Congress

ISBN 978–0–19–005747–3

DOI: 10.1093/oso/9780190057473.001.0001

Printed by Sheridan Books, Inc., United States of America

For Lou

Contents

Acknowledgments ix
List of Abbreviations xiii
A Brief Note on Sources xv

    Introduction: Blood, Gore, and the Costs of War   1

1. Bad Air and Boiled Horsehair: The US Civil War   14
2. From Pestilence to Penicillin: The World Wars   47
3. Blood Is King: The Medicine of Counterinsurgency   90
4. Soldiers' Hearts: Reckoning with Psychological Trauma   124

    Conclusion: Unraveling the Costs of War   154

Notes 173
Bibliography 201
Index 227

Acknowledgments

The person who inspired this book is anonymous.

In 2012, I received reviews for a paper I had submitted for peer review related to my second book, on international humanitarian law. The paper was on why we no longer see peace treaties at the conclusion of interstate war. The second referee report requested that I engage with Steven Pinker's then-new(ish) book, *The Better Angels of Our Nature: Why Violence Has Declined*. Pinker's book was on my bookshelf. I had been planning to read it . . . one day. But the reviewer's report accelerated that process. The first several chapters are mostly about interpersonal violence: how we treat our pets, homicides, and even spanking children. But the second half of the book is about war—a subject I know well—and, specifically, argues that there has been a decline in war. As I was reading (all 696 pages), I became increasingly frustrated. The empirical basis for Pinker's claim that war was in decline was a decline in war fatalities. But over the same time period he studied, medicine has improved significantly. Thus, war casualties are being shifted from the "fatal" to "nonfatal" column.

Annoyed at both Pinker and the reviewer, I wrote the longest response memo to the journal I've ever written, explaining why I didn't think that Pinker's argument spoke to my own paper on peace treaties but also, more generally, laying out my objections to the claim that war was in decline. That response memo formed the core of a subsequent article—a rejoinder to Pinker (and others who argue that war is in decline)—that represented my first foray into a new research agenda on military medicine. So: thank you, Reviewer 2, whoever you are.

There are many others—friends, colleagues, and family—who contributed to this volume and whom I *can* thank by name (as well as those I will have surely neglected to mention, and to whom I sincerely apologize). I conducted the bulk of the research and writing for this book at the University of Minnesota, and am grateful for support and friendly conversations from colleagues such as Bud Duvall, Paul Goren, Andy Karch, Ron Krebs, Nancy Luxon, and Kathryn Pearson. Helen Kinsella has been a steadfast friend and reader throughout. I have been remarkably fortunate to have Dipali

Mukhopadhyay, a twice colleague, share her thoughts on the project and connections in the policy world. Mark Bell deserves special credit for putting up with multiple texts of some undeniably gross descriptions (not to mention photos) of goings-on at various military medical conferences. Beyond Minnesota, I thank Adam Montgomery, Emily Mayhew, and Paul Wise for a series of extremely useful conversations. Linda Bilmes, Mary Dudziak, Helen Kinsella, Sarah Kreps, Emily Mayhew, and Alex Wright lent their time to participate in a book workshop in December 2022, and I thank them for their generous and thoughtful feedback. Page Fortna supplied me with cookies, chuckles, and feedback as I completed the first full draft of this book. "Lucky" is too small a word to describe my great good fortune in having Page as a friend and colleague.

Several students have provided excellent research assistance along the way. At the University of Notre Dame, Alison Hostetler, Jeremy Graham, and Jonathan Leslie joined me on early forays into these topics. At the University of Minnesota, Lew Blank, Thomas Tretheway, Apoorva Malaarvannan, and John Stack dug up obscure facts and figures about military medicine and veterans' benefits. Leah Costik and Jack Sewpersaud deserve special mention for helping with citation and fact-checking; I am grateful to have had them alongside me as I crossed the finish line.

I could not have written this book without the support of colleagues in the military medical community, including Paul Nelson, Todd Rasmussen, Tracey Koehlmoos, Steve Trynovsky, Manny Menendez, Stacy Shackelford, P. K. Carlton, John Holcomb, and others who preferred not to be mentioned by name. Archivists at the National Library of Medicine in Bethesda, the Harvard University Countway Library of Medicine History of Medicine Reading Room, and the National Archives in College Park and in downtown Washington, DC, were generous and kind in helping me find what I knew I was looking for and pointing me to other sources I didn't realize I needed to consult.

Financial support was crucial to the completion of this book. A grant from the Harry Frank Guggenheim Foundation, combined with support from the College of Liberal Arts at the University of Minnesota, relieved me of teaching for one year as I began research on this book in earnest. Additional support from the College of Liberal Arts as well as the Carnegie Council on International Ethics enabled me to push key chapters forward, especially Chapter 4, on war-induced psychological trauma. A two-week stint at Dartmouth University's Dickey Center for International Understanding provided the headspace and deadline I needed to complete a first full draft. I was deeply honored to be selected as an Andrew Carnegie Fellow in 2021; fellowship support from the program allowed me a year of focused writing to complete this book.

I am delighted that this book is published in Oxford University Press's Bridging the Gap series. David McBride has provided excellent guidance from the start, and the series editors have been extremely supportive. Jim Goldgeier, in particular, always seems to have had this project in back of mind, as a steady stream of Twitter DMs on military medicine attest. David Lobenstine was an outstanding developmental editor, skillfully blending kindness with ruthlessness. Working with him made the book much better. I also thank Emily Benitez and Meghan Schaffer at Oxford University Press, as well as the staff at Newgen, for expertly shepherding this book through the production process. Sue Warga provided excellent copyediting, and Enid L. Zafran prepared the index. The terrific cover design is thanks to the talents (and patience) of Rachel Perkins. Portions of this book are derived from "Life and Limb: New Estimates of Casualty Aversion in the US," *International Studies Quarterly* 65, no. 1 (2021), copyright Oxford University Press, available at https://doi.org/10.1093/isq/sqaa068, and "PTSD and Veterans' Benefits in the United States: An Historical Backgrounder," copyright Modern War Institute, available at https://mwi.usma.edu/ptsd-veterans-benefits-united-states-historical-backgrounder/.

Friends and family have patiently heard me discuss this book over the course of many years. Special thanks to my "Minnesota mom" friends (my term, not theirs)—Abbie, Jenifer, Kaitlin, Kim, Sonal, and Stacy—for all their support and good cheer. My mother, Maydene, my sister, Shaena, and my in-laws, Richard and Natalie, have heard many versions of the book's key argument, often on repeat. But my most constant interlocutors have lived with me—and this book—through middle school, high school, and the COVID-19 pandemic. My son, Tag, "shared" an office with me, forcing me to take much-needed breaks. My daughter ,Vi, provided the first artist's rendering of a book cover while also refusing to remove sticky notes from all the books with gross pictures.

Finally, my husband, Lou Ciccone, has been my constant cheerleader. I would not have been able to take the time and trips necessary to write this book had it not been for his willingness to support the project. He has heard about every up and every down, and always knows just what to say. He has pitched in more times than I can count, from internet sleuthing to page proofing. His only failing has been an unwillingness to hear all the disgusting bits about military medicine. I promise the next one won't be as icky. I dedicate this book to him, with love, admiration, and too many thanks for words.

List of Abbreviations

AEF	American Expeditionary Force
AVF	all-volunteer force
BWRI	Bureau of War Risk Insurance
CAPE	Cost Assessment and Program Evaluation
CASEVAC	casualty evacuation
CAT	Combat Application Tourniquet
CBRN	chemical, biological, radiological, and nuclear
CCATT	Critical Care Air Transport Team
CFR	case fatality rate
COIN	counterinsurgency
CRS	Congressional Research Service
DNBI	disease and nonbattle injury
DoD	Department of Defense
DoDTR	Department of Defense Trauma Registry
DSM	*Diagnostic and Statistical Manual of Mental Disorders*
GAR	Grand Army of the Republic
IAVA	Iraq and Afghanistan Veterans Association
IED	improvised explosive device
JTTR	Joint Theater Trauma Registry
JTS	Joint Trauma System
LER	loss-exchange ratio
MDUSAWW	*The Medical Department of the United States Army in the World War*
MEDEVAC	medical evacuation
MSHWR	*The Medical and Surgical History of the War of the Rebellion*
MRE	meal, ready-to-eat
MST	military sexual trauma
OEF	Operation Enduring Freedom
OIF	Operation Iraqi Freedom
PPE	personal protective equipment
PTSD	post-traumatic stress disorder
R&R	rest and relaxation
STD	sexually transmitted disease
TBI	traumatic brain injury
TCCC	Tactical Combat Casualty Care

THOR	Trauma Hemostasis and Oxygenation Research
USPHS	United States Public Health Service
USSC	United States Sanitary Commission
VA	Veterans Administration/Department of Veterans Affairs
VFW	Veterans of Foreign Wars

A Brief Note on Sources

Of the many primary (and secondary) sources consulted in the research for this book, two series require special mention for citation purposes.

The first series, *The Medical and Surgical History of the War of the Rebellion*, is a six-volume set produced by the US Army Surgeon General's Office and is the United States Army's official medical history of the Civil War. Various editions of these volumes are numbered differently. I refer to the entire series as *MSHWR* and to specific volumes by volume and part number. These numbers correspond to each part of the series as follows:

- Volume I, Part 1: *Medical History* (1870, prepared by J. J. Woodward)
- Volume I, Part 2: *Medical History* (1879, prepared by J. J. Woodward)
- Volume I, Part 3: *Medical History* (1888, prepared by Charles Smart)
- Volume II, Part 1: *Surgical History* (1870, prepared by George Otis)
- Volume II, Part 2: *Surgical History* (1877, prepared by George Otis)
- Volume II, Part 3: *Surgical History* (1883, prepared by George Otis)

The second series, *The Medical Department of the United States Army in the World War*, is a seventeen-volume set produced by the US Army Surgeon General's Office and is the United States Army's official medical history of World War I. While the entire series was written under the supervision of Surgeon General M. W. Ireland, authors vary by volume, each of which covers a different topic. I refer to the entire series as *MDUSAWW* and to specific volumes by volume and part number. These numbers correspond to each part of the series as follows:

- Volume I: *The Surgeon General's Office* (1923, by Charles Lynch, Frank W. Weed, and Loy McAfee)
- Volume II: *Administration American Expeditionary Forces* (1927, by Joseph H. Ford)
- Volume III: *Finance and Supply* (1928, by Edwin P. Wolfe)
- Volume IV: *Activities Concerning Mobilization Camps and Ports of Embarkation* (1928, by Albert S. Bowen)

- Volume V: *Military Hospitals in the United States* (1923, by Frank W. Weed)
- Volume VI: *Sanitation* (1926, by Weston P. Chamberlain and Frank W. Weed)
- Volume VII: *Training* (1927, by William N. Bispham)
- Volume VIII: *Field Operations* (1925, by Charles Lynch, Joseph H. Ford, and Frank W. Weed)
- Volume IX: *Communicable and Other Diseases* (1928, by Joseph F. Siler)
- Volume X: *Neuropsychiatry* (1929, by Pearce Bailey, Frankwood E. Williams, Paul O. Komoroa, Thomas W. Salmon, and Norman Fenton)
- Volume XI: Part 1, *Surgery: General Surgery, Orthopedic Surgery, Neurosurgery* (1927, edited by Frank W. Weed)
- Volume XI, Part 2: *Surgery: Empyema, Maxillofacial Surgery, Ophthalmology (United States), Ophthalmology (American Expeditionary Forces), Otolaryngology (United States), Otolaryngology (American Expeditionary Forces)* (1924, by Edward K. Dunham, Robert H. Ivy, Joseph D. Eby, George E. deSchweinitz, Allan Greenwood, S. J. Morris, and James F. McKernon)
- Volume XII: *Pathology of the Acute Respiratory Diseases, and of Gas Gangrene Following War Wounds* (1929, by George R. Callender and James F. Coupal)
- Volume XIII: *Physical Reconstruction and Vocational Education and the Army Nurse Corps* (1927, by A. G. Crane and Julia C. Stimson)
- Volume XIV: *Medical Aspects of Gas Warfare* (1926, by Wilder D. Bancroft, H. C. Bradley, J. A. E. Eyster, H. L. Gilchrist, Samuel Goldschmidt, Paul J. Hanzlik, Robert A. Lambert, A. S. Loevenhart, E. K. Marshall, Walter J. Meek, A. M. Pappenheimer, James E. Poore, Torald Sollman, Jesse Tarr, F. P. Underhill, Alfred S. Warthin, and D. W. Wilson)
- Volume XV, Part 1: "*Statistics: Army Anthropology*" (1921, by Charles B. Davenport and Albert G. Love)
- Volume XV, Part 2: *Statistics: Medical and Casualty Statistics* (1925, by Albert G. Love)

Introduction

Blood, Gore, and the Costs of War

On January 15, 1865, less than a year after enlisting in the Union Army, Private James Spaulding of the 112th New York Infantry was shot in the left thigh. His regiment had sailed aboard the *Atlantic* to assault Fort Fisher, the Confederacy's last remaining major coastal base, located just south of Wilmington, North Carolina.

Spaulding was—at least initially—one of the lucky ones. The battle was messy and grueling, the casualties abundant.[1] His injury was, all things considered, relatively minor, and the wound was dressed. Within a few weeks it became infected and, according to his medical record, was treated with "solution of the permanganate of potash and tonics." Two months later, Spaulding's leg began to hemorrhage. The bleeding was ultimately controlled via a series of procedures, none of which would have been performed with sterilized instruments or even in a particularly clean environment. In this weakened condition, still recovering in the hospital, Spaulding was stricken with dysentery. According to the final postoperative report: "The patient continued to sink under this complication, and died June 15 1865, five months after the receipt of the original injury and about two and a half months after the operation of ligating the artery. At the time of his death the wounds were nearly healed." James Spaulding was twenty-three years old.[2]

Spaulding had been shot by a minié ball, a cylindrical bullet vaunted for its speed, and the most common type of bullet used in the most common type of rifle (the Springfield) of the Civil War.[3] The spin of minié balls meant that they often produced extensive internal wounds; in the wake of their trajectory they also brought dirt and fabric into the body. The initial injury, in other words, was often followed by infection.

Had Spaulding suffered a gunshot wound in World War I instead of the Civil War, his injury likely would have been treated with clean gauze and water instead of unsterilized bandages, dramatically reducing the risk of infection. (On the transatlantic sea journey back to the United States, however, he might well have become another victim of the 1918 influenza pandemic.) If he had suffered a gunshot wound—or, more likely, been hit by artillery—during World War II, he would have been transported to a medical facility via motorized truck or train—rather than by foot or a horse-drawn carriage—and therefore would likely have received medical attention sooner. If he sustained his injury early in the war, he would have been given a transfusion of plasma after the surgery. If the injury was sustained in the closing months of the war—by which time penicillin was widely used by US forces and doctors had shifted to using whole blood for transfusion—these medical innovations would have further increased his chances for survival.

If we jump forward a century and a half, from 1864 to 2014, and Spaulding was fighting in Iraq or Afghanistan, he probably already would have been wearing a Combat Application Tourniquet (CAT) that he could have tightened as soon as he was shot (or, more likely, as soon as he was injured by an improvised explosive device, or IED); he also would have been very quickly evacuated to a higher-level medical facility. A helicopter would have taken him to be treated by a forward surgical team in under an hour. After receiving damage control surgery, he would have been transported on a plane staffed with critical care nurses, ventilators, and many liters of blood—a flying ICU—either to Landstuhl Regional Medical Center in Germany or to a facility such as Walter Reed National Military Medical Center in Bethesda, Maryland. He would have crossed continents and received an extensive operation within a day or two, rather than the many days it took in 1865 for him to travel from Fort Fisher in North Carolina to McDougall Hospital in New York Harbor, where he eventually died.

With all these changes, Spaulding's odds of survival would have been at least three times higher in 2014 compared to 1864. He likely would have survived to be able to take advantage of some version of the GI Bill, and then lived long enough to marry and have children, who could also take advantage of his veterans' benefits.[4]

But survival would come with complications. No matter what happened, Spaulding likely would not have lived the life he had planned prior to his military career. His leg might have been amputated. Even with modern prostheses, the road to recovery is long, and he would have required significant support and sacrifice from family and friends. He might also suffer from additional conditions, such as traumatic brain injury (TBI), post-traumatic stress disorder (PTSD), or other damage from blast injury. He would likely be reliant, in one way or another, on disability compensation and medical care from the veterans' health system for the remainder of his life.

James Spaulding's alternative biography highlights the startling successes of US military medicine since the country's founding. To put it simply, the military has gotten incredibly good at keeping its soldiers alive. That is a story that has been rightly celebrated—a clear victory, particularly amid the fog and destruction of war. But the consequences of this success are surprisingly complicated. As we think beyond the immediacy of trauma care, we find that these improvements have important downstream consequences, which have received far too little attention. The human—and financial—costs of war are vast. Military might is incredibly expensive, of course, and it almost seems trite (though of course also true) to say that death is always a tragedy. But amid these truisms lies a much less acknowledged reality: the costs of war are radically different today than they were a century and a half ago. The modernization of medicine, combined with an enduring commitment "to care for him who shall have borne the battle," as Lincoln promised in his Second Inaugural Address, are profound developments; nonetheless, they have generated enormous, and largely unintended, consequences. Dramatic improvements in military medicine, alongside the various surges in veterans' benefits in the United States, have increased the long-term costs of war in ways that we have failed to reckon with—until now.

War and Its Costs

Two main, related claims combine to form the argument of this book. First, many more military personnel today survive the wars they fight compared to the past—a consequence of persistent improvements in military medicine. I review the state of medicine at the start of each major war from the Civil War till today, as well as military medical developments throughout these conflicts. I examine various aspects of military medicine, from data collection to evacuation to trauma care. Documenting developments and advances—and, sometimes, regressions—over time reveals an overall trajectory of impressive improvements in US military medicine.

Second, US military veterans' benefits have also been on an upward trajectory, especially since World War II. How to fulfill the nation's obligations to its population of (invariably aging) veterans has been a vexing issue throughout US history. I trace the pendulum-like development of veterans' benefits systems, from the remarkable largesse of post–Civil War pensions and the attempt to reduce veterans' benefits after World War I to the steady increase of veterans' benefits after World War II. Nearly from the passing of the first GI Bill in 1944, veterans' benefits have been sacrosanct in US politics. Even amid the extreme political polarization in recent times, there has been bipartisan agreement on the importance of ensuring and, more often than not, increasing, veterans' benefits.

Improvements in military medicine mean that more people return home than would have in previous wars. But surviving injuries that would not have been survivable in past wars often means returning home indelibly changed. Military veterans bear these costs of war upon their person. Their families also bear the costs of war—in time taken off from work, in having to take on additional financial responsibilities, and, most important, in the emotional pain of seeing a loved one hurt. This is not, of course, to diminish the pain of losing a loved one forever. Comparing harms is neither possible nor desirable. The human costs of war encompass both the dead and the wounded.

The history and trajectory of US military medicine is astounding for many of its achievements. But what has gone mostly unnoticed is that these achievements have increased the long tail of war's burden. More wounded, and more severely wounded, return home. US veterans' benefits have expanded just as military medicine has improved. Thus, the financial costs of war are also increasingly borne by the government. The aim of this book is not to suggest that either the medical improvements or veterans' benefits be rolled back. Rather, my argument is that, insofar as we think about the decision to go to war as a cost-benefit calculation, the United States will get the costs part of the equation wrong if we continue to ignore war's long-term and less obvious burdens.

Excavating the Costs of War

The obscuring of the long-term costs of war has not necessarily been by design. Nor have these kinds of costs always been hidden. Sometimes they have been anticipated: one of the objections to the United States entering World War I, for example, was concern about creating a new generation of pensioners.[5] But even then, an overconfident military medical community assured Americans that this war would be a "safe" one. According to historian John Kinder, "safe-war" advocates argued that "by the time US troops entered the line of fire, combat would be little more dangerous than civilian life."[6]

This interplay speaks to the first of three factors (and arguably the most bedeviling one) that have hidden the long-term costs of war: the challenges of assessing these costs prior to fighting. As we'll see repeatedly, the United States historically has done a poor job of anticipating costs. In some cases, such as the invasion of Afghanistan following the attacks of September 11, 2001, the decision to go to war is made too quickly to allow for a proper cost assessment. But even when the run-up to war is much longer—oftentimes because there is debate about whether to go to war—the costs are poorly understood. Rarely do the wounded and future pensioners figure into these equations. Anticipated costs have been underestimated time and again. For example, the George W. Bush administration anticipated that the 2003 Iraq War would cost up to $200 billion. In 2008, Linda Bilmes and Joseph Stiglitz counted the costs at $3 *trillion*. Since then, Bilmes recalculated one portion of her and Stiglitz's original estimates—the disability and medical care costs for veterans of the Afghanistan and Iraq Wars—and the result was approximately $400 billion higher, twice the upper limit of the Bush administration's original estimate for the war's *total* cost. Bilmes's revision was driven by the unanticipated number—and unprecedented rate—of the returned wounded (which was caused, of course, by dramatic improvements in military medicine).[7]

The second factor that has obscured the long-term costs of war, especially recently, refers to the smaller size and volunteer nature of the US military today. In 1973, the United States moved away from conscription—the draft—to an all-volunteer force (AVF). Since then, the size of the military has decreased dramatically, from over 3 million in 1970 to less than half that number today.[8] Less than one-half of 1 percent of the US population serves in the military today, and all who serve do so voluntarily. Not only is the military smaller, but recruits are more geographically concentrated. Combined, these changes mean that a historically small sector of the US population has close ties to the military. The consequences of this shift were clear in a national survey I conducted a few years ago: I found that people within military networks understand the long-term costs of war associated with the war wounded, but those without close ties to the military—in other words, the great majority of US citizens, as well as our political leaders—were much less able to appreciate these downstream human costs of war.[9]

Third, the nature of the timing of improvements in military medicine challenges our ability to understand and, especially, anticipate changes to this long tail. That militaries tend to prepare to fight the last war is a common refrain. This kind of preparation includes assumptions about all aspects of war, including military medicine and the attendant expected array of casualties. But with each war the United States has fought, military medicine has improved. What this means in practice is that the proportion of the wounded to killed tends to increase over time. While the dead are memorialized, the wounded are meant to rejoin their lives as they were before the war.

These historical shifts have dramatically altered the ways in which war impacts our lives. But there is a very different element that we must also consider here: we have a hard time appreciating the costs of war simply because for a long time our measures of costs have been faulty. Assessments of the human costs of war have tended to focus on war fatalities. This tendency may be most visible in the war memorials present in towns and cities across the United States. But it is also on view in the political analysis of war. Consider the theory of casualty aversion—the notion that as casualties go up, public support for war should decrease—which has been the most enduring link between public opinion and the use of military force in the scholarly literature. This argument was most prominently launched fifty years ago by John Mueller, who identified an inverse logarithmic relationship between the number of US casualties and public support for the Korean and Vietnam Wars.[10] Several polls around recent wars have supported the notion that the US public is casualty averse. One study found a fourteen-point decrease in support when casualties were mentioned in pre–Iraq War polls, and in 2016 the Chicago Council on Global Affairs reported a marked preference for the use of drones or even piloted aircraft—where the likelihood of casualties is extremely low—over the deployment of ground troops to combat terrorism abroad.[11]

Ever since Mueller's original claim, scholars have been refining his thesis, focusing on the timing of casualties, the notion of "proximate" casualty aversion, and the demographics of the military, among other factors. The recency of casualties as well as casualties close to home might matter most in inducing casualty aversion; the authors of one study argue that had there been fewer casualties of the Iraq War, President Bush would have won a larger share of the vote in the 2004 presidential election.[12] Another angle on the casualty aversion hypothesis speaks to who participates in the military and thus bears the most direct costs of deployment. In this vein, Michael

Horowitz and Matthew Levendusky find that reinstating the draft would decrease support for military deployment; they attribute this finding to the fact that with a draft, casualties would be distributed randomly across society, rather than concentrated, as they are today, within the relatively tiny population that participates in an all-volunteer force.[13]

But all this scholarship, again, rests on an assumption with far-reaching consequences: it defines casualties almost exclusively in terms of fatalities.[14] This is somewhat surprising given that, a half century ago, Mueller included both the dead and the wounded in his definition of casualties,[15] including in at least some of his data analysis. It is also surprising because the dictionary definition of "casualties" very clearly includes the dead and wounded, and has done so for centuries.[16] Webster's offers the following definition of "casualty" in the military context: "a member of the armed forces who is lost to active service through being killed, wounded, captured, interned, sick, or missing."[17]

This oddly narrowed definition of "casualty" is mirrored in general public opinion surveys, as well as broader cultural conversations. The wounded were not mentioned in any of the various questions fielded from January through July 2015 compiled by the website Polling Report on the possibility of deploying ground troops in Iraq and/or to fight the Islamic State.[18] In a review of nearly a thousand questions fielded by organizations including Pew/*USA Today*, Gallup, NBC News/*Wall Street Journal*, Fox News, CNN, CBS News/*New York Times*, and ABC News/*Washington Post* on the Afghanistan and Iraq Wars, I could not find a single example of a question that referenced the wounded.[19]

The focus on war dead makes, of course, a certain emotional sense. The wounded have a chance to recover. The dead do not. And for much of human history the number of war wounded was not necessarily much higher than the number of war dead. So a focus specifically on the former would have been odd. And yet the last century and a half has seen an initially slow, but recently explosive, shift in this proportion. As a result, the returned wounded constitute an increasingly important—but often ignored—sector of the costs of war.

There is another small, but pernicious, obstacle to our enlarged understanding of war's costs: data availability. We know that the George W. Bush administration was reluctant to release data on US fatalities following the start of the Afghanistan and Iraq Wars for fear of the "Dover effect"—the possibility that public support for war might decline as we see images of military coffins being unloaded at Dover Air Force Base.[20] There is a less discussed alternative possibility: what we might call the "Walter Reed effect." Seeing soldiers with multiple amputations, facial disfigurement, and other, more severely debilitating injuries is testament to the miracles of modern military medicine but also reveals an especially saddening aspect of the consequences of war. It should not be surprising that many governments—including the US government—have been shy to offer much information on the war wounded.

But if we want to truly understand war today, we must expand our focus to include the wounded. Military historians agree that for centuries the wounded-to-killed ratio held steady at around 3:1.[21] The wounded-to-killed ratio is determined by dividing the number of military personnel wounded in action who survived by the number of those killed in action. It does not include the disease and nonbattle injury (DNBI) rate, minor wounds followed by a return to combat within seventy-two hours, or other types of casualties (e.g., soldiers dying or suffering from malaria or automobile accidents are excluded from this ratio). Recent years have seen a dramatic shift in medical care in conflict zones that has translated to a more than threefold increase in this statistic, as seen in Figure I.1. At its peak during the Afghanistan War, the official US wounded-to-killed ratio was nearly 11:1.

Though the larger story is one of astonishing success, the trajectory itself has rarely been linear, or simple. Like most advancements in human history, the story of medical improvements in war is reflected in a jagged line, with periods of intense breakthroughs, periods of minimal change, and even some periods of backward progress.

Path of the Book

I have been studying military medicine for the past ten years. As a political scientist by training, I approach this subject with humility; I am not "that kind of doctor." Nor am I a historian. I therefore began this project expecting that I would learn a great deal about both military medicine and its history. I was right. Reading through the six-volume official medical history of the Civil War, the seventeen-volume official medical history of World War I, the more scattered official medical histories of World War II, numerous official accounts of Korea and Vietnam, and then various medical articles more recently written about Afghanistan and Iraq has allowed me to peer into the process of repairing war-torn bodies and minds. Thumbing through

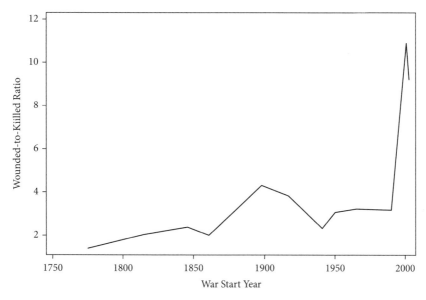

Figure I.1 US Wounded-to-Killed Ratios, 1775–2003
Deaths are battle deaths and died from wounds and do not include deaths from disease or accidents.
Source: Blum 2020.

the papers of various military doctors in dusty archives gave me a sense of their day-to-day challenges and triumphs. The work of scores of historians of military medicine has helped put these primary sources in perspective. Walking the halls of major military medical conferences provides a window into how military medical personnel—doctors, nurses, physician assistants, pharmacists, and others—assess their own successes and failures, as well as how they view the future of their field. At the exhibition floors of these conferences, I was able to climb through up-armored ambulances, try on prototype helmets meant to reduce the incidence of TBI, and conduct (pretend) surgery using augmented-reality goggles. Conversations with military personnel, from clinicians to administrators, have been especially informative when I was writing this book. Many of the people interviewed for this book have been practicing military medicine for decades; they have had a front-seat view of its recent trajectory. I was even able to participate in a military medicine wargame.

Like any book, however, this one has limitations. One is that my analysis does not account for the reasons for war—in other words, the perceived and anticipated benefits. In our rapidly changing world, and particularly in a global economy that has become less focused on agriculture and more dependent on internationally traded services and manufactured goods, it would seem logical that the benefits of war have changed too.[22] However, bearing in mind that states go to war for many reasons beyond territorial conquest, the literature as a whole does not suggest a systematic shift between the Civil War and today in the expected benefits of war; countries continue to fight for access to raw materials as well as for electoral boosts for politicians on tenuous ground at home. Many fewer scholars have focused on the costs of war, even though those costs, as I show, clearly are shifting. If the benefits of war have remained the same but the costs have risen, then this mismatch requires interrogation.

Another limitation speaks to data quality. While this is a book about war casualties, counting casualties is always fraught. The reality is that we will never know for certain how many dead and wounded a given conflict produces; the best we can do is come to a good estimate. Reports from the field bear this point out repeatedly. In the first pages of the *Medical and Surgical History of the War of the Rebellion*—the six-volume official medical history of the US Civil War—the authors point out that they are working with disparate casualty counts; all they can do is try to reconcile them.[23] The United States has a much better casualty data collection system today than in the mid-nineteenth century, but today's system is by no means perfect. For example, medics in the field might be just as likely to write a patient's medical history in marker on their chest as they are to fill out a Tactical Combat Casualty Care (TCCC) card and send the information back to the Department of Defense Trauma Registry (DoDTR). And even if governments had perfect information on casualties sustained—which they do not—they would not necessarily release those data. We see this dynamic playing out in modern wars such as the one between Ukraine and Russia, where casualty counts have become part of the larger information warfare landscape.[24]

Given this constraint, my focus in this book is on providing a qualitative—rather than quantitative—account of the trajectory of US military medicine and veterans' benefits. While I do use the wounded-to-killed ratio throughout, inconsistencies in means of counting casualties across wars limit me to this statistic because it is the most comparable. Assessing veterans' benefits over time is even more challenging. The institutional architecture around veterans' benefits has evolved significantly over the course of US history, including since the Civil War. These bureaucratic changes make it extremely challenging to provide a comparable, generation-by-generation account of changes in veterans' benefits. Thus, I once again take a more qualitative approach, focusing on the combination of improvements in medicine—which mean that more veterans will survive—and changes in the nature of benefits.

I also set a critical boundary around this book by focusing on a single country. The United States is of course not the only country to have benefited from improvements in military medicine. The country's first military medical system was, unsurprisingly, of British design. Dominique-Jean Larrey, Napoleon's medical director, was a pioneer in the field of medical evacuation with his "flying ambulances"—horse-drawn carriages that brought casualties to the rear much more quickly than had been possible in prior conflicts. Japan's military at the start of the twentieth century set a new standard for hygiene and sanitary practices.[25] Today, military medical guidelines are shared among allies and even adversaries. NATO countries train together on military medicine, and rival countries such as Russia have shared military medical knowledge and even adopted systems created in the United States, such as TCCC guidelines.

While developments in military medicine have diffused around the globe, tracing these changes in one country affords important advantages. Limiting the scope of the project makes it both more manageable and also more digestible. The key players in military medicine and veterans' benefits change. But many of the institutions remain the same, or close enough.

The United States is also a good case for a study of the history and consequences of military medicine because it has been at war for so much of its history. The country has been at war for the majority of the lives of most Americans alive today.[26] Over the course of these conflicts, more than 1 million US military personnel have been killed, and more than 1.6 million more have been wounded.[27] War is a crucible for medicine. Countries—like the United States—that are often at war thus face many opportunities to improve military medicine.

Focusing on a country such as the United States also helps expose some of the long-term political consequences of improvements in military medicine, especially in connection with developments of the veterans' benefits system. One reason veterans' benefits have expanded in the United States—especially since World War I—is because of the medicine. Veterans groups such as the American Legion, Veterans of Foreign Wars (VFW), and, more recently, the Iraq and Afghanistan Veterans Association (IAVA) have lobbied vigorously to get doctors, researchers, and the government to pay more attention to war-specific illnesses, from Gulf War Syndrome to lung cancer to respiratory illness. More surviving veterans also means greater membership for these groups, many of which have become vocal members of key congressional constituencies.

Perhaps the most important reason to focus on the United States is that it has engaged in so many wars of choice. As a great power—and, for many years, the single global superpower—the United States has enjoyed relative flexibility in deciding whether, when, and where to commit its armed forces. But the process of costing out these decisions ahead of time has been flawed. Focusing on the US case therefore provides an opportunity to offer an important corrective to how we think about the long-term costs of war.

This book focuses on the three sets of wars arguably most transformative to United States military medical history: the nineteenth-century Civil War, the twentieth-century world wars, and the twenty-first-century counterinsurgency wars. The United States has of course been at war for much of its history; therefore, many wars are not discussed here. I focus on these three sets of wars because they are among the most important in terms of both size of mobilization and medical developments. The Civil War remains the most consequential in US history in terms of the percentage of the (white male) population that served, died, and was wounded. Compared to the Revolutionary War era, the US military medical system was much better staffed and supplied, especially because the US military had learned from its experience in the War of Independence.[28] Many fewer soldiers and sailors served in the 1898 Spanish-American War as well as the "frontier wars" of the nineteenth century that enabled western conquest. Similar to the Civil War, the world wars meant a massive mobilization. These wars also occurred after the development of modern medicine (including the germ theory of disease), providing a crucial contrast to the Civil War era. Finally, while many fewer troops were mobilized for the Afghanistan and Iraq Wars than were, for example, during the Vietnam and Korean Wars, the twenty-first-century counterinsurgency wars mark a much greater contrast in terms of both medicine and the political logic behind veterans' benefits. The country's other military involvements, in between these three sets, are referenced in what follows, because each war inevitably influences the next. But the combination of mobilization, medical advances, and to some extent the duration of conflict made these three sets of wars crucial as historical pivots in the changing costs of war.[29]

Finally, a word on what I mean by the "costs of war." My focus in this book is on the costs of war that emerge from the United States' own military casualties. But these costs represent only a narrow slice of the actual—and, ultimately, unknowable—costs of any war, which inevitably extend beyond the military itself. In the US Civil War, for example, researchers attribute to the fighting the deaths of 50,000 civilians, as well as devastating property damage, especially in the South.[30] As the United States emerged as a great power on the world stage, its military reach extended—and so did the costs its wars inflicted, not just on opposing militaries but also on ordinary people and places across the globe. The firebombings of Tokyo and Dresden during World War II killed over 100,000 civilians. Consider too the human and environmental impact of the use of napalm during the Vietnam War. Or the dreadful physical, psychological, and material toll exacted by US drone strikes in various countries in the Middle East, from Yemen to Libya to Pakistan, which continues to mount. My focus here on US military personnel is in no way meant to diminish the devastation that they have inflicted around the globe. Rather, my intention is to offer an alternative understanding of a story that we think we know well. By focusing on the medicine of one military—for much of the last century, the most powerful military in the world—we can gain new perspective on the fragility of human life, the astonishing efforts to preserve life, and the numerous benefits and costs of that ongoing effort.

Private Spaulding's tale likely would have had a very different ending today. But saving a life is not the end of the story when it comes to the long-term costs of war. With each major war the United States has fought, medicine has improved. More people return home, often with wounds they would not have survived in past conflicts. The human costs of war have shifted with better military medicine, and this shift is reflected in increased veterans' benefits over time. Properly assessing future costs of war requires understanding the causes of these past changes.

The people and policymakers of the United States have been systematically underestimating the costs of war because we have not attended to these shifts. And if war appears less costly, it makes it easier to go to war. Correcting the cost side of the cost-benefit equation might not prevent military action. But clear-eyed assessment should at least make us more cautious about waging war. It should force us to reckon with the costs alongside the benefits, and the ways that those costs will inevitably impact not only our lives but also the world we leave for our children and grandchildren.

1

Bad Air and Boiled Horsehair

The US Civil War

Mose Triplett had a colorful military history. He joined the Confederate Army on May 30, 1862, when he was eighteen years old. While his unit, the 26th North Carolina, was decimated at Gettysburg, Triplett missed the battle due to illness—an incessant feature of the Civil War. Recovered, he deserted on June 26, 1863.[1] Just over a year later, Triplett joined the Union Army as a member of the 3rd North Carolina Mounted Infantry.[2] Known as "Kirk's Raiders," for their commander, the 3rd fought at Morristown, Waynesville, and Asheville.[3] The 3rd was disbanded in 1865, and Triplett was discharged. He died in 1938 at the age of ninety-two, leaving his much younger second wife, Elida, a widow.[4]

Triplett's story is unusual not only because he switched sides but also because he managed to end the war relatively unscathed, at least physically. Had he been wounded at Gettysburg, or even Waynesville, his story might have ended quite differently. By any account, medical care during the Civil War was a grim pursuit. Nearly all our enduring images of the war offer a bleak portrait. Anonymous renderings of buckets of amputated limbs outside a battlefield surgery. Walt Whitman's poignant lamentations for the wounded young men he treated as a nurse during the war.[5] Dirty buckets of water in the PBS television series *Mercy Street*. The images are stark and unrelenting.

Histories of the war, including the six-volume official *Medical and Surgical History of the War of the Rebellion* (*MSHWR*), paint a similarly sad picture. The *Medical and Surgical History* was conceived as early as 1862; it was the brainchild of Army Surgeon General William Hammond but ultimately was overseen by Hammond's successor, Joseph K. Barnes, and authored by Assistant Surgeons General J. J. Woodward and George A. Otis. The original goal was to remedy the "insufficient and defective" data being received on the sick and wounded of war.[6] Published from 1870 to 1888, the set covers topics from "typho-malaria" and "gunshot wounds of the lower extremities" to the "alvine fluxes." Neither Barnes nor Woodward nor Otis, though, lived to see the final fruits of this labor. Others took it over and completed the series. Their legacy—and that of the *Medical and Surgical History*—is long. It was the first official medical history of a United States war; it set a precedent for similar efforts in future wars and serves as an invaluable source for scholars of Civil War medicine.

The sheer breadth of the Civil War also altered Americans' understandings—both during and after the war—of what veterans like Triplett and their families were owed by the country. Indeed, the medical history of the Civil War is inextricably linked to the history of its veterans, if only because so many of the medical case histories were furnished via the Pension Bureau. The care of veterans became a crucial part of the federal bureaucracy—one sign of a broader shift toward the belief that veterans should be rewarded for past service, especially if they had been injured.[7]

Military service during the Civil War—regardless of which side you fought for—bore many risks beyond getting shot or bayoneted on the battlefield. Indeed, immediate death (whether via gunshot, blade, or cannon) was less common than the other, more attenuated ways that soldiers died. Disease, especially dysentery and typhoid, accounted for the largest portion of deaths by far. And if you were wounded during battle, the medicine that you would have received was so primitive that in the decades following the war the medical community regularly described it as medieval.[8]

The war, nevertheless, forced a series of medical advancements, especially with respect to logistics and organization. Jonathan Letterman famously devised an ambulance system. General hospitals were built amid heated debate as to their proper architecture, generating a vision of a hospital system that would—eventually, as medicine improved further—be reproduced for civilians.[9] Women left home to nurse on the battlefield and in hospitals, setting the stage and standard for a new profession for women working outside the home. The United States Sanitary Commission (USSC), a predecessor to the American Red Cross, not only provided food and comfort to soldiers but also argued strenuously for a reorganization of the Union Army's Medical Department and, more generally, for cleaning up military encampments.

These two features of the Civil War—the prevalence of disease and the development of new medical support systems—are emblematic of two halves of military medicine: the care provided to individual patients and the infrastructure that supports that care. We tend to focus on what happens to the body—the sources of our ailments and injuries, as well as the treatments. But what happens *around* the body is equally important. Patients cannot be diagnosed without data; they generally require some sort of transportation to reach medical care; and doctors and nurses work in hospitals that may serve their populations well or poorly. Some of the most important advances in Civil War military medicine would not have been noticed or known by most patients and their families, while the most apparent failings were very much at the surface. Thus here, and in the chapters that follow, I provide an overarching view of medicine in war, exploring both what happens to the body and how those bodies are cared for.

Prewar Assessments of the Costs of War

The decision to go to war is never taken lightly. Leaders know in advance that lives, livelihoods, and—in the case of the Civil War—the fate of nations are at stake. Lincoln biographer David Donald described Lincoln's state of mind as he deliberated whether and how to send reinforcements to Fort Sumter in the spring of 1861: "The strain under which Lincoln labored in arriving at this decision was immense. All the troubles and anxieties of his life, he told [his good friend Orville Hickman] Browning, did not equal those he felt in these tense days."[10]

Both sides weighed the costs and benefits of going to war. According to economic historian Gerald Gunderson: "At the beginning of the Civil War, the federal government conducted an intensive process of budget formation which was designed to project the cost of the war. The Treasury and War departments and Congress all readily agreed that the war should last less than one year, require 300,000 troops, and cost about $265,000,000."[11] It is unclear whether Confederate leaders ever arrived at such exact estimates, although they certainly would have considered costs and benefits as well. For the South, Gunderson argued, the economic costs that would come with the abolition of slavery were deemed too high to risk incurring, regardless of the eventual cost of war itself.

But both sides also severely underestimated the length and size of the war. As James McPherson wrote: "The United States has usually prepared for its wars after getting into them. Never was this more true than in the Civil War."[12] The war preparations that took place prior to April 12, 1861—when Confederate forces fired on Fort Sumter and the war began—were in retrospect almost laughably lacking. Lincoln called initially for 75,000 troops for ninety days, while the Confederacy requested 100,000 for one year.[13] Both authorizations represented a fraction of the dead, let alone the total number of troops in each army. The war was expected to last three months.

This kind of underestimation of the costs and duration of war is common and has inspired myriad studies of the causes of war.[14] A major school of thought, based on the "bargaining theory of war," suggests that one reason potential belligerents go to war is poor information, or information that is not shared, especially with the opposing side. As James Fearon writes in a seminal article: "Leaders know things about their military capabilities and willingness to fight that other states do not know, and in bargaining situations they can have incentives to misrepresent such private information in order to get a better deal."[15] By this logic, if the Union and Confederacy had fully understood each other's capabilities and resolve—and the associated costs of fighting—in advance, they would have settled on a compromise and avoided conflict.[16] But this argument also assumes they had a solid grasp of their own costs.

Even in a fantasy world, where we could accurately forecast what war will exact from us, forecasters make choices about which information they seek out and which they do not. Our projections, in other words, are laden by our biases and blind spots. In the best-case scenario, both sides would have been at least somewhat realistic about the toll of war—in other words, they would have acknowledged, but undercounted, the dead and the wounded. Prewar Civil War estimates, however, were far from the best case. An official history of US military mobilization describes Secretary of War Edward Stanton's projections for the size of the Army as faulty precisely because "he grossly underestimated future casualty losses of the Army."[17] And according to Margaret Humphreys, a major historian of Civil War medicine, "It does not seem to have occurred to the leadership on either side that the war would produce casualties and that the gathering of men in great camps would provide a field day for infectious diseases."[18]

Likewise, neither Washington nor Richmond appears to have planned financially for those veterans who would survive the war. In part, this lack of planning may have been due to prevailing norms about what veterans were owed. At the time, veterans of past US wars, such as the War of 1812, received disability and pension payments of under $10 per month.[19] Decision-makers in 1861 cannot be faulted for hewing to this narrow construction of veterans' benefits; in part because they thought the war would be brief, they did not expect that it would produce many veterans. Nor did they expect the ballooning of the pension system that would begin soon after the war ended.

Lincoln admitted to poor prognostication in his second inaugural address in March 1865: "Neither party expected for the war the magnitude or the duration which it has already attained." While pre–Civil War decision-makers drastically underestimated both the short-term toll and the long-term costs, they did get one thing right: they were confident that the proportion of the wounded to the dead would remain consistent with previous wars. The wounded-to-killed ratio for the Revolutionary War was just under 1.4 to 1. In the decades following, that ratio widened slightly—2:1 for the War of 1812 and 2.4:1 for the Mexican-American War—but did not increase substantially. The Civil War wounded-to-killed ratio is estimated at between 2:1 and 2.5:1 for the Union and 2:1 for the Confederacy.[20] This statistic reflected the medicine of the time, which offered few effective responses to disease or injury. Death was an expected outcome in nineteenth-century war.

Bodies at War

The Civil War ravaged soldiers' bodies more from the inside out than from the outside in. As had been the case for centuries, disease was the scourge of war. Doctors offered various diagnoses and treatments, all of which were compromised by a lack of understanding of the germ theory of disease, which would not become common knowledge for decades to come. The state of mid-nineteenth-century medical knowledge also limited treatment of war wounds; in an era before antiseptics and antibiotics, surgeons had only limited, but often extreme, options for treating war wounds. The results were grim: for those Civil War soldiers who made it home after the war, relatively few returned as they had left.

Soldiers, Doctors, and Disease

From a twenty-first-century perch, it is difficult—if not impossible—to conceive of the vast landscape of disease during the US Civil War. Disease was by far the biggest killer in the war, both ubiquitous and poorly understood. As historian Andrew Bell puts it, the US Civil War was "a pestilential nightmare."[21] While medicine during the forty-eight months of fighting did see some advancements, disease was one area where treatment and comprehension remained fairly static.

Disease is endemic to war for several reasons. First, militaries typically draw in populations from different parts of a country. Not every recruit will have been exposed to every childhood illness. In an era when immunization did not exist (with smallpox being somewhat of an exception), new recruits, from rural areas in particular, were more likely to be exposed to diseases than if they had stayed home. From measles to mumps, many diseases are widely inoculated against today, and rarely a problem. In the mid-nineteenth century, however, these highly contagious diseases could enfeeble entire units.[22] Indeed, early in the war, military officers who assumed that farm workers would make better soldiers than their urban counterparts were quickly disabused of that notion when farmboys were laid low by diarrhea, measles, and mumps, rendering rural soldiers unable to train and fight, and often returning from a hospital to the battlefield much weaker than when they joined.[23]

Second, the combined exigencies of the human body and military life leave a wide-open door for gastroenteric illness. An entire volume of the *Medical and Surgical History* is devoted to the "alvine fluxes"—diarrhea and dysentery—and with good reason. These were the hallmark illnesses of the Civil War, generating at least 1.7 million cases in the Union Army alone. In the first year of the war, nearly one-third of all sick Union troops suffered from diarrhea or dysentery, and thousands of Union troops died from one or the other.[24] All told, almost three-quarters of Union soldiers contracted dysentery at some point in the war (see Table 1.1). Poor and poorly cooked rations were one culprit. But the main cause of disease was the frequent use of unsanitary water, which had been polluted by runoff from human and animal waste. Latrines were not dug sufficiently far away from camp, and feces-contaminated water was used for drinking and cooking in the camp. Soldiers sometimes noticed a difference in how their coffee tasted when they were downstream from the horses.[25] Doctors—and, frequently, members of the USSC—could and did advocate for keeping cleaner camps, including maintaining a minimum distance from latrines. But neither regimental doctors nor USSC inspectors had the authority to enforce sanitary standards.[26] More important, the germ theory of disease was in its early stages but had not yet been fully developed or publicized. Thus, there was no clear logic connecting the expulsion of human and animal waste upstream to dysentery outbreaks downstream. This situation created such a vicious cycle that the position sick armed men took in battle was often referred to as the "soldier's crouch." Poor sanitary conditions produced dysentery outbreaks,

Table 1.1 Diseases and Treatments

Disease	Incidence	Treatments
Diarrhea-dysentery	711 per 1,000 annually	• Laxatives (Epsom salts, castor oil, calomel [until banned by Hammond]), ipecac • Opium • Quinine (administered because of a belief that diarrhea was malarial)
Typhoid	242 per 1,000 annually	• Dover's powders and other opiates for diarrhea • Hot fomentations, blisters, cupping for abdominal pain • Cold compresses for fever • Turpentine (administered orally) for intestinal ulcers
Malaria	522 per 1,000 annually	• Quinine • Mercury (for bowels) • Opium
Yellow fever	1,355 cases in total	• Calomel (mercury)

Sources: MSHWR, Vol. I, Part 1, 191–92; George Worthington Adams, *Doctors in Blue: The Medical History of the Union Army in the Civil War* (Baton Rouge: Louisiana State University Press, 1952), 226–28; Andrew McIlwaine Bell, *Mosquito Soldiers: Malaria, Yellow Fever, and the Course of the American Civil War* (Baton Rouge: Louisiana State University Press, 2010), 3, 33; Michael A. Flannery, *Civil War Pharmacy: A History of Drugs, Drug Supply and Provision, and Therapeutics for the Union and Confederacy* (Binghamton, NY: Pharmaceutical Products Press, 2004), ch. 6.

which were then reinforced by diarrhea so uncontrolled that soldiers would not have been able to reach sanitary facilities in time even if they were able to leave their positions.

Third, militaries often fight on unfamiliar terrain that comes with diseases to which invading military personnel will lack immunity. For example, British troops suffered from malaria contracted in the Middle East and Southern Europe during World War I (and then subsequently brought it home).[27] Similarly, dengue, endemic to tropical climates, afflicted US troops in the Caribbean and Asia over the course of the twentieth century.[28] As Benjamin Bagozzi shows for the civil wars that emerged around the globe in the decades after World War II, rebel forces are typically less likely to contract malaria because they tend to remain in a circumscribed geographic area;

government forces, on the other hand, are more vulnerable, primarily because they are fighting in epidemiologically unfamiliar terrain.[29]

During the US Civil War, at least 15,000 Union soldiers succumbed to malaria, which was classified as "intermittent fevers" for the frequent high temperatures it created (often with chills and diarrhea); many soldiers contracted malaria more than once.[30] While doctors recognized the unhealthy consequences of camping near swamps and marshes, they did not understand their cause. Civil War physicians variably ascribed malaria to odors emanating from the soil or a gas in the air.[31] While mosquitoes were a nuisance, they were not viewed as disease carriers; three decades later Ronald Ross would discover that the female *Anopheles* mosquito is a carrier of malaria, in that it takes blood from an infected person and then passes the parasites on by biting an uninfected person. Prior to this discovery, of course, medical personnel were oblivious to the danger of housing infected and uninfected patients in close quarters.[32]

A related and widespread presumption was that Black soldiers, whether from North or South, were immune to malaria.[33] According to Andrew Bell's history of mosquito-borne diseases in the Civil War, this assumption contributed to the decision to free the slaves. Bell quotes Treasury Secretary Salmon P. Chase making a medical argument in favor of emancipation: "We cannot maintain the contest with the disadvantages of unacclimated troops."[34] Bell further writes: "For Chase a federal emancipation scheme would not only swell the Union ranks but would do so with men who could better endure the disease-ridden swamps of Mississippi."[35] Black soldiers were then placed in malaria-prone areas around New Orleans and the Mississippi River.[36] Doctors eventually came to question the connection between race and disease.[37] While some Blacks had some immunity from having lived in the South, the malaria rate among Black Union soldiers was ultimately slightly higher than for white soldiers.[38]

The causes and consequences of diseases also combined. Soldiers parched from malarial fevers drank contaminated water and then contracted dysentery.[39] Conversely, soldiers already ill from diarrhea could be further weakened by contracting malaria in hospitals.[40] The combination of diseases was so prevalent that an entirely new category—"typho-malarial fever"—was invented to describe the various and often overlapping symptoms of fever, diarrhea, and "rose-colored lenticular spots on the skin." These all indicated typhoid fever, as it was understood at the time, but also a slightly less severe and somewhat briefer fever accompanied by chills that could be treated effectively with quinine and appeared to follow a seasonal pattern.[41] In the final volume of the first series of the *Medical and Surgical History*, which focused primarily on the "continuous fevers," Charles Smart (taking over for J. J. Woodward, who spent a good deal of his career on this topic) struggled to identify the boundaries around various disease classifications, in large part because so many soldiers were suffering from more than one illness simultaneously. Poor (by today's standards) data collection created significant challenges to assessing the incidence of "typho-malarial fever." Ulceration of Peyer's patches (aggregated nodules of lymphatic cells in the small intestine) was considered a necessary indicator of typho-malarial fever. But there were a number of cases where autopsies revealed inflammation but not ulceration, such as that of Corporal E. J. Innes of the 6th Michigan Cavalry, and others where no information on the state of Peyer's patches was reported, as with the case of Private Warren Burton of the 28th Alabama.[42] Modern medical science has rejected the classification of "typho-malarial fever"; while it is possible that soldiers may have been afflicted simultaneously by both typhoid and malaria, the likelihood is that most diagnosed with "typho-malarial fever" in fact suffered from typhoid alone.[43]

Nineteenth-century understandings of the causes of disease, not surprisingly, led to suboptimal treatment. Physicians in early and mid-nineteenth-century America were beholden to the "heroic" theory of illness. Illness was thought to be caused by imbalances of bodily "humors" or by "miasmas" in the air that entered the body. Prescribed treatment followed this logic; bloodletting and sweating were common responses in the early nineteenth century, although bloodletting was not used very frequently during the Civil War. Leeches were sometimes used to treat dysentery, although the famous "blue pill" (hydrargyrum cum creta, perhaps better known as mercury with chalk) was administered more commonly.[44] Mercury was administered orally to treat yellow fever, as was lead.[45] As Table 1.1 (which summarizes data from the Union Army over the course of the entire war) shows, laxatives in particular were a very common treatment for many kinds of illness.

As the war went on, doctors saw the value of quinine as both treatment and prophylactic for malaria.[46] Bell reports that the Union medical staff administered more than 19 tons of quinine to military personnel, which was especially important as the army moved south.[47] But supply issues intervened, especially in the South. As they saw increasing numbers of troops under their care fall prey to malaria, Union and Confederate doctors sometimes used raw cinchona bark (from which quinine was extracted) when supplies of the drug ran out.[48] Between the naval blockade of the South and the depreciation of Confederate currency, the price of quinine increased 125-fold (from $4 to $600 per ounce) in the South over the course of the war.[49]

Especially at the start of the war, medical supply issues were exacerbated by poor military logistics. At every army camp, medical supplies were controlled by the quartermasters, the military officers in charge of supplies. Quartermasters, though, were ill-equipped to estimate the amount of medical supplies needed; supplies would, therefore, often run short. The United States Sanitary Commission, a relief society created by a group of New York City women, raised funds to offset these shortages.[50] Although the USSC confronted various related distribution and bureaucratic challenges (internally as well as externally), the commission made substantial contributions to remedy deficits of food, clothing, and medicine for Union troops throughout the war.[51]

Even so, the supplies were wanting, by today's standards, and not just in quantity. Doctors' kits included quinine, calomel (mercurous chloride), and the "blue pill." As the following quote from a Confederate surgeon shows, doctors did not necessarily exercise a great deal of discrimination in recommending a treatment regimen:

> Diagnosis was made by intuition, and treatment was with such drugs as we chanced to have in the knapsack. . . . On the march my own practice was further simplified, and was, in fact, reduced to the lowest terms. In one pocket of my trousers I had a ball of blue mass,[52] in another a ball of opium. All complainants were asked the same question, "How are your bowels?" If they were open, I administered opium; if they were shut I gave a plug of blue mass.[53]

Quinine was prescribed for fevers beyond malaria, opium was overprescribed and so created a class of addicted veterans, and toxins such as mercury and lead were viewed as useful even though they exemplified the phrase "the cure was worse than the disease." Limited supplies were matched by limited knowledge. Though doctors were beginning to identify correlations between a particular disease and the efficacy of their very limited bag of tricks, there were no systematic guidelines for how to treat the most common diseases.

Again, from a twenty-first-century vantage point, it is not surprising that these prescriptions often did as much harm as good. At the extreme end, giving mercury for yellow fever and using turpentine topically for malaria[54]—the former could cause gangrene of the mouth and the latter skin blistering—sounds horrifying today.[55] The rate of death from disease in the Civil War was thus due not only to a lack of understanding of the causes of disease but also to a subsequent lack of knowledge of how best to treat disease.

The heroic theory of medicine applied to all illnesses, not just those spread from person to person. Malaria (and another mosquito-borne disease, yellow fever) accounted for more than 1.3 million illnesses and 10,000 deaths, and at least a quarter of disease cases.[56] By the end of the war, military doctors' understanding of malaria had advanced very little beyond its nomenclature—meaning "bad air," from the Italian. While doctors recognized some seasonality to the disease, they attributed it to odors emanating from soil in swampy areas, miasmas, or gases in the air.[57] Likewise, typhoid fever was attributed to "bad air, improper food, exposure to wet and cold, great fatigue, anxiety, and other depressing and insalubrious causes."[58] Even decades after the war, as the *Medical and Surgical History* was published, not all doctors had accepted the germ theory of disease. Reading the official history with modern eyes is frustrating because the authors—writing after the war—seem tantalizingly close to grasping the infectious nature of malaria. On one page of the final volume on diseases, published in 1888, Major Charles Smart writes that there is "no illustration on the records of direct contagion from one individual to another." A few pages later, though, the same author acknowledges the likelihood of a germ causing typhoid fever, and seems clearly conversant with the germ theory of disease.[59]

At times, the lack of understanding of how disease was spread could serve militaries well, if unintentionally so. In 1864, a group of Confederate conspirators hatched a plan to infect the Union Army by selling a chest of clothing worn by southerners who had succumbed to yellow fever.[60] Had the clothes, which were duly purchased by a Union supply officer blissfully ignorant of this plot, come from typhus patients instead of yellow fever sufferers, the plan might have had some success.[61] But because yellow fever is spread by mosquitoes and not surfaces such as cloth, that dreaded disease did not overtake the Union Army.[62] Nonetheless, this effort was a harbinger of the yellow fever outbreaks of the Spanish-American War, thirty years in the future, during which Walter Reed would establish that yellow fever was transmitted not by infected surfaces such as clothing but by the *Aedes aegypti* mosquito.

Civil War medicine is often deemed "barbaric" by today's standards. It is of course unfair to judge physicians of the nineteenth century by the standards of the twenty-first, just as it would be unfair to judge today's physicians by the standards of our twenty-third-century descendants. The supposed barbarism of Civil War medicine is typically depicted by images of buckets of amputated limbs next to saw-happy doctors, a stereotype that, as we'll see, was occasionally well deserved. But when it came to surgeries such as amputation, Civil War doctors were in fact much better equipped with scientific knowledge than they were when confronting disease. Insofar as the Civil War occurred during the "medical Middle Ages," it was the treatment of disease that was most medieval.

Weapons, Wounds, and Surgery

In his account of the First Battle of Bull Run (or the Battle of Manassas, as it was named in the South), Confederate officer Lt. Col. W. W. Blackford described a stereotypical scene of battlefield surgery:

> Along a shady little valley through which our road lay the surgeons had been plying their vocation all the morning upon the wounded. Tables about breast high had been erected upon which screaming victims were having legs and arms cut off. The surgeons and their assistants, stripped to the waist and all bespattered with blood, stood around, some holding the poor fellows while others, armed with long bloody knives and saws, cut and sawed away with frightful rapidity, throwing the mangled limbs on a pile near by as soon as removed. Many were stretched on the ground awaiting their turn, many more were arriving continually, either limping along or borne on stretchers, while those upon whom operations had already been performed calmly fanned the flies from their wounds.[63]

Blackford's words paint a grim but not fully accurate picture of Civil War medicine. To be sure, amputations were common, but they were not performed thoughtlessly. Anesthetics were used, although not in a way that would be wholly recognizable today. What the Civil War medicine stereotype does get right, though, is both the prevalence of disease and, as a result of new weaponry, the severity of injuries sustained.

From the War of Independence through the Mexican-American War, muskets and bayonets were the weapons of choice in the United States. While rifles were available, they were not generally used in battle because they required a long reloading time. In 1849—one year after the Mexican-American War had ended—French military officer Claude-Etienne Minié invented a new bullet for rifles that would redefine the weapons and wounds of the Civil War. While known as the minié or "minny" ball, this new bullet was in fact cylindrical (and was often referred to as "conoidal"). Its shape and size made it easier and faster to load, which in turn made the rifle more appealing, ushering in a shift away from muskets and toward longer-range "rifle muskets." Guns, such as the Springfield rifle, that used the minié ball became the dominant weapon of the Civil War, displacing the previously crucial role of cavalry and bayonets. Soldiers no longer had to attack at close range—either on horse or with a blade. With quick-loading rifles, infantry could see and shoot farther than with muskets.

From a military standpoint, the minié ball conferred the advantage of speed. But from a medical standpoint, as we have seen, the minié ball was disastrous: it brought additional foreign (and usually quite dirty) substances, such as fabric, into the wound, and it wrought extensive damage internally. There were few clean wounds from a minié ball.

Rifles were not, of course, the only weapons used in the Civil War. Artillery—which in the mid-nineteenth century referred primarily to wheeled cannons—had not advanced much in previous years. From a tactical perspective, one of the major downsides of artillery lay in poor targeting. Soldiers hit by artillery were very likely to be killed instantly, but the artillery of the time made relatively few direct hits. Springfield rifles, on the other hand, were much more accurate. Shots that hit the head or the trunk, the two parts of the human body most vulnerable to a killing wound, were typically fatal. By contrast, injuries to arms and legs were much more survivable—and, therefore, more likely to be treated and recorded by medical personnel. So while the Civil War saw its share of other kinds of injuries, from concussions and fractures to poisoning and blast injury, injuries to the extremities accounted for more than 70 percent of the cases that were seen by medical personnel and which, therefore, made it into compilations of data on the war wounded such as the *Medical and Surgical History*.[64]

Part of the reason for this distribution of injuries was that Civil War soldiers wore no personal protective equipment (PPE). Centuries earlier, knights went into battle with suits of metal armor. But because armor could be pierced by bullets, the gunpowder revolution made such armor obsolete; the difficulty of moving in armor was no longer worth the protection it afforded. By the mid-nineteenth century, militaries were more likely to wear uniforms—typically, without helmets—that did not protect the body from anything more than a sunburn or insect bite, if that. A major consequence of the lack of PPE in the Civil War was that the heads and torsos of soldiers were left unprotected. Even those who survived their injury for long enough to receive medical attention did not necessarily live for much longer.

When combined with the "medieval" state of Civil War medicine, the destruction wrought by the minié ball meant that amputation was often the most medically sound course of action. Amputation required keeping the patient still. Stereotypes about "screaming victims" notwithstanding, anesthetics *were* used in the Civil War. Chloroform and opium were administered widely (as was, admittedly, whiskey). Visitors to the Civil War Military Medicine Museum in Frederick, Maryland (the site of a Civil War hospital), can see the equipment used to anesthetize patients. While the chloroform-dampened cloths typical of the Victorian era were in use, so were tools that more closely resemble anesthesiologists' equipment today. For example, a chloroform-filled sponge would be placed at the top of a cone held over a soldier's nose and mouth, a rudimentary precursor to the mask through which anesthetics are administered in today's hospitals.

Widespread use of anesthesia was relatively new in mid-nineteenth-century America. This newness is reflected in the surgical reports from the field collected in the *Medical and Surgical History*. Time and again, surgeons described successful use of anesthesia, especially chloroform. In reporting on a series of amputations he conducted and oversaw, surgeon H. P. Stearns wrote: "The anaesthetic employed was chloroform. No deaths from its use were reported."[65] Stearns's report was typical; surgeons appear to have been asked to assess chloroform's results. With rare exceptions—such as when pure, as opposed to diluted, chloroform was used—the typical report was that the anesthetic had been used with no negative results.[66] It is clear from these reports that doctors administered the drug carefully and were especially attentive to any negative side effects.

The primary effects of Civil War anesthesia were quite different from our twenty-first-century associations with such drugs, and account at least partially for the stereotype of screaming patients and sawed-off limbs. What we would call today general anesthesia was not available to Civil War surgeons. Local pain relief, which was akin to anesthesia, was sometimes available in the form of powdered morphine. Chloroform, which was used much more widely, made patients insensible to pain but also put them in a sort of excitable fugue state in which they must have resembled "screaming victims" (especially to those in line for treatment).[67] The postoperative calmness to which Blackford refers attests to the efficacy of anesthesia; the pain of amputation would not have been borne so quietly otherwise.

A second classic stereotype of Civil War medicine embodied in Blackford's comment is the reference to piles of mangled arms and legs. Amputation was the hallmark treatment for wounded Civil War soldiers and has sparked numerous studies—of its execution, its place in medical history, its tertiary consequences like "ghost pain," and even its effects on gender relations in the Reconstruction era, especially in the South.[68]

A large market for artificial limbs emerged after the Civil War for a reason: amputation was by far the most common surgical response to gunshot wounds to the extremities. While most Civil War soldiers were killed by disease, most injuries were caused by gunshot. If the injured soldier was shot in an arm or a leg, the likelihood of survival was much greater than if the head or torso was hit, and the likelihood of amputation was quite high. In a chapter entitled "Wounds to the Lower Extremities," for example, the *Medical and Surgical History* reports that more than half the cases—5,452 of nearly 9,000—were treated surgically, most with amputation.[69]

Amputation was not the only medical option available to Civil War surgeons. "Conservation"—in which the wound was cleaned and closed, and then the limb was splinted—excited great debate among doctors at the time.[70] Excision, or the removal of some of the bone, was also practiced in a number of cases. The mortality rate for conservation and excision, though, was not only higher than for amputation but also worse in the US Civil War compared to other wars of the nineteenth century. Doctors at the time attributed this difference at least partially to the time pressures of medical treatment on the battlefield as opposed to in civilian practice, although this distinction does not help explain why conservation led to poorer outcomes in the Civil War compared to other nineteenth-century wars.[71] Nonetheless, as George Washington Adams notes in his medical history of the Union Army, in retrospect doctors who preferred amputation to conservation were on the right side of history, at least until the Thomas splint used so widely in the world wars was developed.[72]

Brutal imagery notwithstanding, Civil War doctors learned a great deal about amputation during the war. They learned that ligation of vessels could stop hemorrhage, although the success rate of ligation was low.[73] They learned that the closer to the trunk a wound was, the higher the likelihood of death following amputation (this was especially an issue with hips). The best that could be done for such patients—if time and resources permitted—was to offer palliative care. And they learned that "primary," or immediate, amputation was much more likely to be successful than intermediary or secondary amputation.

Even though doctors had good medical reasons to prefer amputation to the alternatives, the mortality rate for amputation was high by today's standards. Civil War leg amputations had a mortality rate of 32.9 percent.[74] While this number was commensurate with other wars of the time, it compares poorly to the world wars, which had an amputation mortality rate just over 4 percent, and especially to the most recent counterinsurgency wars, when the amputation mortality rate was closer to zero.[75]

A crucial reason for these high mortality rates was the high frequency of postoperative infection. The most common causes of post-amputation fatality were gangrene, pyemia, erysipelas, tetanus, and exhaustion (what we would call "shock" today). In the pre-antibiotic, pre-germ-theory era, doctors had few tools at their disposal to prevent such infections. Often, success was by happenstance, such as when doctors noticed that patients healing in the open air were more likely to survive than those in poorly ventilated buildings. While they did not understand the cause, observing this correlation led directly to support for pavilion-style hospitals (discussed below), as well as for ventilation in general in hospitals. In a similar vein, embargos on the Confederacy meant that silk for sutures was unavailable. As a substitute, Confederate surgeons used horsehair, which was boiled to make it more pliable.[76] Boiling the horsehair also sterilized it, therefore reducing the risk of infection. Without knowledge of the germ theory of disease, however, Confederate doctors had no way of connecting success in surgery with sterilization.

Especially given the state of medicine at the time, amputation was often the best recourse in treating the most frequent type of injury. While the image of a pile of mangled arms and legs offers a horrifying picture of Civil War medicine, amputation rates are often high in war because extremities are so vulnerable to injury and because patients can often (especially today) survive such surgeries. In the end, stereotypes aside, Civil War doctors appear to have made reasonable decisions given the tools and knowledge at their disposal.

The Logistics of Medicine

The men in charge of military medicine at the start of the Civil War were ill-suited to the task. Their experience was limited to the short-lived Mexican War and, more significantly, the sporadic "Indian Wars." These ongoing battles between the US government and indigenous populations—which play a curiously minor role in official military medical histories—presented a different set of medical problems compared to the Civil War, in part because of the nature of fighting.[77] Indeed, aside from the crucial difference in advances in medical knowledge, some of the medical problems in these conflicts might bear a greater resemblance to the United States' twentieth- and twenty-first-century counterinsurgency wars. Ira Rutkow suggests that the relatively minimal demands of frontier military medicine produced a subpar Medical Department, led by Thomas Lawson, an out-of-touch and aged surgeon general who had been appointed by Andrew Jackson.[78]

Lawson died soon after the war started. His replacement, the equally "ossified" Alexander Finley, was soon taken to task by members of the USSC.[79] Prominent Sanitary Commission leaders including Frederick Olmsted (the famed designer of New York's Central Park) were consistently stymied in their efforts to lend aid to the military. In a letter to his wife detailing a trip to Washington, Olmsted wrote:

> I do not get on very well; do not accomplish much & shall not I fear. The army men on the Commission can not be seen at an average expense of less than five hours & it is hard to get their pretence of attention for five seconds when you get access to them. They do nothing but discourage & obstruct.[80]

Olmsted, along with Sanitary Commission president Henry Bellows, led an effort to improve battlefield evacuation, among other procedures. But the bigger effort was to replace the leadership of the Medical Department. Following a series of often controversial machinations, Finley was replaced as surgeon general by William Hammond.

Beyond specific personalities, at a high level the bureaucracy around medical care was also deeply problematic at the war's start. The surgeon general led the Union Army's Medical Department, but hospitals and evacuation were under the purview of the Quartermaster Department, while supplies were controlled by the Subsistence Department.[81] Coordination among the three departments was challenging, to put it mildly.

The United States had never fought a war on this scale before, and the medical infrastructure was simply not up to the task when war began. I use the term "medical systems," alongside "medical logistics" and "medical infrastructure," to refer to all of the elements that enable actual care by medical personnel to be delivered to actual patients. Medical systems include hospital buildings where patients are treated, the human resources departments that hire the people to do the treatment, and the ambulances that get the patients to the places where they can be treated. These systems frequently figure in the background in the United States today, because those of us fortunate to have at least decent health insurance largely take these elements for granted. It often takes a crisis—think of the images of body bags stacked in the back of a Detroit hospital in the early days of the COVID-19 pandemic—to force us to see how these medical systems are of profound importance.[82] From ambulances to hospitals to nursing, improvements in the medical systems (rather than the medicine itself) over the course of the Civil War represent signal achievements. And, as we'll see, many of these innovations endured through at least the world wars.[83]

Evacuation

Nowhere were these innovations—and challenges—more evident than with respect to medical evacuation. Once ill or injured, it was no small feat for a Civil War soldier to get medical care, especially in the early years of the war. Stories like those of Oliver Wendell Holmes Sr.—traveling to Maryland to search the fields for his injured son (and future Supreme Court justice)—were common and true, if not necessarily typical.[84] The Union Army's ambulances in 1861 consisted of a limited number of carriages, pulled by horse or mule.[85] According to the late historian Richard Shryock:

> No adequate ambulance services and field hospitals were available as late as 1862. At Second Bull Run, for example, the Union Army was supposed to have 170 ambulances but actually went into battle with 45—most of which broke down. Several days after the battle, in consequence, 3,000 wounded still lay where they had fallen.[86]

There were no dedicated ambulance personnel. Instead, each Army regiment typically had a six-member band, whose music gave rhythm to drills and lifted morale during off-hours. When fighting broke out, members of the band would be temporarily reassigned as stretcher-bearers. Sometimes civilian contractors would be hired as stretcher-bearers. In the heat of battle, however, stretcher-bearers often either could not be found or refused to perform their duties; typically, they ran away.[87]

A major impediment to the development of a modern ambulance system at the start of the war was the fact that ambulances, as well as medical supplies, lay in the quartermaster's domain, rather than under the purview of the medical director. Quartermasters did not prioritize or understand the exigencies of medical care. Medical directors did. Thus, the person ostensibly in charge of medicine had no say over the vehicles that would be best able to deliver that medicine. The issue of who "owns" evacuation vehicles would resurface in future wars, such as when the Army and Air Force debated which service should be charged with control over helicopters in the Korean War. In the Civil War, ambulance drivers often would give rides to officers and their baggage or other cargo, as the quartermaster preferred.[88] Unsurprisingly, this system meant that injured soldiers, such as Holmes, could lie on the battlefield for days, if not weeks. These unhelpful ambulances also impacted manpower beyond just the loss of wounded soldiers; knowing that there was no reliable system to transport their wounded comrades, soldiers would often bear their wounded friends to the rear themselves, and not necessarily return to battle.[89]

With respect to the optimal use of ambulances in battle, the United States was behind the times. Dominique-Jean Larrey, who eventually became Napoleon's chief surgeon, is credited with inventing "flying ambulances" during the Battle of Metz in 1792. These *ambulances volantes* were not aircraft; what made them different was how—and, especially, how quickly—they were deployed in battle. Positioned near the front lines, these wheeled carriages were driven directly to injured soldiers, who were then loaded in and taken to field hospitals. Notably, *ambulance volantes* were also staffed with medical personnel.[90] In the decades following Larrey's invention, the importance of providing immediate care for the war wounded was widely publicized in Europe, between Henri Dunant's memoir, *A Memory of Solferino* (based on his observations during the 1859 Austro-Sardinian War, and a key inspiration for the creation of the International Committee of the Red Cross), and Florence Nightingale's *Notes on Nursing* (based on her experience in the Crimean War). Both figures increased the public's understanding of the value of military medicine in mid-nineteenth-century Europe.

This knowledge had also crossed the Atlantic; Nightingale's work in particular was well known and widely read in US medical circles.[91] It inspired the members of the Sanitary Commission, who lobbied for Hammond's hiring, which, in turn, led to Jonathan Letterman's appointment as the medical director of the Army of the Potomac in 1862.[92] Letterman's hiring was a turning point for Civil War military medicine. Letterman took a systemic approach to medicine, and his innovations—especially in evacuation—continue to be hailed as some of the most consequential of the war. Letterman's reforms focused initially on the ambulance service. He mandated that there should be at least one ambulance for every regiment with fewer than 200 soldiers, and three for regiments of 500 or more. Dedicated ambulance drivers and stretcher-bearers for every regiment were also crucial to Letterman's scheme; from that point, unqualified band members would no longer be expected to remove the wounded from the field. Nor would the lines be depleted by nonwounded soldiers taking their wounded comrades to medical aid stations.[93] From Antietam to Fredericksburg to Gettysburg, the Union Army's marked improvement in medical evacuation was deemed no less than miraculous.[94] Letterman also standardized and shrank medical kits for Army doctors so that they could be carried onto the field. And he streamlined and improved the rations system, with a particular eye to addressing outbreaks of scurvy caused by poor diet.[95]

Particularly as the war progressed and protocol was established, evacuation occurred in clearly demarcated stages. Injured soldiers were first taken to field hospitals—essentially, aid stations set up at an Army base or along the edge of a battle, some of which might be tented and many of which would be moved during the course of a battle. If they needed additional care, soldiers would then be transported to regimental hospitals farther back from the front. Longer-term care meant a stay in one of the many general hospitals in the rear, such as Philadelphia's Satterlee Hospital in the North or, for the Confederate injured, likely Chimborazo Hospital in Richmond.

Over the course of the war, medical evacuation expanded to include rail and ships. Once again, the US Sanitary Commission was instrumental, outfitting railcars and ships for the purpose of caring for the wounded. The contrast between the first and last rail evacuations was immense. After the Battle of Fair Oaks in the early summer of 1862, for example, "surgeons packed living and dead like freight into boxcars with nothing to ease the jolting and bumping."[96] By the end of the war, railroad cars had been fitted with beds and other supplies to ease the transport of wounded troops. For the fighting proximate to the Atlantic coast, a series of ships were eventually retrofitted as floating hospitals—rudimentary, to be sure, but an enormous improvement over waiting for help in the field.[97]

Several logistical issues confronted soldiers during the chain of evacuation, especially at the start of the war. For example, regimental surgeons often refused to treat soldiers not of their regiment. Local doctors had signed up to treat local patients. Restricting care in this way was problematic not only because many of the wounded were not treated in a timely manner but also because the standards for hiring doctors, not to mention the medical training of those doctors, were quite uneven at the start of the war. Part of the challenge, as with the war in general, was in finding men. The Medical Department had a mere 114 doctors on staff in 1861.[98] Following the Medical Reform Bill of 1862, the Medical Department raised standards for hiring medical personnel (although not in a way that would make it easier to hire women physicians, discussed below) and replaced the smaller regimental hospitals with larger division-level hospitals.

Staffing and Hospitals

A separate, but no less important, set of logistical issues referred to the construction and staffing of general hospitals. Hospitals were few and far between at the start of the Civil War and were primarily meant to treat the indigent. The Civil War was a crucible for nineteenth-century American medicine not just because of surgical advancements but also because of the increasing acceptance of hospitals as a part of military, and then civilian, life. While at the start of fighting any structure (a school, a home, a barn) would do as a hospital, eventually the Medical Department understood that large military hospitals must be built. With little architectural precedent to guide them, doctors' input may have been especially crucial to builders. Although there was much about disease they did not understand, Civil War physicians had observed that patients treated in the open air did better than patients housed in poorly ventilated spaces, as we have seen. Thus was conceived the "pavilion hospital," where patient wings would branch off from a central hub or line. Each wing was to be well ventilated. By effectively siloing each ward (wing) and improving air circulation, medical personnel believed that they would improve the health of their patients.[99]

Philadelphia's Satterlee Hospital was a prime example of the pavilion model. Inspired by Florence Nightingale's analysis of the Crimean War, Satterlee Hospital was the pride of the Medical Department. It could serve more than 3,500 patients by the end of the war and, in many ways, was a self-enclosed city, with a barber shop, several laundries, and monies set aside to fill unexpected needs. It represented the best hygienic practices of the day, including ventilation and a new type of latrine.[100]

Satterlee also exemplified the many staffing issues faced by the Medical Department, especially when it came to women. As Margaret Humphreys has chronicled, the Civil War transformed women's relationship to medicine.[101] Prior to the war, women tended to their ill in the home. Once the war started and, especially, once troubling reports of poor medical care and supply trickled out, women shouldered their way into Civil War hospitals. Among them was Louisa May Alcott, whose *Hospital Sketches* provide an intimate portrait of "Nurse Periwinkle's" experiences at "Hurly-Burly House" before she fell ill and returned home.[102] One consequence of the new hospital system created for the war was the development of the profession of nursing, and the role of female nurses outside the home in particular.

Very early in the war, the nursing staff consisted primarily of convalescent patients; especially in the South, men who were admitted to the hospital but able to give some aid frequently served as nurses.[103] While such ambulatory patients, as well as volunteers like Walt Whitman, continued to serve as nurses for the duration of the war, the service was ultimately taken over by women. In *Hospital Sketches*, Alcott objected strenuously to the use of convalescent patients as "a source of constant trouble and confusion" because they were physically incapable and, indeed, reflected poorly upon the women. "Constant complaints were being made of incompetent attendants, and some dozen women did double duty, and then were blamed for breaking down."[104]

Women entered Civil War medicine via three primary routes. First, they founded sanitary commissions and ladies' aid societies to help supply soldiers at the front. Jane Schultz reports that more than 20,000 women—from North and South—were part of such efforts.[105] Feeling that sewing for soldiers was insufficient, women organized more. Although Reverend Henry Bellows served as the first president of the US Sanitary Commission, it was actually inspired by the dozens of women who authored an open letter "To the Women of New York, and Especially to Those Already Engaged in Preparing Against the Time of Wounds and Sickness in the Army." The gender norms of the time, though, meant that male leadership was a practical prerequisite for successful lobbying.

Second, a small group of women led the nursing charge. Here, women like Mary Ann Bickerdyke, Dorothea Dix, and Clara Barton are best known for their efforts. They raised supplies but also offered individual medical care. Tales of "Mother" Bickerdyke corralling lounging soldiers to locate cauldrons and cooking ingredients "so that her boys could be fed" abound. Dix, who ran the Office of Army Nurses, was a stern but respected taskmistress.[106] Barton, in addition to providing field care, is best known for setting up communications systems so that soldiers and their families could be in touch, and families could be notified of any deaths.

All three women challenged gender norms of the times in noticeable and clever ways. Bickerdyke and Dix, especially, are painted (mostly by male authors) as well-loved bullies in both contemporary and historical accounts of Civil War medicine. McPherson describes "Mother Bickerdyke" as "a large, strong, indomitable yet maternal woman [who] swept through the camp like an avenging angel."[107] Similarly, Bollet reports that Dix was sometimes referred to as "Dragon Dix," while also acknowledging her "soft and musical voice" and dedication to treating the wounded.[108] Barton apparently sought to avoid controversy and carved out her own niche in the field. While they have been lauded for their work, their challenge of the era's patriarchal systems typically goes less noticed.

Third, these nursing pioneers led many other women—particularly poorer women—to become nurses themselves. The most common path for women in Civil War medicine was as nursing staff—as opposed to major figures like Bickerdyke and Dix, who set the rules for and selected nursing staff. Class differences intervened such that doctors were less welcoming to "women of society" than to poorer women or nuns; the former often challenged doctors' authority, while the latter were more obedient and considerably less demanding.[109] By the end of the war, Dix was overseeing more than 3,000 nurses, although getting them properly paid and pensioned was often a different story.[110] One of the most important professional developments of the Civil War was opening up the medical field to women; nursing became a respectable profession, which had important implications for women's financial independence and, decades later, their role in World War I.

A fourth path—as physicians—was mostly foreclosed. There were few women physicians during the Civil War. Elizabeth Blackwell had earned her medical degree before the war and directed initial efforts toward organizing the Women's Central Association for Relief, a predecessor to the US Sanitary Commission. Doctors such as Blackwell, Mary Edwards Walker, and Esther Hill Hawks faced constant questioning of their credentials. They were offered the least desirable posts, such as Dr. Hawks's assignment to the 54th Massachusetts, an African American regiment. But they served with distinction.[111]

From ambulances to hospital design to nursing, the systems stood up during the Civil War would have far-reaching effects. They represent the best of Civil War medicine. As the war went on, soldiers benefited greatly from these reforms. These changes, however, did not generate dramatic improvements in case fatality rates (the proportion of those who receive care and survive) over the course of the war. As Bollet notes, the increasing number of wounded combined with long service and substandard diet created a population of less healthy soldiers who were unlikely to survive their wounds even with these other wartime advancements.[112] The medical science of the day created a ceiling to the benefit that could be derived from the dramatic improvements in Civil War logistics.

Data Collection

In the introduction to the first volume of the *Medical and Surgical History of the War of the Rebellion*, J. J. Woodward, assistant surgeon for the United States Army, writes, "From these Monthly Sick Reports, mainly, the tables in this volume have been prepared. They cannot be regarded as complete. There is probably no one month during which all the regiments and detachments, actually in service, are represented."[113] Woodward spends much of that introduction attempting to reconcile different accountings of the dead and wounded in the war. An 1870 report from the adjutant general, for example, lists 303,504 killed,[114] which adds upward of 20,000 fatalities to an 1866 report from the same office.[115] Additional disparities emerge when the adjutant general's reports are compared with those from the quartermaster general, which counted just over 315,000 Union graves from the war.[116] The surgeon general's estimate of war fatalities was the lowest, at 282,955.[117] Woodward ultimately generates his own estimate (304,369) by picking and choosing from these sources.[118] Throughout, the only thing that's clear is the cloudiness of the data.

War is a messy business, and collecting data in war is exceptionally challenging. The Civil War was not the first American war in which doctors attempted to collect systematic medical data. After what was at best spotty data collection during the War of 1812, regular reports were sent to the surgeon general, including during the 1846 war with Mexico. But the quality of these reports was poor, and it is not clear whether similar reports were filed during wars against indigenous peoples in North America.[119] The sheer scale of the Civil War, however, meant that the associated data collection effort was unprecedented. Medical doctors facing deluges of patients might see the benefit of what today we call "charting," but when balanced against the pressures of treating a flood of emergent cases, good record-keeping is rarely the top priority. During the Civil War, military doctors faced additional challenges that undermined record-keeping. Medical forms changed during the course of the war. Doctors did not always understand what data should be collected. They also didn't necessarily agree on diagnoses, which meant that different doctors might label diseases differently—for example, one doctor might diagnose a patient with malaria, while another would diagnose the same patient with typhoid. Add to these inconsistencies disasters like the fires that destroyed Confederate military medical records during Richmond's evacuation, and we can readily see that data collection in the Civil War, like the medicine itself, would not have met today's standards.[120]

I raise this point to underline the danger of relying on a purely quantitative assessment of Civil War medicine—and, indeed, military medicine writ large. The data we have—collected by Civil War military medical personnel, the authors of the *Medical and Surgical History*, members of the United States Sanitary Commission, the Pension Bureau, and independent advocates like Clara Barton—are invaluable. But even their authors recognized that they were incomplete. What is more, we can have no doubt that biases pervade the data we do have; the missing elements in the data are not random.

For example, historians of medicine often rely—with care—upon the numbers presented in the *Medical and Surgical History*. These volumes were based principally on field reports from war surgeons, the Pension Bureau, and documentation and artifacts held by the Army Medical Museum.[121] These sources are likely to undercount those who may have died in the field and whose remains were not recovered. Alfred Bollet notes exactly this phenomenon, pointing out that over 70 percent of wounds reported in the *Medical and Surgical History* were to the extremities. While extremity wounds were no doubt common during the Civil War, what this statistic really reflects is the fact that soldiers suffering more severe wounds deemed untreatable at the time were triaged such that they did not make it to a hospital and enter the ledgers of the wounded.[122] Likewise, wounded soldiers who then deserted and went home are less likely to be included in official counts of the injured than those who received care in military hospitals; many in the former category, however, applied for pensions and thus could have been captured by the Pension Bureau. In other words, it seems quite likely that the dead were undercounted vis-à-vis the wounded. Below, I present numbers, but I do so with caution; we should tread carefully and not draw conclusions only from the numbers.

A critical feature of Civil War data collection speaks directly to the role of race. On page 1 of the *Medical and Surgical History*—just as Woodward launches into a discussion of issues around data accuracy—we see a clear example of contemporary assumptions made by white doctors about race:

> The propriety of endeavoring to present separately such facts as it has been possible to collect, with regard to the sickness and mortality of Colored soldiers, would appear too obvious to require extended remark in this place. Aside from all considerations of a scientific or historical nature, motives of humanity would seem to dictate that the statistics should be presented in the form most likely to render them serviceable as a contribution to our knowledge of the influence of race-peculiarities on disease.[123]

Throughout the six-volume set, casualty rates for Black soldiers are consistently reported separately from casualty rates for white soldiers. As Humphreys argues in her pathbreaking book, *Intensely Human*, Black soldiers began the war less healthy than their white counterparts and saw subsequent declines as a result of substandard healthcare during the war. "Much of this mortality, however, can be traced to specific choices made by officers, bureaucrats, and other authority figures, who proved poor stewards of the men in their care," she writes. "Their decisions, great and small, careless and deliberate, doomed these soldiers to early graves."[124] Jim Downs extends this argument in *Sick from Freedom*, pointing out that emancipated slaves faced a host of health problems caused by a lifetime of poor treatment and preexisting conditions, the absence of a social safety net, racism in the healthcare profession, and the myriad epidemiological challenges faced by war refugees.[125] Substandard healthcare for Black Americans, not surprisingly, continued after the war. Indeed, doctors in the postwar Pension Bureau systematically discounted disabilities suffered by Black soldiers.[126] While the contemporary raconteurs of Civil War military medicine made these distinctions because they assumed physiological differences between Blacks and whites, recently historians have used these various statistical tables to demonstrate the differential effects of structural racism on health.

Given all these issues, we should not take any numbers as gospel. Nonetheless, they offer helpful ranges in assessing the human costs of war. The "official" total death toll of the Civil War—adding both sides—is 620,000—although more recent estimates suggest that the number could be as high as 850,000.[127] According to the *Medical and Surgical History*, between 279,000 and 304,000 Union soldiers died; modern analyses based on excess mortality, however, imply a much higher statistic. A somewhat questionable contemporary southern source claimed that 200,000 Confederate soldiers died—likely a considerable underestimate.[128] Accounting for the wounded is much more challenging. One recent estimate suggests a total of about 475,000 wounded for both sides but also claims fewer than 200,000 fatalities total.[129] The wounded-to-killed ratio for the Union forces, for which we have much better data—and which enjoyed the medical advantage in the war—was likely around 2:1.[130] For every injured soldier that died, another two (or so) survived, but with wounds or chronic illness that often lasted the duration of their lives.

Veterans' Benefits

For its first eighty-five or so years, the United States had an ambivalent relationship to the notion of veterans' benefits. Pensions were used as a lure to swell the ranks during the War of Independence but ultimately were paid out at a much lesser rate than originally promised. Often, the prevailing attitude in the early nation invoked Cincinnatus, the Roman citizen-soldier who hung up his weapons and returned to the field, apparently without complaint. Instead of the thanks of a grateful nation, this attitude held, veterans should be thankful for the chance to have served the nation.

Veterans pushed back against this view. Sometimes the pushback referred to promises made, as in the case of the Revolutionary War. Sometimes, as in the Civil War, veterans argued a much more foundational claim: that the state bore responsibility for them, especially the wounded. The case for pensions was manifold. The most compelling argument was economic—the idea that compensation was due to replace labor lost as a result of injury or death (not to mention as a form of back pay for farmers having left their fields to fight). But many veterans, and their families, also made a moral argument that such service incurred a debt, even aside from injury or death.

In addition to the overarching debate about whether veterans were owed anything, there was a corollary debate: what did a veteran need to do during war in order to qualify for benefits thereafter? Who among veterans deserved benefits became a major political issue in the wake of the Civil War. These controversies were part of a throughline that had begun in previous wars and would continue forward. Additional lines of debate were drawn along the questions of whether—and which—veterans were owed medical care or money, if they were owed anything at all.

Medical care, and care more broadly, could be provided via a new kind of institution: veterans' homes. While facilities for disabled veterans were relatively new in the mid-nineteenth century—the first US Naval Home was built in 1833, and a US Soldiers' Home opened in 1851—these homes would proliferate after the war.[131] Indeed, the new kinds of hospitals built during the Civil War laid the foundation for these homes. The sea change in the role that hospitals would play in American life, prompted by the Civil War, meant that homes for invalided veterans made much more sense in 1865 than they would have in 1798 or even 1846. The majority of the homes were primarily residential, although one (in Bath, New York) was meant to serve as a medical facility.[132] All told, over 100,000 veterans were housed in these institutions between the end of the Civil War and the turn of the twentieth century.[133] While veterans' homes organized by the USSC and other similar organizations ran on charitable donations, many of these were temporary. The more permanent federal facilities were funded by the government, initially via fines of military personnel and later through congressional appropriations. By 1930, the homes had cost the government over $250 million.[134]

By orders of magnitude, however, the much greater cost to the federal government was in pensions to Civil War veterans. Soldiers throughout the North had been recruited with promises of bounties (signing bonuses) now and pensions later, in addition to the opportunity to fight for their country. For example, a poster for the Hillhouse Light Infantry in New York promised a $163 bounty, nearly half of which was to be paid after an honorable discharge.[135] Another poster, for Col. J. Richter Jones's Pennsylvania regiment, exclaims "Pension! Bounty! Extra Pay!" at the top, explaining below that "recruits will be mustered in at once and entitled to extra pay and, in case of death their families will receive a pension from the State in addition to that from the General Government."[136] Having some assurance that their families would receive payment in the event of their death was a critical inducement for many Union volunteers.

Following the war, pensions offered to Union veterans were controversial on several fronts. First, and not surprisingly, only Union veterans were eligible for pensions from the federal government. While a number of southern states attempted to provide benefits for Confederate veterans, their resources were much more limited than those of the federal government.

Second, benefits were at first restricted only to those who could show that they had a disability resulting from their wartime service. This approach was similar to the one the United States had taken after previous wars. But what "counted" as a war-induced disability was very much subject to bias and interpretation. According to historian John Kinder, the determination of disability was highly subjective and unsystematic, requiring character references, and disqualifying most Black veterans, as well as those whose injuries were not visible.[137]

With the passage of the 1879 Arrears Act, however, Civil War veterans could essentially receive lump sum back payments for pensions. These payments were often fairly large, setting off a chain of new applications for pensions that, in turn, created political incentives to expand such benefits.[138]

Third, and partly as a result of the 1879 law, benefits for Union soldiers slowly expanded to include all veterans with disabilities (removing the requirement to establish a service connection for the injury) and then to all Union veterans, regardless of disability status. These benefits, which were issued primarily in the form of monthly pension payments, grew so far and so fast that by 1880 they accounted for more than 10 percent of the federal budget.[139] But the share of the budget devoted to pensions would only grow. The 1890 Dependent Pension Act removed the requirement that disabilities be service-related; as long as a soldier had served at least ninety days and "could not earn a living by his own labor," he could draw a pension.[140] With an aging Civil War veteran population, this meant that almost every Union veteran was eligible for a pension. Widows and other heirs of veterans were also eligible. According to Theda Skocpol, "By the time the elected politicians—especially Republicans—had finished liberalizing eligibility for Civil War pensions, over a third of all the elderly men living in the North, along with quite a few elderly men in other parts of the country and many widows and dependents across the nation, were receiving quarterly payments from the

United States Pension Bureau."[141] By 1893, the share of federal income devoted to these pensions had grown significantly, to over 40 percent.[142]

Those payouts, however, came with a price: pensioners were increasingly viewed with resentment and, at times, as fraudulent. Even aside from resentment and complaints about corruption, Civil War pensions seemed to put the country's financial health in jeopardy. Yet these grumblings, though abundant, never translated into a decrease in Civil War pensions.

The resistance to paying veterans was repeatedly overcome, in large part because of the growing political clout of veterans.[143] The veteran lobby was best represented by the Grand Army of the Republic (GAR), founded in 1866 and a precursor to today's American Legion and similar organizations. Shrouded in secrecy and ritual, GAR meetings sought to replicate the discipline of camp; in many ways the primary mission of the organization was nostalgic. It soon became clear, though, that organized veterans could wield serious political power. In 1890, the GAR boasted 500,000 members, almost all white, at a time when half the more than 60 million people living in the United States did not have the vote, and the voting rights of another 7.5 million remained restricted, especially in the South. Being seen as unsupportive of this constituency was a recipe for losing reelection bids in northern states. The veterans' bloc helps explain the expansion of the pension system, as well as a series of monuments and the ubiquitous presence of the US flag in classrooms around the country.[144]

By 1910, Union veterans qualifying as invalids were receiving pensions worth, on average, $271 per month.[145] For reference, in that year a union carpenter in Chicago made less than half that amount, at just over $110 per month.[146] Nearly a half century after the war had ended, close to 75,000 widows and dependents also were receiving pensions.[147] Monthly payments for widow and dependent pensions were much lower than for invalided veterans. Sophia Boner, for example, was the mother of Private James Boner, who died of wounds at the Battle of Tolopotomy Creek in May 1864.[148] James Boner was unmarried and childless, making his parents his heirs. At the time of her death in 1910, Sophia Boner was receiving a mother's pension of $10 per month.[149] While $10 went much further in the early twentieth century than today, Boner's pension did not come close to compensating for the loss of her son's labor—or his life. Sophia Boner appears to have died destitute, with her daughter appealing to the Pension Bureau to pay her mother's funeral expenses.

The war wounded, and their families, paid a heavy toll. Amputees and other wounded veterans were not able to resume their previous jobs; their ability to be economically productive members of society was often greatly diminished, a fact that threatened the social fabric of the country. Invisible war injuries, including chronic pain, psychological trauma, and opium addiction, could be just as debilitating, and those so injured usually did not get the sympathy evoked by the signature "empty sleeves" of many Civil War veterans.[150] While the post–Civil War image of the lolling, rich pensioner may have been accurate in some cases, other veterans and their families clearly struggled financially. This contrast highlights enduring questions around veterans' benefits—who deserves what, when, and how? Caring for veterans—medically and financially—is an inevitable cost of war, and rightly so. The decision to go to war should, therefore, be conditioned by that inevitability.

Conclusion

Over 600,000 soldiers died during the four years of the Civil War. In the decades after, millions of dollars were paid out in pensions. The United States had never before in its young history reckoned with costs such as these. In 1974, economic historian Gerald Gunderson estimated the financial costs to the Union and to the Confederacy at over $2 billion each ($2.188 billion for the Union and $2.017 billion for the Confederacy): "The cost to the North represents nearly a full year's income while that to the South is nearly as large as the total income they could have earned if peace had prevailed during the duration of the war."[151] As Drew Gilpin Faust notes in describing the politics of post–Civil War pensions, "The meaning of the war had come to inhere in its cost."[152] While the ambiguities within the casualty data—many of which continue to this day—present challenges to precise calculations, the nature and scope of the costs are unobscured, and were clearly a function of the era as well as the war itself.

With the hindsight of more than 150 years, it is easy to see that Civil War medicine suffered from many flaws. Poor preventive care meant that about two-thirds of Civil War fatalities came from disease, rather than from being injured in fighting. A lack of understanding of the germ theory of disease, unavailability of imaging tools such as X-rays, and the complete absence of blood transfusion meant that many lives that would have been saved today were lost, even when soldiers were lucky enough to receive the best medical care of the time. At the same time, amid these many failures, the Civil War prompted some remarkable advances in war medicine. Over the course of the war, a proper ambulance system was created, and its legacy continues today. Nurses were recognized as crucial to medical care in war, paving the way for a new profession for women both on and off the battlefield. And hospitals became a regular feature of war and, ultimately, in civilian life in the United States.

The direct human toll of the Civil War can be counted mostly in terms of fatalities. The Union's wounded-to-killed ratio—a statistic I will use throughout this book—was approximately 2:1.[153] This statistic tells us that approximately two soldiers were wounded for every one killed in battle. Of course, given that disease was the war's main killer, the overall fatality rate for Civil War military personnel was extremely high. One in five Union troops died. The wounded-to-killed ratio for the Confederacy was likely lower but the overall fatality rate higher, with a greater proportion dead of illness and wounds. The loss to these soldiers' families was incalculable.

All these factors—the state of medicine in 1861 as the war began, the military medical logistical revolution forced by the war, and the financial and political demands of veterans after the war—set a baseline for understanding the human and financial costs of war in the United States. The Civil War is crucial to my argument not only because of its magnitude but also because it occurred on the cusp of a revolution in medicine. The medical baseline of the Civil War suggests a sharp contrast with today, when military personnel are much less likely to die, even in the face of more severe wounds from more advanced weaponry. The baseline for veterans' benefits tells a somewhat different story; if the Civil War case provides a low baseline for military medicine, it also provides a high baseline for veterans' benefits. The human toll of the Civil War was enormous. But the downstream costs were due more to an expanded system of veterans' benefits than to a proportionally high number of wounded survivors. By setting subsequent wars against this case, we begin to be able to observe the interplay between these two components of the costs of war.

One of the most poignant reminders of the long tail of the costs of the Civil War is the story of Irene Triplett. Triplett was the daughter of Mose Triplett, the Confederate turned Union soldier who we met at the start of the chapter. Her mother was decades younger than her father when they married;

arrangements where younger wives would care for aged veteran husbands in the expectation of a widow's pension were not uncommon at the time. Mose Triplett was eighty-three years old when his daughter Irene was born. When he died, his pension passed to his widow and then, after her death, to his daughter. Irene Triplett was the last recipient of a Civil War pension. She died in June 2020—155 years after Lee surrendered to Grant at Appomattox.[154]

2
From Pestilence to Penicillin
The World Wars

Disease remained the overwhelming cause of death in war for decades following the Civil War. The so-called Indian wars saw very few US troops wounded in battle, but many were laid low—or killed—by disease, frostbite, and malnutrition. The same general principle held true for the Spanish-American War of 1898, which was infamous for rampant typhoid epidemics, especially in stateside military camps. While the germ theory of disease had taken hold on both sides of the Atlantic by the end of the nineteenth century, US military medical personnel were slow to embrace it wholesale. They still did not understand, for example, that yellow fever was spread by the *Aedes aegypti* mosquito or that typhoid prevention required more than clean drinking water.

The late nineteenth century wars also differed in kind from the Civil War. Rather than ranks of soldiers facing each other across a battlefield, guerrilla warfare was more frequent in the United States' westward expansion. As Army historian Mary Gillet put it: "Just as the experiences of the Civil War were irrelevant to those of the Indian wars, so, too, were the challenges of the Indian wars irrelevant to the demands of modern large-scale warfare."[1] Guerrilla warfare was also standard in the various theaters of the Spanish-American War and, especially, in the subsequent US occupation of the Philippines.

Thus, by the time World War I began, the US military medical establishment had lost its muscle memory for large-scale conventional warfare. On one hand, lessons had been learned about disease prevention, including yellow fever and, especially, typhus. And new tools, such as X-rays and microscopes, were now regularly used to visualize injuries and identify pathogens. On the other hand, it had been decades since the United States had had to evacuate the wounded across a long expanse of land, or stand up the surgical capacity to treat thousands of wounded soldiers.

The world wars ushered in a new era of warfare. Mechanization, as well as the use of weapons such as gas, made war much more deadly. But the early twentieth century also brought a new era of medicine. Knowledge of the germ theory was crucial—eventually—in reversing the proportion of soldiers dying from disease as opposed to wounds. What is more, US medical outcomes in the world wars saw improvement not only in comparison to the Civil War but also relative to each other: military medicine in World War II was much more effective than in World War I. Part of the reason for this relative improvement was the fact that US participation in the Second World War was years longer than its participation in the First World War. Doctors, in other words, had more time to make mistakes and then learn from those errors. But just as important, if the advancement of medicine prior to World War I was slow and cumbersome, the advancement across the world wars was fast and remarkable, saving lives that would have been lost in the past and producing new and unique cohorts of veterans.

Prewar Assessments of the Costs of War

The fact that the United States entered the First World War so late was partly a function of concern about the costs of war. This concern was a legacy of the Civil War pensions system.[2] There was a general desire, as Beth Linker shows, to avoid creating a new generation of pensioners. While concern about long-term costs is evident in congressional debates around the US declaration of war in April 1917, the contours of the attenuated financial burden of war are vague. Members of Congress expressed concern about the "enormous cost" of the war and increased cost of living and war taxes, but with few numbers attached.[3]

By contrast, numbers were abundant in the troop estimates and funding bills coming from Congress pertaining to the immediate financial demands of war. Representative Edward Browne of Wisconsin, for example, estimated that up to 1 million troops might be needed.[4] Most of the projections focused on war finances for the direct costs of war. The 1917 national defense appropriations bill allocated $5 billion.[5] Ultimately, though, the year and a half of fighting cost over $25 billion, which was financed through bonds and taxes.[6]

The possibility of war fatalities and casualties appears not to have been estimated in great detail prior to World War I. The General Staff—the office within the War Department charged with aiding the secretary of war's chief of staff with planning and organization—was understaffed, and though it had been working on war planning documents in the years prior to the United States' entrance into the war, many if not most of these plans were incomplete and based on what were ultimately inaccurate assumptions.[7] In general, postwar analysts viewed the United States as woefully underprepared for the war.[8]

This is not to say that war planners had completely forgotten the long-term consequences of past wars; indeed, the United States was still paying the costs of the Civil War, especially when it came to veterans' benefits. If anything, the overriding goal was to avoid replicating that system. But the solutions were suboptimal. One attempt to soften the financial blow of caring for the war's eventual veterans, implemented at the start of the war, was an alternative to the pension system—"war risk insurance." Under this system, soldiers paid into a government fund and their dependents would receive an allowance during deployment, as well as life and disability insurance in the event of death or injury. Parallel to the institution of the war risk insurance program, the United States decided to invest in the physical rehabilitation of wounded soldiers. The theory, buttressed by an overconfident medical community, was that injured troops could be made good as new. As historian John Kinder notes in his study of disabled veterans, World War I was expected to produce few casualties partly because of advances in medicine.

> As the nation girded itself for battle, scores of newspapers, magazines, and military publications offered up a similar message: that the Great War was, in fact, becoming safer and that, by the time US troops entered the line of fire, combat would be little more dangerous than civilian life. Led by military physicians, government pundits, and pro-war journalists, the campaign to frame World War I as a "safe war" was part of a larger ideological crusade—emerging in the late nineteenth century and culminating in the postwar rehabilitation movement—to eliminate mass casualties from the ledger of American war-making.[9]

Therefore, there would be no need for disability-based pensions. Orthopedic surgeons and physical therapists became integral to the chain of recovery. The US government invested hundreds of thousands of dollars in rehabilitation hospitals, at the military's behest. As Linker puts it, "Rehabilitation proponents aimed to rid the nation of 'war's waste,' a turn of phrase that referred to the human remains of war as well as to the economic cost that the nation had to endure after the battle was over."[10]

The belief that military medicine could save the country from a new generation of World War I pensioners was unjustified, to say the least. Badly embarrassed by the typhoid epidemic of the Spanish-American War, which killed 1,590 soldiers (more than were killed in battle in Cuba),[11] the Medical Department in the years prior to the First World War was understaffed, undersupplied, and poorly trained. In 1907, Army Surgeon General Robert M. O'Reilly complained, "This office is constantly embarrassed by demands for medical officers that can not be supplied, and little can be done in the way of preparedness for great emergencies with a personnel that is not sufficient to meet the little emergencies that occur in peace."[12] A 1916 pamphlet titled *The Fate of Our Wounded in the Next War* lamented the state of medical training and anticipated a breakdown of the Army Medical Corps in World War I similar to that of the Spanish-American War.[13] Perhaps most important, even the advances in medical logistics made during the Civil War had been forgotten: "All that was painstakingly achieved during the Civil War, from battlefield evacuation schemes and echeloned hospital care in divisional field hospitals, to the establishment of a well-oiled machine of hospital supply distribution, had disappeared."[14] Partly as a consequence of poor planning, the government was unpleasantly surprised by the cost of veterans' healthcare after the war.[15]

The twenty-three years between the end of World War I and the country's entrance into World War II saw improvements in war planning and casualty estimation. For example, a 1936 report on war casualties provides tables of estimates for a future conflict. According to the report: "There appears to be no method for computing loss replacements on record.... It is believed that some system should be adopted and made a matter of record for future use." By design, the assumptions were based on the kinds of casualties incurred, and medicine available, during World War I, with a focus on victims of gas attacks and gunshot wounds.[16] While preparing to fight the last war is a perennial—and even understandable—practice, it was clear during the interwar period that the next war would be different. Mechanization was now a given. Armed and armored tanks, which saw limited use in World War I and greater use in the Spanish Civil War of 1936–39 (to which the United States had sent military observers), were clearly going to play a major role in the next war. One implication of this shift was that artillery would be a greater factor in the next war compared to the last. Nonetheless, a 1938 analysis was likewise based on World War I data and assumptions, although it did make some updates, such as the inclusion of possible casualties from fighting in the air given the recent creation of the Army Air Forces—the predecessor organization of today's US Air Force.[17] Just a few months prior to the United States' entrance into the war, a conference of the War Plans Division of the War Department General Staff estimated a 15 percent attrition rate for aircrews, based on the British experience in the war thus far.[18]

These estimates, limited as they were, seem to have had little effect on World War II war planning. In the months prior to the attack on Pearl Harbor, the War Department created numerous documents, such as the various RAINBOW plans and the "Victory Program," which were clear improvements over similar documents prior to World War I. They included more robust estimates of troops needed, although—once again—much less attention was paid to casualties and losses.[19] For war planners, casualties mattered in terms of how many men could be brought to the fight—not in terms of how to care for these men in the short or long term. To underline the point that the requirements of caring for casualties were poorly assessed at the start, the number of military medical personnel requested was based on World War I numbers, rather than the needs of World War II.[20] Medical equipment was "of 1918 vintage."[21] And as medical personnel were setting up a hospital in Bataan in 1941, they opened crates containing "surgical gowns wrapped in newspapers dated 1917."[22]

More systematic attention was paid to casualty estimates prior to World War II than had been done before World War I, but World War I planners had a better handle on the scope, if not the amount, of the future financial burden of war. In neither case did military planners or policy makers have the foresight to predict the long-term costs of war due to improvements in medicine or possible changes in veterans' benefits. This gap was very much reflected in military medical preparedness, or the lack thereof. Military medical preparation for World Wars I and II was at best along the lines of fighting the last war and at worst involved forgetting key lessons from the previous conflict.

Bodies at War

Compared to the Civil War, twentieth-century medicine narrowed the range of illnesses soldiers suffered in the world wars. In part, this was due to a broader set of immunizations, but it was also a function of significantly improved disease prevention and treatment. The global 1918 flu pandemic was, of course, an important exception to this trend. The range of injuries sustained, on the other hand, widened considerably, with the advent of gas attacks, tank warfare, and aerial bombardment. Battlefield medicine improved, to be sure, but could only be delivered to those who survived what were increasingly devastating injuries.

Soldiers, Doctors, and Disease

The illnesses of past wars loomed large for military medical personnel in the world wars. World War I physicians, remembering the lessons of the Spanish-American War, were diligent in administering the new, mandatory typhoid vaccine.[23] Similarly, at the start of the Second World War, doctors prepared vigilantly for the outbreak of a new respiratory pandemic like the 1918 flu, which killed more than 50,000 US soldiers and sailors.[24] But in neither war was past prologue. Sometimes the disruption was due to interwar innovations, such as new immunizations. Other times it was due to changing circumstances. Different theaters of war, for example, exposed military personnel to different pathogens. In the early twentieth century, disease was still the main killer in war. In World War I, more US military personnel died from tuberculosis than from combat injuries.[25] By the end of World War II, the United States had unequivocally reversed its historical wounded-to-*ill* ratio, which had previously consistently seen more soldiers dying from illness than from wounds. As Norman Kirk, who served as surgeon general during the war, put it somewhat gleefully in 1945: "A division of 10,000 men would experience 156 deaths per annum from disease (excluding injuries) in the last war, whereas in this war the division would lose only six men by death from disease, a reduction greater than 95 per cent!"[26] World War II was the first US war where the ratio of death from disease to deaths from battle casualties was less than 1 (it was 0.07:1), and the reason was clear: "improved control of acute infectious disease."[27]

Advances in preventive medicine were crucial to this reversal. At the start of the Civil War, the only vaccine available was for smallpox. Fifty years later, soldiers were vaccinated against smallpox and typhoid fever. In addition to immunizations, understanding of the germ theory of disease led to new practices around sanitation. Towns near US base camps were "cleaned up" by the US Public Health Service (USPHS).[28] Soldiers in World War I were punished for relieving themselves in the trenches.[29] Standing orders required a safe water supply, the building of fly-proof latrines, and that cooks wash their hands.[30] To be sure, these practices were not always followed. Sometimes the basic circumstances of war made compliance difficult. As Lt. Stanhope Bayne-Jones of the US Army Medical Corps wrote his aunt in 1918, "Living on a recent battlefield is not pleasant!"

> The litter of excreta, dead animals and dead bodies—Bosch [German soldiers] unburied in this sort of festering summer weather with the flies like plagues—is what we've gotten used to—but it is a great worry to a doctor. Because of the shelling it is hard to clean up the place.[31]

Concerns about sanitation were directly related to the massive task of providing food for military forces. While previous wars fought in Europe were famous for foraging armies, the US Army shipped most of the food its soldiers consumed across the Atlantic during both world wars.[32] Doing so allowed some control over rations, including nutritional content and caloric intake.[33] The Army's version of appropriate, though, was not always pleasing to the palate. As a World War II Army report noted: "The American army was unquestionably better fed than any in history. However, feeding in combat can never be like that in garrison or cantonment, nor remotely like home cooking. Field rations must be non-perishable, compact, and easily carried by the individual soldier."[34] World War II B-rations—canned and dehydrated foods prepared on the move and meant to be consumed in the absence of refrigeration—were particularly unwelcome, but sometimes were all that was to be had.[35] As a pharmacist's mate on the Pacific island of Peleliu put it:

> But you can't go without food very long and fight at the same time. One of the biggest problems we had was trying to get men to eat who wouldn't. I don't remember what our exact words were. I think I said, "We're not going to get anything better, fellas, so you might as well eat what you've got." There were always rumors that more K-rations and C-rations were going to be brought in or something better was coming up to us. I think these rumors did more damage than anything. Something better didn't come along and we had to eat what we had.[36]

Even so, the food available was more nutritious and better prepared than in previous wars. Milk, for example, was now pasteurized before it was given to troops.[37] While gastrointestinal illness remains a reality of war even today, gone were the hundreds of thousands of cases of "alvine flux" that afflicted soldiers in the Civil War.

In addition to cutting down on gastrointestinal illness, the country's relatively short participation in World War I meant that US forces did not suffer outbreaks of rat- and louse-borne illnesses such as "trench fever," which afflicted thousands of British and French soldiers.[38] Instead, the major disease plaguing US forces in the Great War was influenza. The so-called Spanish flu of 1918 was in fact likely to have first spread in a US military barracks in Kansas.[39] Newly recruited troops from different parts of the country thrown together in poorly ventilated quarters provided a fertile breeding ground for the virus. The number of cases grew rapidly. In late July 1918, seventy-seven members (about 2 percent) of the 5th Artillery Brigade had been stricken. One month later, more than 6 percent of the brigade was ill; that percentage then more than quadrupled, with significant fatalities.[40] During one week in the autumn of 1918, four out of every 1,000 US soldiers in stateside camps died from influenza; it was further estimated that at least one-quarter of Army personnel and up to 40 percent of Navy personnel had influenza at some point during the war.[41] Apparently healthy troops were shipped to Europe, and shipboard outbreaks were common. Naval estimates suggested that nearly 9 percent of all soldiers on transport ships came down with the flu.[42] The medical officer of one such ship estimated at least 2,000 cases on the voyage.[43] The medical staff was not immune: "Doctors and Nurses were stricken by the disease and thus became not only unable to aid but also an added burden to the overworked medical personnel. Every available medical officer, nurse, and hospital orderly was utilized to the limit of endurance."[44] Indeed, many nurses died from influenza on the transatlantic journey.[45]

The Great War and the 1918 pandemic were deeply and causally intertwined. Had it not been for the extensive transatlantic travel associated with the war, the pandemic would have spread to Europe much more slowly. In the same way that globalization—and, especially, the relative cheapness of air travel—facilitated the spread of COVID-19 around the globe, the war itself became a vector for disease in 1918.

Ultimately, estimates suggest that 50 million people globally died from the 1918 pandemic.[46] For comparison, to date, over 6.8 million people have died from COVID-19.[47] Adjusted for world population, about 2.7 percent of the global population died from the 1918 influenza outbreak, while COVID-19 is estimated to have directly killed less than 1 percent of the world's population today.[48] While vaccines have blunted fatality rates from COVID-19, no such medicines were available in the early twentieth century. Doctors understood bacteriology but not virology, and antibiotics were not yet available.[49] The virus ultimately ebbed to the point that it became an annual flu; by 1945 annual flu shots were available across the United States, although they had already been used in the military during World War II.[50]

Advances in immunology in the interwar period meant that US troops were much better protected against disease than their predecessors in World War I. In addition to the protections against smallpox and typhoid fever, World War II military personnel were vaccinated against tetanus and yellow fever. Depending on theater and circumstance, soldiers in World War II also could be inoculated against cholera, plague, typhus, and diphtheria.[51] US forces in the Second World War, though, served for longer and in a much wider variety of places. Malaria, trench foot, and sexually transmitted diseases (STDs)—especially syphilis and gonorrhea—beset troops such that entire platoons could be debilitated at once. Another key distinction between the world wars was that the duration of US participation meant that medicine had time to advance during World War II in ways it did not during the First World War.

Consider malaria. As discussed in the previous chapter, malaria was endemic to the southern United States. None of the theaters of war where US troops fought in World War I were malarial. But malaria presented an enormous challenge in World War II, especially in the Pacific. As Albert Cowdrey, a major historian of World War II military medicine, puts it, "A good case can be made that malaria was *the* disease faced by American forces in World War II."[52] According to an official medical history of the war in the Pacific, by January 1943

> ninety percent of the 1st Marine Division acquired the disease.... From 1 November 1942–13 February 1943 hospital admissions for malaria from Army units alone averaged 420 per 1,000 troops per year. Malaria so depleted some units that General Vandergrift ordered doctors *not* to excuse soldiers with temperatures of 103F or less from frontline duty or patrol missions.[53]

Malaria was also a challenge in the Mediterranean. During the invasion of Sicily, for example, "malaria cases outnumbered battle wounds."[54] The same held true in early battles for the Solomon Islands; in Guadalcanal, entire units fell to malaria.[55]

As the war went on, malaria numbers decreased. This was not due to changes in environment; if anything, US troops were more likely to be present in malaria-endemic areas later in the war. Instead, what changed were prevention and control measures.[56] The overall malaria control program had three key elements. First, the area would be treated for mosquitoes. This treatment involved spraying the newly developed insecticide dichloro-diphenyl-trichloroethane, more commonly known as DDT. Developed during the war, DDT saw increasing use by 1943 and was deemed extremely effective in preventing malaria as well as typhus; malaria rates decreased by as much as 80 percent after malaria control units sprayed an area with DDT.[57] Second, troops were prescribed Atabrine (quinacrine hydrochloride) prophylactically. Atabrine was the mid-twentieth century's version of the quinine used in the Civil War. While quinine might have been preferable, Japan had prohibited the export of Javanese cinchona, thus cutting the world off from a major source of quinine's essential ingredient.[58] The bigger problem, however, was that troops did not want to take Atabrine. Side effects included nausea, vomiting, headaches, loss of appetite, skin yellowing, and diarrhea, especially in the first few days. There were also rumors that it was toxic and could cause impotence.[59] An orange-colored shirt stain was a telltale sign of noncompliance, as troops would store their unswallowed pills in their shirt pockets.[60] In response to noncompliance, doctors adjusted the dosage, from two pills once a week to half a tablet a day; this change alleviated the unpleasant side effects somewhat.[61] Military commanders also threatened to punish officers whose men did not take Atabrine.[62] But neither solution was perfect, and malaria persisted as a challenge throughout the war. Third, troops who contracted malaria were treated with Atabrine and, if their fever was high enough, a saline infusion.[63] But treatment did not necessarily translate into a recusal from duty. At times, the number of troops suffering from malaria was so great as to potentially impair military effectiveness. For example, during the landing in Sicily, soldiers with a fever of less than 101 degrees were sent back to their units rather than kept in the overcrowded infirmary.[64] Additional measures included selecting campsites that were not (or were less) mosquito-infested, draining standing water, and using bed nets.[65]

As a result of these interventions, malaria rates declined dramatically. Cowdrey reports that "in the first six months of the control program, the [Pacific] theater malaria rate in American troops fell from an average of 970 admissions per 1,000 men per year to 148."[66] It is challenging to assess these numbers because cases depended greatly on when and where troops were concentrated. Winter in Italy saw few cases of malaria, but cases exploded in the summer. And as the war went on, the United States devoted increasing resources to the Pacific theater, especially once significant advances had been made in North Africa and Western Europe. Thus, malaria numbers toward the end of the war reflect a military focus on the tropics rather than a medical failure; without DDT, Atabrine, and malaria control units, both rates of malaria and the likelihood of an Allied defeat would have been significantly higher.

Another illness—really, an injury—that was common to both world wars was trench foot. Similar to frostbite, trench foot was classified as an injury that emerged from cold and wet conditions, and it was exacerbated by the compromised circulation to the foot that came with tightly laced boots.[67] "The soldier's feet would swell, turn pale, and become clammy to the touch. Numbness and often agonizing pain rendered the man unable to walk."[68] The best solution was preventive. Soldiers needed to have dry socks and shoes, and also to have their feet inspected regularly. Perhaps surprisingly, given that the First World War is famous for trench warfare, trench foot was a bigger problem for US troops in World War II. One reason for this discrepancy is the timing of the US entrance into World War I; by the time the United States joined the fight, forces were needed more among the trees of Belleau Wood than in the trenches.[69] Even though trench warfare was much less common in World War II, the name "trench foot" stuck to the condition. It was especially common in colder climates, and the winter of 1944–45 was the coldest in Europe for years.[70] There were a number of trench foot casualties from the Battle of Ardennes; the official medical history of the European Theater of Operations reported that "one company of the 11th infantry had only 14 men available for duty, and the chief cause of ineffectiveness was trenchfoot."[71] Likewise for the invasion of the Italian peninsula; Anzio in 1943–44 was cold and wet, and medical staff treated hundreds of cases of trench foot.[72] Unlike malaria, however, there were few innovations in the treatment of trench foot during the world wars. Once available, penicillin could be administered. But amputation was also a distinct possibility.[73] The Army made significant investments in research on protective footwear, but these were uniformly unsuccessful. One such experiment, the "shoepac," was a cure at least as bad as the disease; after wearing it for several days, study participants developed "shoepac foot."[74] As Maj. Gen. Paul Hawley, command surgeon of the European Theater of Operations in World War II, put it, "The plain truth is that the footwear furnished US troops is, in general, lousy."[75] While some in the military accused the troops of misusing equipment, most agreed that what was provided was insufficient.[76] For example, commanders such as Omar Bradley had hoped that the war would end before the winter of 1944–45. Consequently, commanders failed to order proper winter gear for troops, whose feet bore the brunt of this failing during the Battle of the Bulge.[77] It was not until the Korean and Vietnam Wars that there would be improvement in footgear, although even those improvements were marginal.

The military medical community saw more success in addressing the pressing, and perennial, problem of sexually transmitted diseases. Combining large populations of young men with civilians who are battered—both physically and economically—by war has always translated into prostitution near military camps. While the British and French sought to regulate local brothels in the world wars, the US approach was one of resigned Puritanism. US leadership could not condone prostitution in any form, but it also recognized that soldiers and sailors would frequent the local red light district.

The contribution of STDs to the "ineffective rate"—the percentage of soldiers unavailable to fight due to illness or injury—meant that the Army had to pay attention to the issue. In World War I, an extensive educational campaign may have been somewhat successful in keeping US numbers down compared to the British and French.[78] But concern about troop loss due to STDs was sufficiently high that American Expeditionary Force (AEF) commander Gen. John J. Pershing reviewed daily reports with an eye to rates of venereal disease in units, and demanded additional information if the rates seemed unusually high. Medical specialists were dispatched to Europe. One such physician, urologist Maj. Hugh Young, was asked what he was doing in France. His reply: he was there "to make the underworld safe for democracy."[79]

Quips notwithstanding, solving the problem of troop loss due to STDs seemed like a hopeless cause. Just over 10 percent of troops seen by doctors in the First World War were diagnosed with venereal disease; 6,804,816 man-day losses in the US Army were attributed to STDs during the Great War.[80] Early in World War II, the rate hovered at about 40 per 1,000 men.[81]

Gonorrhea, which was known as "the great crippler" because it caused intense pain while urinating, was easier to diagnose and more immediately debilitating than syphilis. This is partly because the more severe symptoms of syphilis, including brain, nerve, and heart damage, often do not appear for years after infection; the more proximate symptom is a painless ulcer on the genitals, for which troops might not seek treatment (especially if they could be punished for having contracted the disease) and a subsequent rash on the torso.[82] Note that US troops who contracted venereal diseases during the world wars were still eligible for veterans' benefits—and continued healthcare to treat these illnesses—by virtue of their service.

Combined, the prevalence of prostitution and STDs during the world wars demanded a strong medical response. Prophylactics were deemed crucial to this effort. Questions of efficacy aside, levels of use were likely low. In addition to a condom, the World War II prophylactic kit included a syringe that was supposed to be used to inject one's penis with Protargol (silver proteinate—an antibacterial believed to be especially effective in preventing gonorrhea) after intercourse (see Figure 2.1).[83] Troops were also subject to

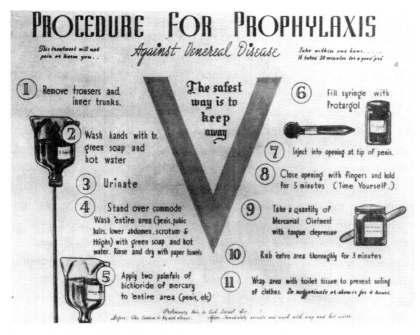

Figure 2.1 World War II Prophylactics Against Sexually Transmitted Diseases
Source: Cosmas and Cowdrey 1992, 145.

"short-arm" inspections by medical officers to make sure the kits were being used.[84]

Continued high rates of STDs, especially in World War II, served as a clear indication of the failure of a prophylactic focus. Penicillin transformed this landscape. The military began to use penicillin in 1943, but widespread use did not start until early 1944. Now soldiers diagnosed with syphilis and gonorrhea could be off duty for days—if that—rather than months while undergoing treatment. The change in recovery time was remarkable. Some doctors, such as Col. Edward Churchill, a consulting surgeon for the US Army and a major figure in World War II US military medicine, disdained troops that had contracted STDs; Churchill would have preferred that troops with combat wounds be prioritized in the use of penicillin.[85] But the physical consequences—and thus the battlefield consequences—were undeniable. For example, in the Italian campaign, which began before the widespread use of penicillin but ended after, the loss exchange ratio—attacker fatalities divided by defender fatalities—between US and Allied attacking troops, on one hand, and German defenders (who did not have access to penicillin), on the other, saw a dramatic decline once penicillin was widely used.[86] Troops that otherwise would have been incapacitated were now available for the fight, and they were in better condition; this combination contributed to victory in Italy. Penicillin, of course, was not offered to Black syphilis patients in the infamous Tuskegee study, even after it was widely available.

While advances in treatment for illnesses like malaria and STDs were dramatic, the military medical community also saw steady progress in treating other wartime diseases. Clothing was treated and DDT used for the purpose of delousing, to prevent the spread of typhus—a practice that was crucial during the liberation of concentration camps in Europe. Measles, mumps, and diphtheria—all common in World War I—saw much lower incidence in World War II; doctors attributed the change to natural immunity gained by childhood infection as well as immunization. And meningitis, a disabling and historically fatal illness that is frequently spread among populations of young people such as those on college campuses or serving in militaries, was, starting in World War II, treatable with sulfonamides. The fatality rate for meningitis dropped from 34 percent to 4 percent between the world wars.[87]

By the end of the Second World War, medical advances in preventive medicine had saved many thousands of lives. Troops were now deployed immunized against a host of diseases that had plagued the armies of the past. The germ theory of disease led to the development of sanitary practices that translated into far fewer gastrointestinal illnesses among military personnel; while not a thing of the past, the "alvine fluxes" that so drastically compromised Union forces in the Civil War merited just a few pages in the medical histories of the world wars, rather than the full volume in the six-volume official medical history of the Civil War. Antimalarial teams sprayed endemic theaters with DDT as military personnel were prescribed Atabrine prophylactically. And soldiers who did fall ill were much likelier to get better. Penicillin, the "miracle drug" of World War II, treated infections among the wounded but also meant that soldiers who had contracted syphilis and gonorrhea could bounce back much more quickly than before. Soldiers' health had never been so good.

Weapons, Wounds, and Surgery

An unfortunate fact of military history is that human beings have become increasingly inventive, finding more and more effective ways to kill each other. This trend is evident not only in the comparison between the Civil War and the world wars but also between the world wars themselves. The most pronounced change was from guns to bombs; the widespread use of artillery by the early twentieth century inflicted very different types of wounds compared to the damage wrought by rifles in the Civil War. But larger explosions were far from the only difference. The use of gas in the First World War was a new and chilling development. Tank warfare in World War II produced a still different array of injuries. And the far-flung theaters of World War II, combined with the advent of aircraft, meant that ship and air wrecks were much more common in the Second World War than in the First. This is to say nothing of the deadliest weapon of all, the atom bomb, which in the final moments of World War II would be used against civilians, not military personnel, but would nonetheless raise a series of as yet unanswered questions for future military medical practitioners.

In terms of the nature of wounds suffered by military personnel, the most important change over time was the shift from guns to bombs. As Figure 2.2 shows, 91 percent of battle injuries suffered in the Civil War were produced by gunshot, with only 9 percent caused by explosives. While gunshot wounds still accounted for the majority of battle injuries in the First World War, this ratio reversed during World War II, when 73 percent of battle injuries were caused by explosives.

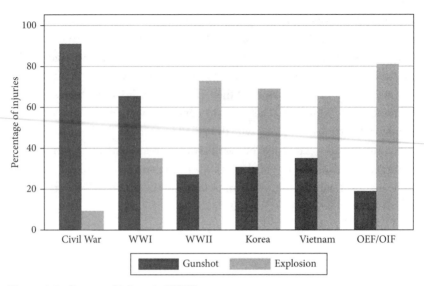

Figure 2.2 Causes of Injury in US Wars
Source: Owens et al. 2008; Brevard, Champion, and Katz 2012, 43, fig. 41.

Howitzers, cannons, hand grenades, and long-range artillery became more frequently used during World War I, and were used against military structures as well as personnel.[88] A single bullet wound—or even multiple bullet wounds—could not compare to the bodily harm wrought by artillery. The machine guns used in the world wars fired many more rounds per minute, often causing massive bodily injuries.[89] Most deaths across the world wars occurred as a result of wounds to the head or trunk, and about two-thirds of cases presented with multiple wounds.[90] Among those surviving to receive medical treatment, the majority—just over 70 percent—in both wars suffered wounds to the extremities.[91] After World War II, in a speech to Denver's Red Cross Blood Center, renowned vascular and cardiac surgeon Henry Swan described artillery wounds he had observed while serving as a captain in the war:

> People do not realize the tremendous size or terrible nature of some war wounds. When a high-explosive shell goes off it is splintered into fragments that whirl through the air and cover a large area. When it goes in it is red hot and it sears and burns. Because it is big and heavy it has a lot of momentum and the body has to take the shock. As such a shell fragment goes in, it takes with it clothing, skin, etc., and carries it into the depths of the body.

I had one soldier who was hit where his pants pocket was, and, scattered throughout the depths of a very deep wound, were parts of his K ration, the key to open the can, and a considerable portion of the "Stars and Stripes" of that morning. When a person suffers that type of injury, if it goes into the chest you have a hole in the chest that you can stick your fist in.[92]

In other words, bombs inflicted multiple different kinds of wounds, often across various parts of the body, in ways that guns did not. A typical victim who might have stepped on a "Bouncing Betty" land mine, for example, could have had his foot pulverized and require amputation.[93] In a grim search for silver linings, one World War II military physician noted: "Thank God for the heat of high-velocity missiles: the main artery in the upper arm, the brachial artery, had been cauterized automatically; otherwise, the man would have bled to death on the field."[94] Maxillofacial injuries also were common in both wars as a result of the shift to explosives.[95] Before-and-after images of such injuries demonstrate the incredible work of reconstructive surgeons.[96] That the case fatality rate (CFR)—the proportion of injured who received care and died—in the world wars improved, despite the increasingly lethal weaponry, is a testament to dramatic advances in military medicine.

Among these advances were improvements in personal protective equipment. During the Civil War, a soldier's uniform offered about as much protection as a pair of jeans and an overcoat. By the early twentieth century (and especially by World War II), one of the two parts of the body most vulnerable to fatal injuries—the head (with the trunk being the other)—was afforded significantly more protection. Helmets returned to the battlefield in the twentieth century. Soldiers began to wear tin helmets in World War I and continued to do so in the Second World War, offering significant protection in comparison to past wars. But helmets were not always used as intended. Maj. Brendan Phibbs reported on his experience in the Second World War: "Lying on the floor, feeling the aid-station building rock under a torrent of high-caliber explosions, waiting for a white-hot fragment to hit and tear, I automatically put my helmet over my crotch; so, I noted, did everybody else."[97] Perhaps more important, helmet design did not always meet the needs on the ground. Evelyn Monahan and Rosemary Neidel-Greenlee relay the story of a World War II doctor who, when told by a visiting Gen. Patton to button the chin strap to his helmet, replied: "Sir, I don't care if you fine me one hundred dollars. I'm a doctor and I can do without the hundred dollars. Don't you know that if I have my chin strap buttoned and a shell hits up here pretty close to us, it will break my neck? So, sir, as soon as you leave, I'm going to unbutton my chin strap again."[98] Nonetheless, helmets were understood to be crucial to survival, so much so that personnel caught without their helmets could be fined.[99] According to Capt. French Moore, "Because of the excellence of the helmets, the bullet was often deflected so that the bullet, instead of penetrating the skull, merely grooved the scalp."[100]

Doctors had more mixed success in dealing with the hallmark weapon of World War I: gas. The Germans used four major types of gas weapons. Lachrymators were primarily eye irritants—tear gases—which produced temporary blindness but did not require evacuation. Sternutators were also nonlethal. They were nasal irritants that could cause short-term sneezing and vomiting. Lung irritants were designed to kill, either by suffocation or by irritating the respiratory system—but because they dissipated quickly, they were hard to deploy effectively. Finally, vesicants, such as mustard gas, were skin irritants that typically caused burns. While not lethal, they were particularly insidious because they could permeate clothing and their effects did not show up until hours after an attack.[101] By using explosive shells as a delivery vehicle for gas, the Germans made gas warfare "one of the most important military developments of the World War."[102] Among those who received medical treatment, over 30 percent had been gassed; nearly 9 percent of US battle injuries leading to death were caused by gas.[103]

Soldiers did have some protection against gas attacks. Gas masks were issued by all major belligerents during World War I. The masks were uncomfortable, but they were widely used once soldiers understood the dangers of a gas attack. Military personnel had to have gas masks fitted and were drilled in their use.[104] Because, however, gas masks were ineffective against mustard gas, the Army began to develop clothing that was also treated against gas. But it was not ready by the time World War I ended. Instead, troops would often carry bars of soap with them to the front so that they could wash off after a mustard gas attack.

The efficacy of gas warfare was striking. Memorialized in paintings such as John Singer Sargent's *Gassed*, which depicts a line of soldiers wearing bandages over their eyes, each man with a hand placed on the shoulder of the man in front of him, presumably en route to an aid station, gas warfare was as effective psychologically as physically. It is perhaps this psychological element—the sense that gas warfare was "out of bounds"—that led to the codification of the 1925 Geneva Protocol for the Prohibition of the Use of Asphyxiating, Poisonous or Other Gases, and of Bacteriological Methods of

Warfare.[105] Despite their efficacy, chemical weapons have not seen significant use in war since World War I, although the Allies were certainly prepared for a reprise in the Second World War.[106]

Another injury specific (although not unique) to World War I was gas gangrene. Caused by anaerobic bacteria that were widely present in the heavily manured fields upon which the war was fought, gas gangrene produced swelling and infection. The weaponry used in World War I often created small entry and exit wounds, which preserved the anaerobic conditions that allowed *Clostridium welchii* bacteria to thrive.[107] The mortality rate for patients with gas gangrene was exceptionally high.[108] If the patient stood a chance at survival, often the only treatment was amputation of the infected limb.

Advances in transportation also led to new weapons of war; these, in turn, presented new medical problems. Tanks, for example, came into widespread use in World War II. While the British experimented with tanks in the First World War, it was not until the Second that armored warfare came into its own. The combination of speed, strength, and protection promised by tanks made them integral to the war; one has only to look at the Blitzkrieg to see how effectively they could be used. But tanks were by no means impervious. Almost as soon as tanks came upon the scene, so did anti-tank weapons, exposing the vulnerability of armored vehicles.[109] Tank crews operated in close, hot conditions, surrounded by metal. The Sherman tanks used by US forces were particularly vulnerable to explosion both because of relatively thin armor and because the tank ran on gasoline—which is much more flammable than diesel.[110] In the worst-case scenario, all that would be left of a victim would be his bones and teeth. Relaying the story of finding the remains of a tank crew, combat surgeon Maj. Brendan Phibbs wrote:

> "So little, all there was left, out of a whole person. I knew him. Friend of mine named Kenny. Why is it so little, what's left?"
>
> "Water," I explained, "we're mostly water so there isn't much left when you burn."
>
> "Kenny, like a tiny black, old mummy, and the teeth white. The white teeth make it much worse. Why aren't they black too?"
>
> "They're different stuff, enamel. Last thing to burn."[111]

Any survivors would suffer extensive burns—even their lips could be so burned that they could not drink. Burn treatment thus quickly became critical to military medicine. In extreme cases, the only option was to wrap the victim's entire body in bandages.[112]

Burns were also a frequent injury at sea when fires would break out in contained areas, especially during an attack. While the use of ships in war was not new, the United States had never engaged in maritime warfare as extensively as it did in World War II—nor has it since. Similar to tanks, the loss of a ship is catastrophic, and often translates into near-complete loss of life, because of both the dangers of the ocean and the challenges—indeed, often the impossibility—of evacuation. Pearl Harbor saw the first such casualties. Even with access to land-based medical facilities—and despite the coincidence of the Pearl Harbor attack with an American Medical Association conference on Oahu[113]—the US military famously lost more than 2,300 personnel, with another 1,110-plus wounded.[114]

There are, of course, stories of shipwreck survival. Lt. Walter Burwell relayed one such story, when the *Suwannee*—on which he served as ship's doctor—was sunk by the Japanese in October 1944. The men had to share life jackets. Despite Burwell's insistence that they not drink salt water, many did; they would fall ill and become "maniacal."[115] While Burwell did not see any sharks, every morning until they were rescued the number of sailors in the group declined.[116] The uniqueness of Burwell's story is the exception that proves the rule; fatality rates for downed ships were generally quite high. The Navy reported nearly 37,000 combat deaths in the war.[117] Recognizing these challenges, naval medicine therefore focused more on problems it could solve, such as treatment of burns.

Aircraft are similar to ships in that a catastrophic attack typically—indeed, by definition—means that the crew is lost. Even apart from attacks, though, flying created a host of medical issues. Limited access to oxygen at high altitudes was chief among these.[118] Hypoxia meant that pilots could suffer confusion or shortness of breath, both of which would compromise them in a dogfight. Flying high also meant flying cold—fighter jets were not fully heated yet flew to 25,000 feet—so hypothermia and cold injuries among airmen were quite common. Carbon monoxide poisoning was another danger in flight. And fatigue in the air was potentially much more deadly than on the ground (or even at sea), presenting military doctors with another challenge in keeping airmen alive and healthy. Maj. Gen. David N. W. Grant—the Air Surgeon during World War II—described the problem as follows:

Low temperature is second only to low pressures as a physiological hazard in high-altitude flight. Anoxia is far swifter than subzero cold but no less deadly. High-altitude frostbite, principally of the hands, constituted a leading cause of battle casualties in heavy bomber operations over Europe, where temperatures of 40 to 50 degrees below zero are "normal" between 25,000 and 30,000 feet altitude. Waist, tail and ball turret gunners in the more exposed portions of the bomber suffered most, since they did not have the benefit of the cabin heating system. A few minutes' exposure of the hand, such as in clearing a machine gun of a jam, is sufficient to produce frostbite, and two or three frozen fingers will incapacitate a gunner as effectively, and sometimes as permanently, as the loss of a whole arm.[119]

Extensive research was conducted to guard against frostbite, leading to an electrically heated suit that could be plugged into the plane. As a result of these measures, frostbite aviation casualties fell significantly.[120] The National Research Council developed an "anti-blackout" suit to reduce the risk of carbon monoxide poisoning.[121] To address low-velocity weapons fired at airplanes, early flak jackets were developed.[122] Flak jackets protected the trunk, but they were not used widely on the battlefield until later in the twentieth century, during the Korean and Vietnam Wars.

Once injured, US soldiers in the world wars could be treated with an array of new tools and practices. Civil War doctors often could do little more than make an educated guess about the injuries and illnesses with which they were confronted. With the development of roentgenology—what we call today radiology, or X-ray technology—in the late nineteenth century, visualization took an enormous leap forward. Alongside the use of new devices such as ophthalmoscopes as well as developments in pathology, doctors in World War I were much better informed about their patients' inner landscapes and, therefore, better positioned to treat them with the best medicine of the time. Many of these innovations, though, were only available in general hospitals at the rear. Dissatisfied with the fact that soldiers had to travel so far for imaging, scientist-turned-radiologist Marie Curie traveled across the front with a mobile X-ray lab in World War I.[123]

Knowledge of the germ theory of disease extended beyond the preventive medical measures described above, and entered the surgical tent. Operating equipment was now sterilized. As a result, postoperative infection rates declined in the First World War. Antiseptics, however, are not antibiotics, and it was not until the widespread use of penicillin in World War II that doctors could be much more confident that patients would not succumb to an illness after an operation.

Another aid to surgery was the use of twentieth-century anesthetics. In the Civil War, medical personnel anesthetized patients by placing a chloroform-soaked cloth over the top of a cone placed above a patient's nose. During the world wars, additional anesthetics—such as pentothal—were available, and could be given intravenously as well as via new technologies such as Boyle's apparatus—a mask connected to a pump connected to anesthetic solutions.[124] As with many medical tools used in war, though, supplies of anesthetics and analgesics often ran low, requiring creative solutions. For example, when opium—a necessary ingredient of morphine—became difficult to procure in World War I, the military requested that the US Treasury Department provide caches of opium seized from smuggling operations.[125] But morphine carried its own dangers. As wounded soldiers moved through the chain of evacuation, they were vulnerable to unintentional overdose as medics at different stages provided the drug. Edward Churchill wrote about World War II:

> Our aid men were equipped with half-grain tablets of morphine and, not infrequently, a soldier brought in by litter bearers would be given two, three, sometimes more doses because his pain had not been relieved. This meant that he did not have enough circulation (because of blood loss) to absorb the injections which were remaining as depot morphine under the skin. Then when the casualty was warmed and perhaps given plasma to improve the circulation, he would pick up these depots of morphine and exhibit serious morphine poisoning.[126]

Once the danger of morphine overdose was better understood, both the Army and Navy mandated that morphine doses be recorded in some way, either in the patient's chart or by writing "M" on their foreheads.[127]

Anesthetics were important not only for pain management but also to sedate patients undergoing surgery. While not as common as during the Civil War, amputation continued to be a critical treatment for extremity injuries during the world wars. DeBakey estimated that amputations accounted for 0.4 percent of the wounded in World War II.[128] New practices of splinting, and new ways to address extremity wounds in general, saved many limbs. Use of the Thomas splint, for example, dramatically reduced mortality rates for thigh fractures in the British Army during World War I; the Thomas splint was used by the US military through the Second World War, and is still used today.[129] Likewise for developments in vascular surgery and the development of blood vessel banks, also during World War II.[130]

These changes resulted in part from the rise of medical specialization, first evident in World War I. By the early twentieth century, the medical profession had gone well beyond the division between doctors and dentists. Roentgenologists, orthopedists, anesthetists (including nurse anesthetists), neurologists, and psychiatrists were typically present in wartime general hospitals, if not further forward. The availability of this specialized care made medicine more complicated, but also more effective.

Expansion of the military medical community also meant that entrenched interests emerged, often leading to intense debates about appropriate medical practices. One such debate emerged in World War II around the use and efficacy of sulfonamides, or sulfa drugs.[131] Sulfonamides were meant to prevent infection in wounds and could be either ingested by mouth or applied topically. But in early 1944, when penicillin started to be used widely, sulfa drugs were deemed an ineffective antibiotic. Penicillin was the first true antibiotic, a "wonder drug" that did more than help soldiers ill with STDs recover more quickly. It also prevented infection in wounds much more effectively than sulfa drugs; penicillin was effective against bacteria associated with pneumonia, influenza, and staphylococcus infections.[132]

An even more intense controversy emerged in World War II around the question of transfusion. Loss of blood leading to shock has always been a major cause of battle death. Plasma was viewed as a solution to this problem; it was seen as a blood replacement and a backstop against shock. At the start of World War II, dried plasma was the default treatment for blood loss. Because it could be dried and did not require blood typing prior to being administered, it was also extremely convenient.[133] By 1943, however, Edward Churchill was arguing strenuously for the use of whole blood in lieu of plasma.[134] Plasma simply could not provide the red blood cells, which carry oxygen, necessary to counter shock and adequately prepare patients for surgery. As Cowdrey puts it, plasma was deceptive:

> Men who had been brought out of shock with plasma often relapsed and died. They could not tolerate movement, let alone anesthesia and surgery. Deprived of red cells, their tissues underwent a kind of suffocation. And their blood loss often was much greater than anyone had realized, because

blood seeped into the wound and the surrounding damaged tissues, rather than out of the body where it could be observed. In short, the condition of the wounded man was worse than anyone suspected, and the value of plasma was less than almost everybody had supposed.[135]

But Churchill faced strong pushback. The American Red Cross, for example, had made significant investments in dried plasma. The National Research Council also had staked its reputation on plasma.[136]

Undeterred, Churchill launched a program for whole blood in the field. Soldiers would donate locally, although long-term storage was an issue.[137] The effects were remarkable, and remarked upon by military physicians. A Navy corpsman on Iwo Jima noted: "You would get color, pink lips again rather than purple."[138] In advance of the invasion of Anzio in 1944, military doctors who understood the importance of whole blood insisted that the Army ship whole blood to them. They declared—as a kind of ultimatum to ensure sufficient supply—that they would not allow soldiers in the unit to donate blood if the Army failed to deliver blood.[139] Their complaints were heard: a blood bank was created in Naples, and the effects on the battlefield writ large were significant. Both penicillin and whole blood began widespread use by the US military at about the same time—in early 1944, during the Italian campaign—and neither was used by the Germans (who, following the Italian government's surrender to the Allies, became the primary opponent in Italy). The loss-exchange ratio (LER) between US and German forces saw a dramatic decline in the period following the use of penicillin and whole blood in the field compared to the period prior. The average LER at the start of the Italian campaign in fall 1943 was 2.88; nearly three US soldiers died for every German. Starting in 1944, however, the LER reversed, with a mean of .82 and a low of .28 during the battle at Lariano in April, when more than three German soldiers died for every American.[140]

The powers that be were now persuaded of the utility of whole blood. But problems of supply, preservation, and transport remained. The Red Cross stood up a massive blood drive campaign stateside. As whole blood gained acceptance, new refrigeration technologies were developed, such as the medical transport box invented by Dr. Henry Blake, which allowed for longer-term transport and storage.[141] And aircraft were drafted to transport blood on the order of 1,000 pints a day by September 1944.[142] Success was also evident in the field. As Henry Swan wrote to his wife in the immediate aftermath of the Normandy invasion: "The fact that we had blood to give as well as plasma has made the difference between life and death in some of these boys. The organization of that blood bank is somebody's great contribution."[143]

Of course, the use of whole blood was not without its issues, one of which exposed the nature of race relations at the time. Black blood donors were originally turned away.[144] When donations from Blacks were accepted, their blood was segregated and used only for Black soldiers.[145] Racism permeated all aspects of the world wars, from the trials of Black medical personnel described below to the mistaken belief that Black skin was less susceptible to the effects of mustard gas than white skin.[146] Casualty data were still segregated by race, reflecting a continuing belief in physiological differences rather than an acknowledgment that Blacks were simply more likely to receive inferior medical care. Such policies complicated, demeaned, and undermined the medical care received by soldiers in the field.

The list of battlefield medical advances in the world wars is long. In addition to improvements in visualization, anesthesia, antiseptics, and antibiotics, the wars saw new policies regarding the secondary closure and debridement of wounds as well as advances in naval and, of course, aviation medicine. Indeed, many of these changes went hand in hand. Better antiseptic practice and understanding of the germ theory of disease—as well as visualization—convinced doctors to wait before closing wounds, until they were confident that all foreign objects and dead tissue had been excised. Improved understanding of the importance of fluids in the body meant that burns could be treated more effectively with rehydration, including and especially at sea and in the air. The same held true for ensuring that fliers had access to sufficient oxygen (more on this below). Military medical practitioners in the world wars were justified in their pride in performance compared to the US Civil War. But their self-congratulation was perhaps excessive. Soldiers still suffered and died from malaria and hemorrhage at rates that would be unacceptable today. In sum, many more lives had been saved—despite the increased lethality of weaponry and as a result of military medical advancements—than would or could have been saved in the previous century. But the advances to come were greater still.

The Logistics of Medicine

Alongside technical advancements in preventive and battlefield medicine, military medical systems improved during the world wars, with meaningful consequences for the care of soldiers, sailors, and airmen. Nursing expanded and became more formalized. Evacuation practices also saw significant advancements, with the development of new transportation technologies like motorized vehicles and airplanes. But these changes also brought challenges that exposed weaknesses in infrastructure around medical care, if not the military as a whole. As military service expanded to women and nonwhites, sexism and racism loomed large in ways that had clear negative effects on military performance.[147] Separately but at the same time, the development of the Air Force generated bureaucratic tensions that would have implications for military medicine for decades to come.

Evacuation

The challenges engendered by advancements in military medical systems were especially evident in the evacuation procedures. By the end of World War I, an updated version of Jonathan Letterman's Civil War–era evacuation system was firmly in place. The chain of evacuation then endured across the world wars. As shown in Figure 2.3, injured soldiers would be taken first to aid stations near the front line, where they would receive first aid and, if possible, be returned to the line. If they required additional medical attention, they would be transported further down the chain, to hospitals of increasing size and with access to greater expertise and better technology. Many of the stops along the way were either temporary structures or preexisting buildings that had been repurposed as medical facilities. US Surgeon Stanhope Bayne-Jones, for example, describes one of his World War I field hospitals as a "fortified cellar," an improvement upon his previous location, which lacked a ceiling.[148]

Capt. Henry Swan's description of the chain of evacuation in World War II is nearly identical to a description from twenty-five years earlier. Injured soldiers would be taken first to a battalion aid station for first aid, then to a collection point, where they would be delivered to a clearing company to be triaged. Soldiers needing additional care would be sent to a field hospital (which was next to the clearing station), an evacuation hospital (about ten miles from the front), or a general or convalescent hospital much farther back (indeed, some were located in the United States).[149]

What changed was *how* soldiers were transported from one part of the chain to another. Revolutions in transportation meant new kinds of

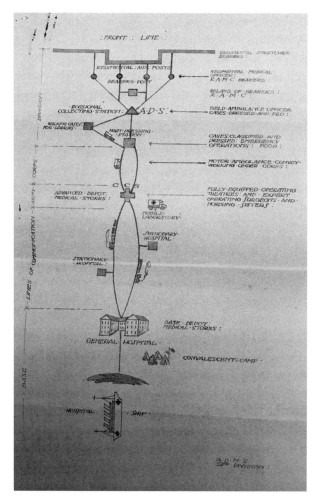

Figure 2.3 Chain of Evacuation in World War I
Source: Stanhope Bayne-Jones Papers, Archives and Modern Manuscripts Collection, History of Medicine Division, National Library of Medicine, Bethesda, MD, MS C 155, Box 8.

ambulances. The most obvious change was that the reliance on horses during the Civil War was replaced, by the end of World War I, with a reliance on motorized ambulances. Like many of the medical advances made in the First World War, the relatively short duration of the United States' participation meant that those responsible for medical transport spent most of their time learning how best to use this new technology.[150] But it quickly became standard; the injured were typically brought to aid posts—the first stop in the chain of evacuation—by litter, then transported via motorized ambulance to the next link and via train to general hospitals.[151]

Even though faster transport conferred clear advantages, it wasn't always an option. Terrain often dictates evacuation practices. The use of motorized ambulances would certainly have been impossible in the trenches of World War I. Stretchers—and stretcher-bearers—were the only way to get the wounded out of the trenches, but doing so posed significant risk. The trenches were narrow and angular, and lines of stretcher-bearers at the top attracted fire from German snipers, as Emily Mayhew notes.[152] Even though US troops engaged in much less trench warfare than the British forces documented by Mayhew, Bayne-Jones recounted several incidents and issues in evacuation of US forces from trenches, from navigating narrow passageways to the lack of litter-bearers to the absence of wooden planks to allow bearers to cross trenches.[153] Similarly, trucks were not always seen as the best solution for evacuation. Sometimes horse-drawn ambulances were better because they could get to harder-to-reach places more easily. But they were also slower and therefore more vulnerable to attack.[154]

Decades later, the Battle of Guadalcanal in World War II saw similarly low-tech innovations: "Medics reinforced Navy issue Stokes litters with planks; to cross ravines, they hoisted them on steel cables strung by the engineers or, using ropes, slid them down muddy slopes like toboggans. Sometimes hospital corpsmen formed a human chain to pull the walking wounded uphill."[155] During Operation TORCH in North Africa, the motorized ambulances considered standard by World War II were useless in the sand; Jeeps—especially "Weasels," which resembled tanks in that they had tracks around their wheels—were much better suited as transport vehicles.[156] Mules were used to transport casualties from challenging terrain in both North Africa and Italy.[157] Even when mechanized ambulances could be used, transport times were less than ideal. In a 1943 letter to a colleague at the Office of the Chief Surgeon of the Army, Dr. Frank Berry described how long it could take for the wounded to reach his evacuation hospital in North Africa:

> How long between time of wounding and arrival at our hospital? Usually 6–15 hours. A very few showed a shorter lapse of time. A minority were in the 15–36 hour period. A very few came to us after having lain on the field for 2 or 3 days. In the northern offensive the wounded were often hard to find and sometimes had to be carried several miles by hand through mountainous country.[158]

At the start of World War II, airplanes were used for evacuation on a limited basis.[159] Initially, aircraft served double duty as troop transports and evacuation vehicles.[160] Thus they were not kitted out for medical evacuation, to save space (nor were they marked with a red cross).[161] Indeed, military leadership did not anticipate the utility of air evacuation. It was not until spring 1944 that specific aircraft were designated and designed for that purpose.[162] Following the invasion of France, air evacuation became so common that it accounted for one-third of cross-Channel evacuation cases.[163] And by January 1945, air evacuation came into its own, having "finally achieved its long promised evacuation rate of over 2,000 patients a month."[164] Air evacuation was a medical advance in several regards. First, it got wounded patients to higher-level care more quickly. Second, some of the injured could not have survived other forms of transportation. Third, often planes could land where motorized ambulances could not reach.

There were two factors—weather and contested airspace—that planes could not overcome. Just days after the invasion of Normandy, bad weather meant that planes could not fly.[165] And air evacuation was not possible at the start of the Anzio invasion because airspace was contested.[166] While these apparently intractable problems limited reliance on air evacuation, they were partly a function of the fact that most of the aircraft used in World War II had fixed wings. Rotary-wing aircraft—helicopters, used more regularly beginning in the Korean War—were better positioned to overcome these obstacles.

Overall, though, military medical personnel clearly preferred air evacuation—when it was available. As World War II went on, doctors began to realize that availability of air evacuation was contingent on the military—and, sometimes, bureaucratic—concerns of the Army Air Forces. Recall that, until 1975, what we know today in the United States as the Air Force was not a separate service but rather a part of the Army. Even during World War II, the Air Force sought independence, and this aim conditioned its position vis-à-vis the Army when it came to evacuation. For example, military missions performed by aircraft were often prioritized over evacuation flights. Likewise, the health and rest of aircrews were put first, meaning that even if planes were available, evacuation flights often did not happen or were extensively delayed. The Army Air Forces also argued that they required their own medical personnel, not only to attend to the specific health needs of personnel such as pilots but also because specialized crews were necessary to monitor patients in flight.[167]

The Army and Navy experienced similar bureaucratic tensions around sea evacuation. Ships used to transport troops from the United States to Europe in the 1940s could then be turned around with the wounded. Like the aircraft, though, most ships were not set up as hospital ships.[168] This issue was further complicated by international humanitarian law. The 1929 Geneva Conventions were meant in part to protect medical personnel and medical transport vehicles from attack. But ships and aircraft that dual-hatted for troop transport in one direction and medical evacuation in the other could not legitimately be said to be out of the fight. The solution was to designate exclusive hospital ships and medical transport planes, but this solution was slow in coming for both military and logistical reasons.

Improvements in transportation technology made doctors understandably impatient to reduce evacuation times. While trauma surgeon R. Adams Cowley is most frequently credited with coining the term "golden hour" in 1976 to describe the optimal window by which injuries should be treated, the concept was in evidence much earlier.[169] Writing in 1944, Churchill referred to a four- to ten-day "golden period" as the "time-lag between initial and reparative surgery."[170] Knowledge of the importance of treatment as soon as possible had also filtered down the ranks, as evidenced by this passage written by Capt. Henry Swan to his first wife:

> The importance of the time lag between the time a man is wounded until he receives definitive surgery has become more and more recognized in recent years. Among the seriously wounded, for the first few hours there is a certain mortality for a given (Army) surgical method;—this is the mortality of the wound itself. After a few hours, 5–8 perhaps, the mortality begins to rise sharply and continues to mount, even though the same surgical treatment is given; this additional mortality, arising from prolonged shock, toxemia, blood loss, infection, etc., is the mortality of *delay* in treatment. It seems strange to us now that this fundamental concept and its vital implications has taken so long to be recognized.[171]

It was, in other words, increasingly understood that fast, safe transport to a facility where a wounded soldier could receive excellent care was his best chance for survival.

Staffing

Once a soldier was evacuated—and, oftentimes, even prior to evacuation—he would be tended to by medical staff, and especially by nurses. Compared to the Civil War, nurses were considered an integral part of military medicine during the world wars, and certainly by World War II. A bill creating the US Army Nurse Corps was passed in 1901; while just over 5,000 nurses served overseas in World War I, ten times that number participated in the Second World War, all of them women.[172] Medical staffing shortages were a constant issue during the war, and nurses filled many gaps. Not only did each nurse oftentimes do the work of several nurses, but they also filled in for doctors with some frequency.[173] From sterilizing bandages to administering medication to assisting in surgery, nurses had become a regular, and essential, part of US military medicine.

The military depended on nurses, but both implicit and explicit sexism meant that it was often difficult to integrate nurses into the military. When special hospitals for women service members were designated at the start of World War II, the surgeon general expected women's sick rate to be higher than men's.[174] Quartermasters were completely unprepared for female military personnel.[175] Uniforms were inappropriate to the climate.[176] Nurses altered army fatigues so that they could wear pants, but had trouble finding shoes that fit properly.[177] Menstrual products were also in short supply. "Feminine products such as sanitary pads were not stocked at most post exchanges and it was up to each individual army nurse to make certain she had a good stand-in—cloth Curity diapers. Where a nurse found and purchased the dozen diapers was totally the woman's responsibility."[178] At the same time, the military insisted that only women could serve as nurses—even when men who were nurses in civilian life joined the force.[179] This restriction may have made it easier to underpay Army nurses and withhold commissioned rank; the situation on both fronts improved with new legislation in 1942, passed with an eye to addressing the challenges of recruiting nurses.[180] While nurses clamored to serve at the front, military leadership was sometimes ambivalent. As Monahan and Neidel-Greenlee write in their history of US Army nursing in World War II: "Eisenhower had strong fears that if the American public discovered that its daughters had gone ashore on D-Day in North Africa, and again in Sicily, there might be such a negative outcry that it would be impossible to assign any army nurses whatsoever to any combat zone."[181] But by the time Allied forces landed on the beaches of Anzio, the tide had turned, so to speak; command had decided that excluding nurses from the landing would be too damaging for morale. According to an official account:

> When the German drive of February was in full swing, and conditions on the [Anzio] beachhead were at their worst, the evacuation of nurses was considered, but only briefly. As a morale factor, their presence was of incalculable value. To remove them would have been very close to an admission of defeat in the eyes of the combat troops.[182]

Ambivalence regarding the role of Black nurses was especially acute, reflecting deep-set attitudes about race in the military. Black nurses were trained separately from white nurses; they also were housed separately, ate separately, and served in all-Black wards. In World War I, trained Black nurses were not even allowed to serve in the war.[183] Segregation was such that separate social events were devised for Black nurses, who also were prohibited from attending dances with white soldiers. Likewise for Black doctors. Deciding whether to hire Black doctors meant deciding whether—really, how—to continue segregation in the Army. Hiring Black medical staff made it easier to maintain wards segregated by patient as well as physician.[184] While these policies shifted during World War II, it is hard not to imagine that the priority given to maintaining segregation compromised care for Black servicemen and -women.

Data Collection

Evidence-based research came into its own during the world wars, especially during (and because of) the United States' longer participation in World War II. Doctors assessed the relative efficacy of sulfonamides versus penicillin, and plasma versus whole blood, using data collected in the field as well as their own experience. The data available allowed a bird's-eye view of progress in military medicine, even in the midst of war. Figures 2.4 and 2.5 below, for example, chart wartime accounts of the differences in actual and expected wound mortality across the Civil War, World War I, and World War II.

At the same time, doctors expressed concern about the quality of data available. Dr. Michael DeBakey, who after the war would become a leading

FROM PESTILENCE TO PENICILLIN 79

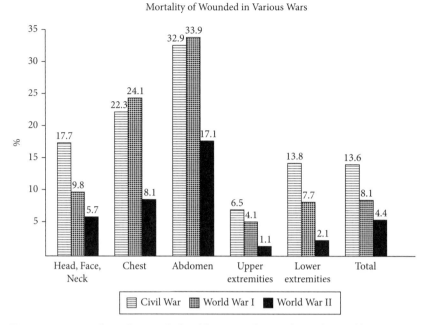

Figure 2.4 Mortality of Wounded Soldiers: Civil War Through World War II
Source: Edward D. Churchill Papers, Countway Library Center for the History of Medicine, Harvard University, H MS/ C 62, Folder 22.

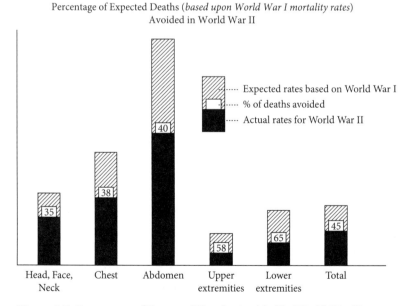

Figure 2.5 Percentage of Expected Deaths Avoided in World War II
Source: Edward D. Churchill Papers, Countway Library Center for the History of Medicine, Harvard University, H MS/ C 62, Folder 22.

cardiovascular surgeon and founder of the National Library of Medicine, complained to Churchill in July 1944 that "although there is fairly complete information on the incidence of communicable disease, data on battle casualties and on non-battle injuries are insufficient in quantity, difficult to collate, and not also of high quality."[185] Doctors did not, however, take issue with the assumptions underlying the continued practice of distinguishing data by race. In a practice carried over from the Civil War, systemic racism continued on view in the labels of casualty columns in the world wars. While doctors in the world wars had improved upon Civil War data collection practices in ways that enabled major updates to medicine in war, they were cognizant of only some of the deficiencies of their data collection efforts.

Veterans' Benefits

Veterans' benefits before, during, between, and after the world wars reflect an enduring tension between the financial burden of supporting war veterans and the obligation to do so. This tension was very much visible in the politics of the times—just as it is today—especially as veterans' service organizations such as the American Legion applied pressure to politicians to support their constituencies. Since World War II, veterans' benefits have been on a mostly uninterrupted upswing. But the period around the world wars saw much more back-and-forth around what such benefits should look like and how much the government owed veterans.

In comparison to the Civil War, veterans' benefits in the twentieth century were initially less generous. The government still had many Civil War veterans on its rolls, and by 1915 the cost of paying those benefits was greater than the cost of the war itself.[186] Conscious of the economic burden of Civil War pensions, many in the United States were reluctant to enter World War I for fear of creating a new generation of pensioners that would stress the national economy.[187] This sentiment warred with a sense of obligation to the future veterans of the Great War. This dilemma was resolved by changing the nature of veterans' benefits. Instead of receiving pensions, veterans could sign up for life insurance, and if they were injured, they would be physically rehabilitated.

Jessica Adler describes a four-part plan for World War I veterans: (1) treatment in military hospitals; (2) disability payments paid out by the Bureau of War Risk Insurance (BWRI); (3) any additional post-discharge treatment to be administered by the United States Public Health Service; and (4) availability of free vocational classes for job retraining for veterans unable to take up their previous occupations due to war injuries.[188] This system encountered bureaucratic challenges almost immediately. The Bureau of War Risk Insurance had been created in 1914 to guard against cargo losses of US merchant vessels. Three years later, coverage was extended to the crew of those vessels. The bureau's preexisting insurance program set the precedent that was meant to govern payments to and care of veterans of the Great War. Both its newness and the rapid change in its mandate led to scrambles and missteps, especially when thousands of veterans applied for healthcare insurance and disability payments seemingly all at once.[189] At the start of the war, the bureau had fewer than fifty clerks on staff. This number had increased to over 3,000 by spring 1918, and they were tasked with processing the 1.17 million applications, primarily for allowances for dependents of deployed soldiers and sailors, that had arrived in the meantime.[190] By the time the war ended in November 1918, the bureau had received an additional 4.15 million insurance applications.[191] As John Kinder explains, postwar wait times for veterans seeking to make claims were unacceptably long; it could take weeks or even months. Consequently, injured and ill doughboys were not receiving the care they needed, and were "languishing" in the corridors of the bureau.[192]

The next link in the chain—the United States Public Health Service, which was tasked with providing veterans' healthcare—was equally weak. The USPHS was significantly older than the BWRI, having been created in 1889. By the early twentieth century, the USPHS was tasked primarily with sanitation and disease prevention. Like the BWRI, it was unprepared for its new task of caring for veterans writ large. USPHS hospitals were understaffed and underequipped, circumstances that produced predictable results; by autumn 1918, their hospitals were "overflowing."[193]

Neither the BWRI nor the USPHS was up to its assigned task. To make matters worse, they jockeyed for position against each other and blamed the other for any failings.[194] In 1921, the two organizations were merged into the Veterans Bureau. While that was a good idea in theory, the bureau's first director, Charles Forbes, was a serial embezzler who threw lavish parties funded by kickbacks received for selling government hospitals to friends at below-market prices. Forbes was ultimately convicted and sent to prison for conspiracy to defraud the government. His crimes were especially scandalous because they wasted funds meant for veterans' care.[195]

While demobilization after World War I did not occur as quickly as soldiers and their families would have liked—partly because the British and French ships that had supplemented US transports were unavailable for the journey home—it did happen at a relatively rapid clip. More than 2 million troops had been deployed overseas. They returned to various ports up and down the East Coast, and were then sent to demobilization centers; the entire process was complete by the one-year anniversary of the war's end.[196] Initially, soldiers evacuated back to the United States were treated at Army medical centers, including at Walter Reed Hospital in Bethesda, Maryland. After 1921, veterans' medical centers were set up across the country via the newly established Veterans Bureau. Discharged soldiers, sailors, and airmen were eligible to receive care for the wounds of war. In response to requests to keep healthcare costs down, doctors working in the system rightly pointed out that they could not limit their care to service-connected disabilities. If a veteran came in complaining of pain from an injury sustained during war but was also found to have tuberculosis, the attending physician could not avoid treating both ailments. This logic helped birth the extensive veterans' hospital system still present in the United States today.

Healthcare for veterans was expensive. By July 1920, the Bureau of War Risk Insurance had paid more than $10 million in compensation claims.[197] In 1922, the US government paid $92 million for veterans' hospitals.[198] The 1923 estimated federal budget allocates twelve percent of total spending to the Veterans Bureau—at a time when the Pensions Bureau was still under the auspices of the Department of the Interior, and therefore represented a separate line item in the budget.[199] The only categories with higher spending than the Veterans Bureau were the military and interest on the public debt. While disability payments from the BWRI were initially not very generous, the monthly amount eventually saw increases as well as expanded eligibility.[200] Liberalizing the compensation system inevitably raised the costs of veterans' care, which began to resemble Civil War–era pensions, albeit on a smaller scale.

As after the Civil War, however, benefits were not distributed equally. African American veterans sometimes received segregated, and substandard, medical care (the Tuskegee Medical Center, later home to the eponymous infamous experiments, was created for African American World War I veterans in the interwar period).[201] Black soldiers receiving treatment in military and veterans hospitals were beaten, especially when (and because) the facilities were not segregated.[202] Veterans service organizations were unwelcoming, closing an important route for advocacy and redress.[203] Racism was clearly visible in rehabilitation practices; artificial limbs, for example, were all white, and clearly designed with white soldiers in mind.[204] It is no wonder that Blacks sought care at lower rates than whites.[205] And women who had served in the war as volunteers, principally as nurses, were denied benefits until years after the armistice.[206]

Even white male veterans felt cheated by their benefits. As Kinder explains, participation in the war had put them back economically compared to those who had not served. Add to this sense of injustice the seismic shifts of the Great Depression a few years later, and the fact that veterans of previous wars had received bonuses, and a cocktail of discontent was well mixed. These sentiments, stirred up by veterans' organizations like the Veterans of Foreign Wars and Disabled American Veterans, led to the Bonus March of 1932, when World War I veterans encamped near Washington, DC, in protest.[207] After two months, the Bonus Marchers were dispatched by Army bayonets and gas grenades; infamously, Gen. Douglas MacArthur pursued them over the Potomac to their camp in the Anacostia Flats, which was then burned.[208]

The US government's violent response to the Bonus March was evidence of a sympathy ceiling for the plight of veterans. By 1930, a quarter of the federal budget was being spent on veterans' care—a callback to the post–Civil War era that World War I planners had so desperately sought to avoid.[209] One reason the number was so high was that disability payments could now be disbursed to veterans who sustained disability in their civilian lives, not just during military service.[210] Franklin Delano Roosevelt, now president, was very much opposed to this kind of pension system for veterans, instead wanting to extend a social safety net to all, not just veterans. On these grounds, he repealed pensions for Spanish-American War and World War I veterans in 1933.[211]

Only a few years later, however, FDR would begin planning for a new cohort of veterans—even before the United States entered World War II.[212] This planning process was meant to address a series of anticipated postwar tensions. On one hand, the government wanted to avoid a flood of demobilized veterans seeking employment. On the other hand, prolonging the demobilization process to prevent this flood would create significant political backlash because it would extend soldiers' time in service until well after the war had ended. Thus, the primary task was to reintegrate soldiers into society as quickly and painlessly as possible without a return to the era of pensions. Temporary unemployment payments, loans for homes and farms, and educational subsidies were the main proposals on the table.

The politics around this new set of proposed veterans' benefits posed a very difficult needle to thread. FDR's New Dealers, recently stymied in their efforts to extend the broad social programs they had created, saw an expansive veterans' benefits system as a window to open when the door to a broader social safety net had been shut. Republicans and southern Democrats—who had shut that door—were concerned about increased government spending and bureaucracy; for example, they feared that educational subsidies would lead to a new agency such as a Department of Education that would interfere unduly with curriculum.[213] Southern Democrats in particular also opposed the egalitarian spirit of the proposal, which would in theory increase the ranks of Black college degree holders and homeowners. The chief aim of veterans' organizations was to ensure that veterans received due care and support.

The American Legion, aided by William Randolph Hearst's media empire, led the campaign for what would eventually become the GI Bill. Two main themes appeared repeatedly in their advocacy. First was the fear of a reprise of the Bonus March, one with millions more armed participants;[214] more generally, the American Legion stoked fears of trained and armed unemployed veterans wreaking havoc around the country. The second theme cast veterans in a softer light and focused on the obligation the country owed to those who had fought so valiantly in the war. These arguments resonated with the public but also with policymakers. New Dealers continued to see an expanded veterans' package as a wedge for greater social programming. Republicans were reassured that the proposed benefits would be limited in time and scope and, moreover, that few veterans would use them. Here, the title of the proposed legislation, the Serviceman's Readjustment Act, is telling: it implied a finite set of benefits, especially when compared with the decades of pensions paid to Civil War veterans in particular.[215]

But the politics around post–World War II veterans' benefits were also different because of the sheer scale of the war—not to mention postwar economic prosperity.[216] And, in contrast to today's political landscape, many members of Congress either were themselves veterans or had sons serving in the war. Politicians understood that, with more than 11 million troops mobilized, it was much savvier to offer benefits that would satisfy soldiers and their families, and also allow veterans to reintegrate into society more easily after the war.[217]

Discussion over the right combination of benefits to offer was heated.[218] Should benefits apply only to the disabled? To those whose education had been interrupted? The result of this debate was the GI Bill, passed in 1944, which reshaped the nature of veterans' benefits and, by extension, society. Historian Arthur Schlesinger described it as a "national turning point" for its scope.[219] Not only would veterans continue to receive healthcare for both service-related and non-service-related disabilities, they would also receive educational benefits, mortgage assistance, and unemployment benefits.[220] After a slow start and subsequent revision of the bill that increased benefits, approximately half of all World War II veterans signed up for benefits under the GI Bill.[221]

Implementation of this plan, however, was not always perfect. As in World War I, the Army after World War II created a "reconditioning program" to ensure that "no casualty is discharged from the Army until he has received full benefit of the finest hospital care this Nation can provide."[222] More specifically, the reconditioning program was meant to "restore to fullest possible physical and mental health any soldier who has been wounded or fallen ill in the service of his country . . . [t]o insure that men are properly prepared for return to civilian life."[223] It was also the case, though, that the Veterans Administration (VA, the Veterans Bureau's successor organization, as of 1930) was not prepared to provide medical care for the tens of thousands of soldiers injured and ill from World War II. Half of veterans suffered from either wounds or a war-induced disability, especially the prolonged effects of trench foot.[224] Thus, the Army's policy solved a problem for the VA; soldiers would remain in Army hospitals until the Army could do no more for them.[225]

Nonetheless, VA disbursements after the Second World War constituted a significant portion of the federal budget. The VA was responsible for veterans' medical issues ranging from tuberculosis to neuropsychosis to prostheses. Improvements in medicine meant that different categories of patients, such as paraplegics and those who had suffered extensive burns, could now benefit from additional care. As Sanders Marble notes in a government study on war rehabilitation: "Advances in medicine and surgery were keeping more patients alive, and more severely wounded ones as well."[226] Additionally, the VA managed the various benefits described above, alongside a significant and continuing pension system from the Civil War through the world wars.

As in the First World War, not surprisingly, not all veterans were treated the same. Nurses, for example, were denied admission to the major veterans' organizations such as the American Legion—which lobbied for veterans' benefits and rights—and were also discouraged from applying for benefits under the GI Bill (even though the bill's original nickname was "a bill of rights for GI Joe and GI Jane").[227] Post–World War II VA hospitals were ill-equipped to serve women veterans, with long wait times for gynecological exams and almost no expertise with respect to offering Pap smears or breast exams.[228] And southern Blacks had few opportunities to take advantage of the key educational benefits in the bill, given the paucity of institutions of higher learning that would accept Black men in the Jim Crow era.[229] They also had trouble obtaining home loans across the country because of common practices like racial covenants and redlining.[230]

Such discouragements did not save the US government much money. Blacks accounted for less than 15 percent of the military, and nurses even less than that. Yet the amount of money spent on veterans was astounding. "Net disbursements from appropriations and trust funds of the Veterans Administration for the fiscal year 1943 ran to $643,406,394, while its budget estimate for the fiscal year 1944 was $1,259,310,500."[231] By 1946, appropriations for veterans were only exceeded by those for the military.[232] Had the United States not been experiencing a postwar economic boom, the trade-offs inherent in spending so much on veterans' care would have been unsustainable. In other words, the costs were high, but the country could afford them.

This was in part because veterans' benefits were also viewed as a benefit to society as a whole. The educational benefits were especially popular, used by just over half of eligible World War II veterans.[233] Glenn Altschuler and Stuart Blumin find that over three-quarters of World War II veterans took advantage of at least one provision of the GI Bill.[234] As Suzanne Mettler points out, in an era of conscription, World War II veterans were broadly representative of the US male population. What this meant was that benefits were fairly equally distributed across social class—albeit not race or gender. The scale of the war amplified the effects of the benefits, as did their nature; the GI Bill went beyond the cash payments and healthcare offered to previous veterans, and instead focused on targeted, even limited, goals such as paying for college and helping veterans buy homes. Mettler's broader point harkens back to Schlesinger's characterization of the GI Bill as a national turning point; she argues that, by improving the economic lot of millions of men—and their families—across broad swaths of the American populace, the GI Bill created a "civic generation" that helped knit together social fabric for decades.[235] The bill also transformed higher education; not only did more US-born students attend over time, but eventually higher education became an increasingly valued export as millions of international students vied for spots at US colleges and universities.[236] Viewed from this perspective, the costs of the "good war" were at least partially evened out by the benefits.

Conclusion

Advances in military medicine are never uniform. Between wars, knowledge is forgotten or lost. Within wars, fatal errors often precede innovation. But in comparing the world wars, both to the Civil War and to each other, the observable improvements are undeniable. Even though military doctors burned by the typhoid outbreak of 1898 failed to prevent the 1918 influenza pandemic, an understanding of the germ theory of disease meant that they instituted new sanitary practices; as a result, many of the camp diseases that ravaged Civil War soldiers were, in World War I and even more so in World War II, now controlled. Even though medical personnel had to be retrained in the chain of evacuation for each new war, they adapted to technologies, such as motorized trucks and airplanes, that greatly decreased transport time and, consequently, increased their patients' odds of survival. Even though intense debate around transfusion delayed the shift from dried plasma to whole blood, the proof of whole blood's advantage eventually won out. Of course, many advances were applied unevenly, with Black soldiers in particular receiving substandard medical care due to systemic racism.

These improvements are less visible in the wounded-to-killed ratios across the two wars. World War I's wounded-to-killed ratio was higher than that for World War II: 3.8:1 versus 2.3:1. This difference, though, has more to do with weapons than with medicine. Simply put, the large bombs used in the Second World War killed many more people outright than did the gunshots of World War I. When and if military personnel reached medical care, however, their odds of survival were much higher in the Second World War than in the First. Here, the case fatality rate may be more informative than the wounded-to-killed ratio. As shown in Figure 2.4 above, the CFR for those wounded in war declined steadily and significantly, from 13.6 in the Civil War to 8.1 in World War I to 4.4 in World War II. Medicine explains the seeming contradiction of a higher wounded-to-killed ratio but a lower CFR.[237] As Army surgeon Capt. Henry Swan wrote to his future wife, Mary Fletcher, in November 1944: "For any comparison of the surgery of this war and the last it must be stated at once that surgical knowledge and therapeutic armamentarium have progressed to an astonishing degree in the intervening years."[238]

The trajectory of veterans' benefits is more uneven than that of military medicine. The enormous pension system that emerged from the Civil War has never been matched since. Reaction to that system is precisely why veterans' benefits were more conservative during and after World War I. And yet, learning from the past did not always lead to fewer benefits. Memories of protests like the Bonus March, combined with the fact that the scale of US participation in World War II was simply on a much higher order of magnitude, meant that politicians had greater incentive to be generous to veterans. A booming economy enabled that generosity. Veterans service organizations, such as the American Legion and the Veterans of Foreign Wars, had become increasingly powerful in their lobbying. So many members of the US population would benefit—either directly or indirectly—from the programs in the GI Bill that the political upsides were extremely high. Thus, while veterans' benefits did not increase consistently from the mid-nineteenth century to the mid-twentieth, the trajectory across the two world wars is undoubtedly upward.

While the provision of pensions for veterans of new wars was uneven from 1865 to 1945, healthcare for disabled veterans has been a benefit throughline. Add to this logic the considerable expansion of veterans' benefits in the United States after the Second World War compared to the First—including home loans, educational support, and the continuation of healthcare—and two key components of the long-term costs of war become clear. First, as a proportion of those deployed who received medical care, dramatic advances in military medicine saved many more lives in the world wars as compared to the Civil War. Second, even though the trajectory of veterans' benefits is more uneven, the amount of money spent on World War II veterans was ultimately much higher than that spent on World War I veterans, in large part because greater numbers of veterans were eligible for more expansive benefits. The growth of the US economy after World War II meant that veterans' benefits would never again approach the share of the federal budget seen in the aftermath of the Civil War. World War II serves as an additional benchmark; from then on, the combination of steadily improving medicine and (less steadily) expanded benefits meant that the hidden costs of war would only increase.

While this book focuses primarily on the costs of war, war brought many benefits to society, beyond US victory. Medical innovations, such as penicillin, were first used widely during war and then became commonplace in civilian life. And, as Suzanne Mettler argues, the expansive benefits from the GI Bill created a "civic generation" whose commitment to American democracy and society sustained the US for decades.[239] But recipients of World War II veterans' benefits, as a group, would become historically unusual in at least two respects: first, the scale of that war has never been repeated in US history, and so we would never again see veterans taking advantage of benefits in such large numbers; and second, with the shift away from conscription at the end of the Vietnam War, the distribution of veterans' benefits across society would look much different. World War II did not generate a distinct "veteran class"—a concern about the pensioners of the Civil War—because so many people had fought. But as we will see, the move away from the draft in 1973 represented a return of this distinction. So while the veterans' benefits of the Second World War reduced some inequalities, they also set precedents that would be adapted in ways that would set veterans apart from the rest of the society in the decades to come.

3

Blood Is King

The Medicine of Counterinsurgency

Advances in military medicine between the Civil War and World War II were undeniably significant. But improvements since then, and especially in the United States' most recent wars in Afghanistan and Iraq, have produced even more startling results. Between World War II and today, the wounded-to-killed ratio has more than tripled, and the case fatality rate has dropped precipitously. Military medicine deserves much, if not most, of the credit.

The United States' singular role in the world since the middle of the last century has meant near-constant military deployments. Indeed, there are only a handful of years since 1945 when the US military has *not* had troops involved in military operations abroad.[1] Most of these conflicts—from interventions that toppled leaders in Latin America in the 1970s to coalition warfare in the Balkans in the 1990s—involved relatively few US troops and, therefore, little in the way of advancements on the medical front. But the two larger wars of the Cold War era—Korea and Vietnam—did see notable improvements in military medicine.

The US entered the Korean War at the conflict's beginning, in 1950—only a few years after the close of World War II. While many of the medical practices that had evolved in the Second World War remained in place, the people did not. Ensuring that enough doctors were available for the war effort was a constant concern in the early 1950s, so much so that it led to a "Doctor's Draft," where eligible physicians and medical students with the least amount of service were called first to the front. Two other major changes emerged out of the Korean War in the arenas of hospital construction and medical evacuation. The Mobile Army Surgical Hospital—popularized in the TV series *M*A*S*H*—was a nimble and effective facility first developed and used widely in Korea. And the images of helicopter evacuation, which became emblematic of Afghanistan and Iraq, have their origins in Korea and Vietnam.

Unlike the Korean War, the ramp-up to Vietnam was gradual, with the first US troops arriving in 1965 (more than a decade after the Korean armistice had been signed) and leaving—in infamous and dramatic fashion—a decade later. Helicopter evacuation came into its own during Vietnam, just as drug use among troops skyrocketed.[2] But the most challenging aspect of the war—from both a military and medical standpoint—was the use of guerrilla warfare by the Viet Cong. While the regular North Vietnamese army employed conventional tactics against South Vietnamese and American troops, with clear front lines and uniformed belligerents, the Viet Cong used hit-and-run attacks and combatants who did not visibly distinguish themselves from the civilian population.

Beyond the increased use of helicopter evacuation, however, there were relatively few medical adjustments made to this new military landscape. Similarly, the Korean War was, in many ways, medically quite similar to World War II—the Mobile Army Surgical Hospital, for example, has its roots in the auxiliary surgical groups first deployed in the Second World War.[3] The US military has been frequently criticized for its reliance on traditional conventional warfare and failure to adopt effective counterinsurgency (COIN) measures in Vietnam—which would have had downstream implications for military medicine.[4] Thus, while both of these conflicts saw improvements in military medicine, these improvements were on a much smaller scale compared to what the United States would achieve in Afghanistan and Iraq. For this reason, while I reference the Korean and Vietnam Wars frequently in this chapter, they are not its focus.

The invasions of Afghanistan and Iraq—known as Operation Enduring Freedom (OEF) and Operation Iraqi Freedom (OIF)—were, almost from the beginning, fundamentally different kinds of wars. With few exceptions, US military history (and thus military medicine) had previously been defined by conventional warfare. But for much of the first twenty years of the twenty-first century, the United States was engaged primarily in COIN operations. Changes in warfare both required and enabled changes in medicine. The improvised explosive devices characteristic of the Afghanistan and Iraq Wars produced new injury patterns—oftentimes multiple and traumatic injuries—that required new strategies to assess and treat patients, both near the fighting and farther from battle. The fact that the United States' opponents in both wars lacked a viable air force, though, meant that air evacuation became much easier than in previous conflicts, where control of the skies was contested. Rapid air evacuation became so integral to the United States' recent wars that the military adopted a "golden hour" policy: casualties were to be evacuated to higher-level care within the first hour after injury, to maximize chances for survival.

Perhaps the most striking, albeit subtle, advance in military medicine during the United States' twenty-first-century counterinsurgency wars has been an unprecedented effort to integrate the various components of military medicine into a more coherent whole. As discussed below, the Joint Trauma System (JTS) has enabled extraordinary data collection, which has in turn informed various changes in policy and procedure. Included among these changes are the golden hour policy, the development of Critical Care Air Transport Teams (CCATTs), an intense focus on hemorrhage control, and the development of new personal protective equipment. All these changes contributed to the rise in the US wounded-to-killed ratio. And while survivors of the Afghanistan and Iraq Wars have returned to a remarkably polarized domestic political landscape in the United States, one of the very few programs that has consistently received bipartisan support is veterans' benefits. The 9/11 GI Bill, for example, substantially expanded the educational benefits so valued (and so widely used) by World War II veterans. This is part of why, as Linda Bilmes and Joseph Stiglitz have argued, Operation Iraqi Freedom can be thought of as "the three trillion dollar war."[5] The costs of our recent wars have increased substantially in both trajectories—medical advancements and veterans' benefits—in ways that will be felt for generations.

Prewar Assessments of the Costs of War

Operation Enduring Freedom began weeks after the attacks of September 11, 2001. The political urgency to respond to these shocking attacks meant that President Bush did not wait for the kind of systematic cost analysis that one might otherwise hope for. For example, the Congressional Research Service (CRS), which has produced analyses for legislators on major policy issues since 1970, did not publish a report on the potential costs of the war prior to its start. Indeed, costs of war were an afterthought at best. In an October 10, 2001, memo titled "Costs of Campaign" to Department of Defense (DoD) comptroller Dov Zakheim, Secretary of Defense Donald Rumsfeld wrote: "At some point we are going to have to figure out what all this is costing us and how we are going to pay for it."[6] By the time Rumsfeld sent the memo, the airstrikes that launched Operation Enduring Freedom had already begun, on October 7; the ground war began nine days later. The overriding initial aim of the invasion was to remove the Taliban from government and ensure that al Qaeda was unable to execute any additional attacks on the US homeland. As President George W. Bush put it in an address to the nation at the start of the war on October 7, 2001: "These carefully targeted actions are designed to disrupt the use of Afghanistan as a terrorist base of operations, and to attack the military capability of the Taliban regime."[7] But experts warned of a long and costly quagmire.[8] British imperial forces had tried unsuccessfully to impose their will on Afghanistan from 1838 to 1919. More recently, the Soviet Union had withdrawn in 1989 after a decade-long, failed attempt to ensure that Afghanistan would be a stable and friendly ally. Ultimately, US forces spent twenty years in Afghanistan, with a mission that evolved from counterterrorism to state-building and stabilization. The true cost of the war to the United States is ultimately unknowable. The hasty US withdrawal in 2021 saw the return of the Taliban and therefore the loss of the measurable gains the United States—and Afghans—had made since 2001.

The lead-up to Operation Iraqi Freedom was much longer. There was significant debate about the wisdom of invading Iraq. Proponents ran the gamut, from those who saw the war as tipping the Middle East into a wave of democratization and those who argued that invading Iraq was essential to protecting the world against terrorist attacks to those who argued that the United States must liberate the Iraqi people from Saddam Hussein's rule.[9] According to those in favor, the war would be short and decisive. Defense Secretary Donald Rumsfeld asserted in November 2002—about four months before the United States invaded—that the war would last five months at most.[10] And Vice President Dick Cheney assured Americans that Iraqis would greet US troops "as liberators."[11]

Opponents of a war in Iraq were skeptical about both war aims and the likelihood of achieving those aims.[12] Many questioned the basic legality of such an invasion.[13] Others argued that the United States should not divert its attention from Afghanistan. Experts on Iraq cautioned that Americans were uninformed about the complexities of Iraqi society and politics, and that US policymakers were naive to place their trust in Iraqi exiles like Ahmed Chalabi.[14] Experts on the broader Middle East worried that invading Iraq would cause a backlash against the US rather than a democratic domino effect.[15] Many also questioned the credibility of the (eventually debunked) claim that Saddam Hussein had a robust nuclear weapons program.[16]

The White House and Congress did consider the potential costs of war in this case, at least to some extent. Prewar CRS reports offered estimates of foreign aid in the billions of dollars that would be needed should an invasion occur,[17] comparisons to the US occupations of Germany and Japan,[18] and a worsening humanitarian situation in Iraq.[19] White House economic advisor Lawrence B. Lindsay suggested a price tag of $100 billion to $200 billion for a two-year war.[20] These estimates were likely based on a report from the Congressional Budget Office, which suggested the United States would have to pay about $150 billion for a one-year war (but did not specify when the war might end).[21] Others, such as Deputy Secretary of Defense Paul Wolfowitz and Vice President Dick Cheney, were more optimistic, suggesting that the war would essentially finance itself.[22] But these projections were vague and the Bush administration was criticized for obscuring the potential costs even before the war started.[23]

Prewar casualty estimates are harder to come by. Once again, in the Afghanistan War, there were no such estimates, or at least none that are publicly available, because of the very short run-up to the war. When it came to Iraq, the military's confidence in its own abilities implied a low casualty rate.[24] Gen. Tommy Franks, who led US forces in the Iraq War, is said to have estimated that there would be somewhere between a few hundred and no more than 1,000 US casualties; the reporting suggests that Franks was talking about fatalities only.[25] Michael O'Hanlon of the Brookings Institution gave a range of 100 to 5,000 US military fatalities and another 500 to 30,000 wounded.[26] The high end of O'Hanlon's estimates turned out to be most accurate (although they still underestimated the wounded-to-killed ratio). According to the Defense Department, 3,490 US military personnel were killed in action during the eighty-nine months of Operation Iraqi Freedom, and another 31,994 were wounded.[27]

Missing from the conversation, as usual, was consideration of the long-term costs of war associated with US military casualties. A large part of the reason for the underestimates of these costs of war was simply that military and civilian leaders, just as they had for nearly a century and a half, proved unwilling to give the topic serious consideration. But another, far more surprising reason is that no one predicted how effective military medicine would be in Afghanistan and Iraq.

The Logistics of Medicine

From the Civil War through Vietnam, medicine scrambled to catch up, often slowly and haphazardly, to the chaos and destruction of war. While doctors, nurses, and medics found themselves in a similar position at the start of the Afghanistan and Iraq Wars, their position changed substantially over the course of those conflicts. During these most recent counterinsurgency wars, medicine took on a more primary role, such that medical considerations began to influence military tactics. This shift is partly due to the length of these wars, which allowed remarkable advancements in medicine. But it is also due to particular innovations—especially those in the realm of medical logistics.

Arguably, the most important of these innovations is the creation of the Joint Trauma System. Especially following the Vietnam War, the military's medical trauma system was behind the times compared to the emergency rescue squads operating in major American cities. This gap was evident in the early 1990s, during the First Gulf War.[28] US trauma surgeons knew from experience in the civilian sector that a proper trauma system could reduce fatalities by up to 20 percent, and sought to replicate such a system in the military.[29]

Col. Stacy Shackelford, who served as director of JTS from 2018 to 2022, describes the US military medical trauma system at the start of the Afghanistan and Iraq Wars as "nonexistent."[30] Stood up in 2003–4, the purpose of the JTS is "to coordinate battlefield care to minimize morbidity and mortality, and optimize essential casualty care."[31] The JTS slogan is "To provide for the right care to the right casualty at the right location and right time."[32] In its early days, the system was wobbly. As John Holcomb, a key figure in the development of the JTS, reports: "We were building it as we were flying it."[33] But as the JTS evolved, military trauma education was centralized and standardized, a weekly morbidity and mortality review call was established, and new data collection efforts were put in place.[34]

Data Collection

There are at least two ways to think about data management in wartime, each of which lines up with a different but related aim. For medical personnel in the thick of battle (or surgery), the priority is the patient. As casualties move through the chain of evacuation, it is important for medical personnel to know what their injuries are and what prior treatment they might have received. This is why, as discussed in the previous chapter, injured soldiers who had received morphine often arrived at their next stop with an "M" written on their foreheads, to avoid overdoses. Likewise for a "T" to indicate the placement of a tourniquet, which should not be left on for too long. For medical personnel tasked with developing clinical guidelines and practices, however, data serve a different purpose. Here, data are meant to inform research. For this purpose, comprehensive data—systematic, comparable, and as complete as possible—are needed.

But data collection in war is hard. Good data collection in war is even harder. For medical personnel, the primary aim of collecting data about casualties is to understand where medicine is succeeding, where it is failing, and how it might be improved. While data collection has of course improved since the Civil War and even the world wars, two basic problems pose a perpetual challenge. The first is missing data; any conclusions you draw are only as effective as the data you are actually able to gather. The more data that are missing, the less useful the existing data are—especially if data are not missing randomly. The second problem is data comparability; that is, the ability to make comparisons across (and even within) wars. Data about a previous war are useful only insofar as they can apply to what happens next. Military medical personnel trained their attention on these problems at the start of the Afghanistan and Iraq Wars.

While the US military has collected systematic data on casualties since at least the Civil War, the extent to which these data could inform practice was limited by the collection process itself. If, for example, data are collected on the incidence of disease but not on the consequences of various interventions, it is hard to use the data for more than summary purposes. As we have seen, there were halting efforts by doctors in World War II field hospitals to collect data that could be used to create evidence-based guidelines. Such efforts were more systematic in Korea and Vietnam. During the Korean War, for example, a series of studies based out of the 46th Surgical Hospital (a support hospital ten miles behind the front) began to shed light on questions around resuscitation, vascular injuries, and renal failure.[35] The Vietnam War saw the deployment of epidemiologists, Special Forces officers, and lab technicians as part of the Field Epidemiologic Survey Team, which traveled to hard-to-reach areas to study diseases.[36] While researchers involved in these efforts emphasized the importance of reprising them in future wars, this advice was unheeded, at least at first. The status of US military medical data collection in the 1990s—during the First Gulf War and the intervention in Somalia—was poor. While there was *a* system in place to collect data on casualties at the start of the Afghanistan and Iraq Wars, the system did not direct practitioners to collect data that could be used to inform new guidelines. A great deal of the data collected was anecdotal rather than systematic.[37]

As the war in Afghanistan began, researchers naturally turned to past wars for guidance. But serious issues of comparability arose.[38] The increased use of body armor by US forces in Afghanistan and Iraq compared to Vietnam, for example, raised questions about how the efficacy of various medical interventions could be understood given that the presence (or absence) of body armor will lead to very different injury patterns.[39] What is more, military medical researchers now recognized that inconsistent definitions of critical categories such as who "counted" as wounded affected basic statistics such as case fatality rates.[40] And these inconsistencies were not just across wars, but also across services in the same military; the Marines, for example, would include the lightly wounded in their analyses while the Army did not, leading to a deceptively low CFR for the Marines as compared to the Army.[41] As one group of US military doctors put it, "The US military went to war in 2001 without an integrated trauma care system to collect and analyze combat casualty care data."[42]

One solution to this problem was the creation of the Joint Theater Trauma Registry (JTTR) in 2002, now known as the Department of Defense Trauma Registry.[43] According to the Joint Theater System Framework document, the overall purpose of the DoDTR is to create a trauma registry that holds data on battle casualties that can then be used to inform evidence-based medicine.[44] Research teams were dispatched to combat hospitals to collect data, which was then registered and deposited with offices such as the US Army Medical Research and Development Command, which could give access to researchers within and without the military, as appropriate.[45] As the registry matured, data collection practices were applied to stages earlier in the chain of evacuation—moving from combat surgical hospitals to prehospital (i.e., field) care.[46] The introduction of the Tactical Combat Casualty Care card in 2007 was crucial to this change, as medics now had a (theoretically) quick and efficient way to transcribe data in a standardized format; certainly, for data collection purposes, TCCC cards were far superior to writing a patient's

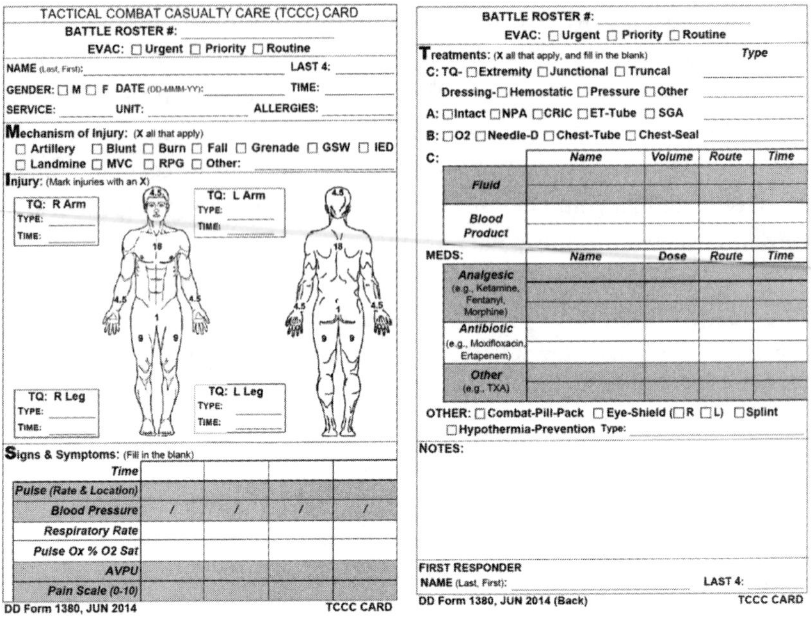
TACTICAL COMBAT CASUALTY CARE (TCCC) CARD
BATTLE ROSTER #:
EVAC: ☐ Urgent ☐ Priority ☐ Routine
NAME (Last, First): LAST 4:
GENDER: ☐ M ☐ F DATE (DD-MMM-YY): TIME:
SERVICE: UNIT: ALLERGIES:
Mechanism of Injury: (X all that apply)
☐ Artillery ☐ Blunt ☐ Burn ☐ Fall ☐ Grenade ☐ GSW ☐ IED
☐ Landmine ☐ MVC ☐ RPG ☐ Other:
Injury: (Mark injuries with an X)

Signs & Symptoms: (Fill in the blank)

Time				
Pulse (Rate & Location)				
Blood Pressure	/	/	/	/
Respiratory Rate				
Pulse Ox % O2 Sat				
AVPU				
Pain Scale (0-10)				

DD Form 1380, JUN 2014 TCCC CARD

BATTLE ROSTER #:
EVAC: ☐ Urgent ☐ Priority ☐ Routine
Treatments: (X all that apply, and fill in the blank) Type
C: TQ- ☐ Extremity ☐ Junctional ☐ Truncal
Dressing-☐ Hemostatic ☐ Pressure ☐ Other
A: ☐ Intact ☐ NPA ☐ CRIC ☐ ET-Tube ☐ SGA
B: ☐ O2 ☐ Needle-D ☐ Chest-Tube ☐ Chest-Seal
C:

	Name	Volume	Route	Time
Fluid				
Blood Product				

MEDS:

	Name	Dose	Route	Time
Analgesic (e.g., Ketamine, Fentanyl, Morphine)				
Antibiotic (e.g., Moxifloxacin, Ertapenem)				
Other (e.g., TXA)				

OTHER: ☐ Combat-Pill-Pack ☐ Eye-Shield (☐ R ☐ L) ☐ Splint
☐ Hypothermia-Prevention Type:
NOTES:

FIRST RESPONDER
NAME (Last, First): LAST 4:
DD Form 1380, JUN 2014 (Back) TCCC CARD

Figure 3.1 Tactical Combat Casualty Care Card (Side 1 and 2)

medical notes on their chest, which had been common previously.[47] As seen in Figure 3.1, TCCC cards provide space to record the location of injury as well as the patient's vital statistics. Filling out the TCCC card is now meant to be a standard practice, according to the 2018 *Emergency War Surgery* manual.[48]

Having systematic data available, through DoDTR, meant that military medical researchers could analyze that data to suggest a series of evidence-based changes in the practice of military medicine. Several policy shifts emerged based on these new data. First in time was the development of the Tactical Combat Casualty Care guidelines. The TCCC guidelines were designed for medics in the field—in other words, for prehospital care. They instruct medics to "mitigate hemorrhage on the battlefield, optimize airway management, and decrease the time from point of injury to surgical intervention."[49] They also reversed several long-standing practices. For example, TCCC clearly recommends the application of tourniquets in cases of hemorrhage, while previous guidelines did not mention tourniquets at all, or even advised against their use (more on tourniquets and hemorrhage control below).[50] As Brian Eastridge and colleagues remarked, "TCCC has revolutionized how combat medicine is practiced in the battlefield."[51]

TCCC guidelines are widely believed to have saved lives, especially in the prehospital setting. In a 2011 study comparing the Army's 75th Ranger Regiment to all US military ground troops, Russ Kotwal and coauthors found that the 75th, which was using TCCC at the time, had a 1.7 percent died-of-wounds rate, compared to 5.8 percent for ground troops as a whole. This result is all the more striking given that the 75th Ranger Regiment is typically forward-deployed into relatively dangerous areas compared to other units.[52] For example, the Rangers participated in key, smaller operations at the start of the invasion of Afghanistan, in the Battle of Tora Bora, and to secure air bases during the invasion of Iraq.

A related set of changes made based on DoDTR data speaks to the issue of hemorrhage management. Hemorrhage was shown, back in 1984, to be the leading preventable cause of battlefield death.[53] Investigators using DoDTR data found that one site in Afghanistan lacked junctional tourniquets (often used for pelvic injuries), an absence that may have led to a number of preventable deaths; based on these data and subsequent analysis, junctional tourniquets became standard issue for medical kits.[54] The DoDTR also informed transfusion practices using blood components. Perhaps most important, data from the DoDTR led the US military medical community to conclude that standard tourniquets should be applied in a prehospital setting, a policy that in turn led to the widespread use of the Combat Application Tourniquet (see Figure 3.3).[55] Perkins credits the DoDTR with more than forty new clinical practice guidelines, and further notes that "these efforts have contributed to survival rates as high as 98% for those arriving alive at military hospitals in Afghanistan."[56]

While the DoDTR represents a new era of military medical data collection efforts, its implementation has been far from seamless. The challenges of data collection in war make it hard for researchers to duplicate the controlled study conditions that are the gold standard for scientific research.[57] The biggest challenge is getting medical personnel to provide data, especially in prehospital settings. In a medical emergency, filling out a TCCC card is necessarily secondary (or tertiary, if that) to providing care; providing the data is also not mandatory.[58] According to one aeromedical physician assistant, TCCC cards are filled in only about 14 percent of the time.[59] One reason is that carrying around physical TCCC cards adds weight to a medic's pack;

another is that handwriting (versus typing) can lead to difficulties in transcription down the road.[60] The system works, but only if people use it.[61] As suggested in the *Emergency War Surgery* handbook, it is sometimes easier to revert to documenting a patient's progress on their chest with marker than it is to fill out a data card.[62]

Col. (Ret.) John Holcomb, a dean of US military medicine today and a key figure in the development of the DoDTR, wrote along with coauthors in 2007: "Critical review of deaths due to trauma is a cornerstone of the evolution of trauma care systems. This type of analysis defines the direction of future research and identifies areas in need of improvement, not only in the deployed medical system, but in the civilian medical sector as well."[63] As the authors note in the same article, many medical advances, such as the availability of diagnostic tools like CT scanners (invented in the 1970s), improve the ability to collect good data on casualties today.[64] But some of the most dramatic recent improvements in military medicine rest on research that was itself based on new data practices—rather than hardware like CT scanners—implemented by the military In Iraq and Afghanistan.

Evacuation

The revolution in data collection created several key changes pertaining to evacuation and logistics. A seminal 2011 study showed that 87 percent of deaths occurred in the prehospital setting—before an injured service member reached a medical facility.[65] Giving every injured US battle casualty "the optimal chance for survival" became the prevailing aim of JTS, and caused the military medical community as a whole to train its attention on the question of how to improve prehospital care.[66]

Understanding how many deaths could have been prevented if medical interventions had been administered prior to arrival at a medical facility led to the development of new guidelines for care, such as the TCCC system, amendments to how echelons of care were designed along the chain of evacuation, and evacuation practices themselves.

How military casualties move through the chain of evacuation today represents a continuation of practices developed in Korea and Vietnam. Air evacuation was central to both wars, but also evolved across them. Helicopter evacuation saw its first significant use in Korea, where numerous casualties would be evacuated to hospitals via helicopter. Still, helicopters were very much an adjunct to motorized ambulances and railroads; they were also small, undersupplied, and prone to malfunction.[67] The use of helicopters for evacuation became commonplace in Vietnam, in large part because of the challenges of terrain—dense jungle and lack of a road network that could support motorized ambulances.[68] Indeed, the "Dust-off" call sign and the nomenclature "MEDEVAC" originated in the Vietnam War, as did the use of hoists and other tools to board casualties.[69]

The fact that the United States had air superiority in Afghanistan and Iraq—as well as Vietnam—meant that air assets could be used more easily for evacuation. This is not to say that air evacuation was invulnerable to attacks; indeed, the lack of tree cover in the Middle East compared to Vietnam may have made it more so. Consider the tragic case of Pedro 66 in 2010, for example, when a MEDEVAC helicopter with that call sign came under fire in Afghanistan and crashed en route to delivering medical aid, gravely injuring the pilot and co-pilot, who themselves then required evacuation. While the surviving crew did ultimately receive medical care, the second-level evacuation procedure was surrounded by confusion, and it is as illustrative of the bureaucratic and logistical tangles of war as it is of the courage of military medical personnel.[70] Even so, these assets were less vulnerable than a truck ambulance, many of which were armored only in the cab and could be felled by IEDs.

In terms of speed, air evacuation is a clear improvement over the horse-drawn carriages of the Civil War and even the first motorized ambulances of the world wars. But this speed required some on-the-fly adjustments to the traditional chain of evacuation. Injured troops would be evacuated by helicopter either from the point of injury or a "Role 1" battalion aid station where they would have received first aid care according to TCCC guidelines. Depending on circumstance, however, the evacuation crew might overfly the "Role 2" field hospital, where forward surgical teams were meant to provide damage control surgery, and take the patient directly to a "Role 3" combat support hospital. As a result, personnel from certain facilities (like Role 2s) would sometimes be sent to other hospitals as the fighting ebbed and flowed.[71]

The JTS saw additional room for improvement in air evacuation. At the start of the Afghanistan and Iraq Wars, casualties loaded onto aircraft received limited medical attention; a medic might be on board, but that medic would have had limited training. As part of the move to focus on prehospital care, personnel with more advanced training began to staff MEDEVAC helicopter flights. (The same philosophy—albeit now in a posthospital phase—led to the creation of Critical Care Air Transport Teams for fixed-wing casualty evacuation flights). Today, injured personnel on both helicopters and fixed-wing planes are attended to by a three-person ICU team.[72] In other words, some version of the hospital travels with the patient. While this innovation is not historically unique—for example, during World War II nurses often traveled with the injured being evacuated by air, and medical care was delivered on flights in both Korea and Vietnam (albeit at times in a somewhat slapdash manner)[73]—it was resurrected in the Middle East, and of course takes advantage of decades of medical advances. For example, CCATTs often use sophisticated ventilation equipment, transfuse blood, and otherwise monitor critically ill or injured patients during flight. Having trained medical staff aboard evacuation flights is associated with decreases in battlefield mortality by as much as half.[74]

The focus on prehospital care is justified technically by the data analysis overseen by the JTS. But doctors have always known that delivering care sooner than later is better for severely injured patients. As mentioned in the previous chapter, World War II's military doctors understood that they needed to treat patients within a relatively short window if they were to survive. Likewise for military medical personnel in Korea and Vietnam, who celebrated the use of air evacuation precisely because it cut down time to treatment. The intuition behind the "golden hour" between injury and treatment, in other words, had been widely shared for decades.[75] But again, systematic evidence matters, and it was precisely this kind of evidence that led Defense Secretary Robert Gates to mandate in 2009 that care be delivered within the golden hour.[76]

Subsequent to Gates's mandate, average evacuation times from point of injury to a field hospital fell from two hours to under one hour in Afghanistan. In the years since, the CFR also fell—from 13.7 percent to 6.7 percent. Note that this change overlapped with the Afghanistan "surge" of 2009; even though there were more casualties, a higher percentage were being saved. The golden hour policy became so embedded that it created its own military implications; once the policy was in place, personnel could only be deployed within a radius where they *could* be evacuated to a higher-level medical facility within an hour. While today's trauma physicians debate whether the "golden hour" is more or less apt than the similar concept of the "platinum fifteen minutes," the policy has been credited with saving hundreds of lives.[77]

Bodies at War

Unconventional warfare, as well as changes in the structure of the military, produced a different set of injuries in Afghanistan and Iraq compared to previous wars. Bombs were still more frequent than guns, but the nature of bombs had changed; there was less in the way of artillery and much more in the way of IEDs. In the inevitable back-and-forth between weapons and wounds, US troops under attack arrived healthier and better armored. Thus, they were ex ante more likely to survive. And their odds of survival increased even further due to advances in preventive and battlefield medicine.

Soldiers, Doctors, and Disease

New data practices were immediately informative in describing the military's rate of disease and nonbattle injury. By 2005, data confirmed what had been previously established on a more anecdotal basis in past wars—that the DNBI rate tends to be quite high at the start of an overseas deployment, as military personnel adjust to a new physical environment and roles.[78] Troops entering each new theater of war confront new illnesses. Union troops in the Civil War contended with malaria and yellow fever in the South. Allied troops during World War I fell to the 1918 influenza epidemic. Epidemic hemorrhagic fever (aka hemorrhagic fever with renal syndrome), spread mostly by infected rats, afflicted thousands of United Nations troops during the Korean War.[79] Malaria and hepatitis A, among other tropical diseases, were common among US forces in Vietnam.[80] During the Vietnam War, the twelve-month rotation of troops meant that new troops regularly, if temporarily, succumbed to local diseases as they acclimated to the new environment.[81] While not all illnesses particular to Afghanistan and Iraq were predicted ahead of time, they were ultimately managed such that disease was not a large contributor to the military's casualty count, especially compared to past conflicts.

The United States' recent wars in Afghanistan and Iraq were both different from and similar to previous conflicts when it came to disease outbreaks. While the frequency of childhood immunizations in the twenty-first-century United States means that vulnerability to many illnesses—diphtheria, tetanus, pertussis, measles, mumps, and rubella—has decreased, these immunizations are to some extent tailored to the United States. As in previous wars, additional immunizations—particularly against hepatitis

A—were administered to troops as they deployed, to counter the disease's prevalence in the Middle East.[82] In invading Afghanistan and Iraq, US troops were vulnerable to illnesses (still) endemic to the region, such as leishmaniasis and Q fever (*Coxiella burnetti* infection). Indeed, it may well have been US military actions that upset sand fly habitats, leading to outbreaks of leishmaniasis. While none were fatal—for US troops—all can be, and were, debilitating. But unlike the local population, US soldiers were cared for by a vast medical infrastructure that prevented more severe outcomes.[83]

HIV posed a somewhat greater challenge to US military personnel. Unlike in previous theaters, the disease was not contracted primarily via contact with local populations upon deployment; instead, troops testing positive for HIV typically seem to have contracted it either just before or just after deployment, during windows that were often missed by screening tests. From a military perspective, HIV outbreaks were especially consequential because of their impact on the supply of blood for transfusion.[84]

Either Napoleon Bonaparte or Frederick the Great—no one seems to know which—is famously said to have quipped that "an army marches on its stomach." For the United States in Afghanistan and Iraq, the issue was not so much food—which was supplied from home, often in the form of prepackaged meals ready-to-eat (MREs)—as potable water. Keeping troops well hydrated is critical, even in rainy environs. But it is also difficult. The provision of ice in Vietnam, for instance, was extremely challenging given differences between local sanitary practices and the requirements of the US Army.[85] In arid areas of Iraq and especially Afghanistan, providing sufficient water became a major logistical challenge. Initially, the Army purchased bottled water from local commercial outlets, but at a relatively high cost. More than once, troops deployed forward in the unrealized expectation that water would follow. Ultimately, the Army began bottling its own water, ensuring quality and supply, and significantly lowering costs.[86] One downstream consequence of the rampant use of water bottles, however, was their disposal in burn pits—areas where trash was burned in the open air—that generated toxic fumes; many Afghanistan and Iraq veterans now suffer long-term respiratory illness as a result.

With immunizations, treatment, and preventive measures such as bottling water, the "disease" part of DNBI was relatively low in OEF and OIF. But nonbattle injuries as a whole have been on the rise. One reason for this trend stems from the mechanization of the military. Vehicular accidents are simply more common and produce a large number of nonbattle injuries. According to one study, the major causes of nonbattle injuries among US military personnel in Iraq were (in order) military vehicle accidents, falls, drug use, and sports/physical training.[87] There were more evacuations due to musculoskeletal nonbattle injury than for any other category, although these injuries would have been much less likely to produce death than a battle injury.[88] And even though these injuries were unrelated to battle, the fact that they were incurred in service meant that injured troops were eligible for veterans' benefits to continue to treat them after returning home.

Preventive care is essential to military medicine. But the overall prewar fitness of the troops, combined with an aggressive immunization campaign, meant that relatively few fell to disease, especially compared to past wars. There were certainly improvements in preventive care in the Afghanistan and Iraq Wars. But there was also simply less to do to advance an already well-functioning part of military medicine.

Weapons, Wounds, and Surgery

The shift from guns to bombs that began in World War II has continued through the more recent counterinsurgency wars. But instead of artillery, booby traps and improvised explosive devices became the primary causes of battle injury in Afghanistan and Iraq.[89] Especially when US troops were operating in armored vehicles, antitank weapons were also used. This is not to say that there were no gunshot wounds sustained—there were, of course—but blast injuries, which typically injure a body in multiple ways simultaneously, were much more common, and also increasingly varied.

The 2018 *Emergency War Surgery* handbook lists the primary causes of injury for US troops in Afghanistan and Iraq. By far the most common, at just over 60 percent, are IEDs. The next most frequent cause is gunshot wounds, at just under 20 percent.[90] This spread reflects the nature of operations in Afghanistan and Iraq. Rather than front-line fighting, Afghan and Iraqi insurgents were much more likely to emplace homemade bombs that could be detonated from a distance as US troops arrived on the scene, either in a vehicle or on foot.

IEDs cause a complicated set of injuries. As shown in Figure 3.2, these weapons cause injury from missiles, pressure, and toxic gas if the person injured is in a vehicle. Explosions release shrapnel, which can penetrate flesh, into the vehicle. Blast pressure forcefully pushes soldiers' bodies in a

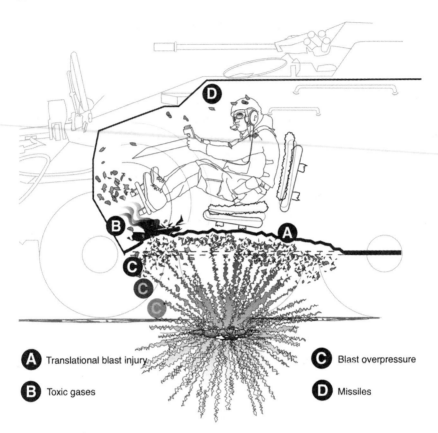

Figure 3.2 Blast Injury
Source: Cubano 2018, fig. 1-10.

confined space, often producing bone fractures.[91] And IEDs would activate the vehicle's fire suppression system, releasing toxic acid into an enclosed area smaller than a New York City subway car.[92] These types of injury were common at the start of operations in Iraq, when troops were "mounted" in vehicles. Dismounted IED injury is also typically multifactorial, although without the same pressure and toxic gas effects. But these injury patterns changed as troops increasingly used personal protective equipment.

The two parts of the human body most vulnerable to a fatal wound, as we know, are the head and the trunk. In the Civil War and much of World War I, soldiers wore little in the way of protective equipment. By World War II, helmets were standard issue. Flak jackets became more common during the Vietnam War, but soldiers engaged in combat tended to avoid wearing PPE because it was uncomfortable. According to one US military doctor serving in Vietnam: "If our combat troops . . . were to wear the helmet, we believe that about 1/3 fewer significant combat causalities would need to be admitted to neurosurgical center."[93] In the United States' most recent counterinsurgency wars, personal protective equipment became much more central to the daily lives of soldiers, and thus to the medical personnel that treated them.[94]

The exhibition hall aisles of military medical conferences such as the annual meetings of the Military Health Systems Research Symposium or the Special Operations Medical Association contain numerous displays of body armor (as well as mangled mannequins). Compared to the flak jackets of the Vietnam era, the Outer Tactical Vest (and its successor, the Improved Outer Tactical Vest) affords significantly more protection against high-velocity weapons and IEDs; it is also more maneuverable and compatible with various holsters for small arms. The general consensus among trauma researchers is that historically low levels of US mortality in Afghanistan and Iraq are thanks in significant part to the use of improved body armor. For example, two military orthopedic surgeons present a case of a patient with welts on his chest: "These welts represent likely fatal wounds had he not been wearing his personal protective equipment."[95] Because body armor worn over the torso protected the trunk, extremities were at greater risk. In previous wars, bomb fragments penetrating the chest would be fatal. In Afghanistan and Iraq, it was much more likely that the injured were at risk of dying because they were bleeding profusely from an arm or leg—or both. It is this combination of weapons and wounds that made hemorrhage the main cause of preventable battle death in Afghanistan and Iraq (as well as Korea and Vietnam).[96]

Helmets are just as crucial. During the Vietnam era, US troops wore helmets very similar to those used in the Second World War. Today's helmets weigh less, accommodate equipment like night vision goggles and headsets, and, most important, afford more protection. While helmets often protected troops from fatal head injuries, the combination of blast injury and this specific PPE frequently produced one of the so-called signature injuries of these twenty-first-century counterinsurgency wars: traumatic brain injury. TBI is typically caused by a blow to the head, but it can also be caused by an object penetrating the head, especially when brain tissue is penetrated.[97] To understand why survivable TBI has become so common today, consider two scenarios. In the first scenario, a soldier without a helmet (or with a weakly armored helmet) is in a tank that runs over a land mine and thus experiences blast injury; in this case, the soldier is likely to sustain a fatal injury to the head (as well as other parts of the body) as a result of some combination of shrapnel, overpressure, or impact to the head from the blast. In the second scenario, a soldier with a modern helmet is in an armored personnel carrier that runs over a mine or an IED. Here, the soldier is more likely to survive, but to have been concussed. Because this second type of scenario was relatively common in Afghanistan and Iraq, TBI has also become a commonly diagnosed condition. Note also that research on brain injuries has increased over time precisely because these kinds of injuries—which, as discussed in the next chapter, frequently occur alongside psychological and psychiatric illness—have become more survivable.[98]

Another advance in PPE emerges from a new focus on "life, limb, and eyesight." Again, because of other advancements in military medicine, new injury patterns emerge among survivors. Eye injuries accounted for about 10 percent of combat injuries in Afghanistan and Iraq.[99] While not typically fatal on their own, ocular injuries often produced disabilities that meant personnel could not return to duty.

While the solution—safety goggles—seems obvious, it was not an easy one to implement. Goggles stopped IED fragments from entering the eye, and by 2014 they had been mandated for all International Security Assistance Force personnel in Afghanistan.[100] But getting to that point was challenging; not only did appropriate goggles have to be designed, but military personnel had to be persuaded to wear them. Overcoming this challenge included education programs as well as designing and adopting goggles that were more "fashion-forward"—typically, yellow-tinted wraparound goggles angled toward the face.[101]

The most common injury pattern, though, implicated multiple parts of the body. According to the DoD's *Emergency War Surgery* handbook, just under 70 percent of injuries catalogued from 2007 to 2017 were coded as "polytrauma."[102] Dr. Robert Mabry, a former command surgeon in Joint Special Operations Command whose military medical field experience began in Mogadishu, Somalia,[103] recounts the story of a Marine on foot patrol in Helmand Province in Afghanistan who in 2015 stepped on an IED. "The blast blew off his forearm and both legs below the knees, and threw him about 30 feet. He also sustained a concussion and internal injuries."[104] An array of medical professionals was deployed to treat this Marine, who ultimately survived his injuries.

While IEDs were common to both theaters, the primary weapons used and wounds sustained did differ. In Afghanistan, for example, US troops often conducted COIN operations on foot rather than in armored vehicles after the initial toppling of the Taliban regime in 2001.[105] What this meant was that troops were now vulnerable not just to IEDs but also to gunshots that would not have been able to penetrate armored vehicles. While the COIN phase of the Iraq War also began shortly after Saddam Hussein's regime fell to the initial invasion in 2003, the rural landscape of Afghanistan combined with a long-standing gun culture saw relatively more gunshot wounds inflicted (and sustained) in the Afghan theater than in Iraq.[106]

Better body armor protected troops from many immediate, fatal wounds. But wounds were nonetheless sustained, and could then become infected. Indeed, many of these infections—often from drug-resistant bacteria—were contracted while patients were receiving medical care.[107] Thus, the multifactorial injury pattern was further complicated by additional, albeit unintentional, harms rendered while receiving care.

Another set of wounds was often sustained by only one segment of the deployed military population: women. With the move to the all-volunteer force in 1973 and the ability of women to serve in combat roles in ground forces much more recently (during the Obama administration), women served in Afghanistan and Iraq in ways they had not in previous conflicts.[108] They could not be sequestered in the way that women nurses were in the world wars, and indeed did not seek such separation from their male colleagues. While sexual assault has always occurred in military operations, we know much more about it in recent conflicts.[109] The first Defense Department report on sexual assault in the military, sometimes referred to as "military sexual trauma" (MST), was released in 2004. According to the Defense Department's *2021 Annual Report on Sexual Assault in the Military*, 8.4 percent of active-duty women and 1.5 percent of active-duty men reported some type of sexual assault.[110] This number is noticeably lower than what a series of scholars have estimated, especially for women, with ranges from 9 percent to 33 percent. That figure goes even higher (43 percent) when female veterans are included.[111] Studies of older cohorts—for example, women who served in the Vietnam War and since—have found that nearly half of survey respondents reported physical or sexual assault.[112] In her analysis of the veterans' healthcare system, Suzanne Gordon quotes a social worker affiliated with the Veterans Health Administration's women's clinics: "The majority of [Afghanistan and Iraq] veterans have MST but won't tell you about it. Many of them just want to put it all behind them."[113]

The physical and psychological consequences of sexual assault have been studied much more for women than for men. They include vaginal and perineal trauma, STDs, chronic pain, menstrual problems, and gastrointestinal disorders.[114] Sexual assault is also correlated with higher rates of PTSD onset, a topic discussed in the following chapter, as well as eating disorders.[115] Studies of male victims of military sexual trauma reflect similar results in terms of long-term physical and psychological consequences.[116] Even beyond sexual assault, the few studies that have been conducted on female service members suggest a higher level of fatal casualties and a greater need to invest in trauma care for women.[117]

One final logistical factor—unrelated to military medicine, but with significant implications for the nature of the long-term costs of war—affected the distribution of injuries across individuals. The increased use of military contractors meant that uniformed military personnel were much more likely to be in combat and less likely to serve in the kind of support roles that could now be taken over by contractors. This is not to say that contractors did not serve in combat roles; rather, it is to say that contractors were often subbed in for military personnel in support functions.[118] In other words, compared to past wars, the proportion of military personnel in harm's way was higher in Afghanistan and Iraq.

This new array of injuries led to a significant reorientation of battlefield medicine. As discussed in the next chapter, mental health professionals are now regularly embedded with military units. We have new diagnostic tools and treatment options for TBI. But hemorrhage remains the overwhelming focus.

Blood is king in battlefield medicine today. Prioritizing blood has happened slowly, as over the past half century several major studies demonstrated that the great majority of preventable battle deaths have occurred due to blood loss.[119] In 1984, Ronald Bellamy showed that 38 percent of preventable battle deaths in Korea and Vietnam were due to hemorrhage. Nearly three decades later, an article by Eastridge and colleagues demonstrated that most preventable deaths occurred in the prehospital setting—again, due to hemorrhage.[120] The importance of blood is visible in the TCCC guidelines, the extensive research on blood products and practices reported at major military medical symposia, and even the creation of organizations such as the Trauma Hemostasis and Oxygenation Research (THOR) network.

While tourniquets had been used historically for limiting blood loss, military doctors were often opposed to the use of tourniquets because they were frequently misapplied, hidden under blankets, or otherwise kept on for too long; in such cases, rather than saving the limb, the tourniquet could doom the limb.[121] One World War I British surgeon went so far as to refer to tourniquets as "an invention of the Evil One."[122] While recognizing their utility, doctors who served in Korea also described the tourniquet as "fraught with danger."[123] At the start of the Afghanistan War, battlefield trauma care guidelines recommended *against* the use of tourniquets.[124] One reason was that past tourniquets were of rudimentary design, and at the start of the Afghanistan War the military was still issuing World War II–era tourniquets.[125] But new scientific research forced a revisiting of these guidelines. One early intervention has been the invention, distribution, and widespread use of the Combat Application Tourniquet, beginning in 2003 (see Figure 3.3).[126] Sometimes referred to as the "ratchet" or "one-handed" tourniquet, the CAT is different because an injured person can apply and tighten the tourniquet without assistance. Thus, other members of the unit, who might still be under fire, can focus on combat rather than delivering medical care. The CAT was so popular during the Afghanistan and Iraq Wars that military personnel often walked around base with the tourniquet (or sometimes even more than one) loosely applied; the thought

Figure 3.3 Combat Application Tourniquet
Source: Crown 2016b.

was that if they were hit, they could quickly tighten the tourniquet. Studies justify—and perhaps inspired—this widespread use, with data suggesting that these new tourniquets have saved many lives.[127]

Tourniquets are especially useful for wounds to the extremities, where the pressure can help stem bleeding. But there are many wounds where standard tourniquets cannot be usefully applied. Injuries to joints, such as the shoulder or pelvic area, and the torso require specialized "junctional" tourniquets, which are wide enough to compress both sides of a joint (see Figure 3.4). There have also been key advances beyond the development of new types of tourniquets in the last two decades, including hemostatic powders and dressings such as QuikClot Combat Gauze, which activates the body's natural clotting factors, and Celox Gauze, which creates a seal over an injury.[128]

Preventing additional blood loss, whether via tourniquets or hemostatic dressings, is of course just a temporary solution to the problem of hemorrhage. The longer-term solution requires replacement of fluids, especially blood. As we have seen, US forces began to use whole blood for transfusion in World War II. But the challenges of typing and screening for infection in the field raised doubts about relying on whole blood. Whole blood was also tricky to store. One of the benefits of airpower in the Korean War was

Figure 3.4 Junctional Tourniquet
Source: Crown 2016a.

that aircraft could be used not just to evacuate casualties but also to transport fresh blood; subsequently, Vietnam saw innovations in blood storage equipment such as the Styrofoam blood box.[129] And doctors in the Korean War had begun to experiment with fluids—like dextran, serum albumin, and modified fluid gelatin—to try to reduce the high hepatitis infection rates that sometimes resulted from whole-blood transfusions.[130] By the 1960s, the thinking around transfusions had begun to change—even though doctors in the Vietnam War recognized the importance of using whole blood. Instead of whole blood, civilian hospitals had switched to crystalloids[131] and/or blood components for initial transfusion. The advantage of crystalloids, such as lactated Ringer's solution, was that they were much more readily available than blood and could still bring blood pressure back up.[132] Another advantage was cost. But the great disadvantage was that pumping patients full of crystalloids was at best a temporary measure. Their blood pressure would rise but, as Col. Stacy Shackelford muses ruefully about her medical residency, "these people would swell up massively like balloons and we made sure they got compartment syndrome by closing their abdomen as well.... It's hard to think, back in those days, how many people could have survived that didn't survive."[133] In other words, the overreliance on crystalloids in trauma surgery killed patients.

Col. (Ret.) John Holcomb hypothesizes that the need for platelets for chemotherapy in civilian hospitals was another factor that drew military medicine away from whole blood and toward blood components. Additionally, it was more lucrative for blood bankers to sell blood components than to sell whole blood.[134] These components—plasma, red blood cells, and platelets—were an improvement on crystalloids, but they came with their own problems. One issue centered around the ratio of blood components. Was it better to use more red blood cells than plasma, or to use them in equal amounts?[135] By the time the Afghanistan and Iraq Wars began, reliance on blood components had become the norm in civilian trauma, and this was carried over into military medicine. For deployed troops, another issue was one of convenience, especially for forward medics. Multiple components require multiple containers, taking up space in what is already a very full rucksack. And the containers could be fragile. One Army physician assistant shared a common quip about freeze-dried plasma—"I need 5 units of plasma. Can I have 10?"—because the bags in which frozen plasma was transported would break so often.[136]

By the early 2000s, the US military was ready to consider switching back to whole blood for transfusions. But it had been a long process. During the Battle of Mogadishu in 1993, US medical personnel had used a walking blood bank, where troops in the field would donate blood on the spot, similar to that used in World War II. At the time, it seemed revolutionary, frighteningly so. Holcomb was a major at the time, and reports that "I thought I was going to go to jail" for using whole blood in a forward setting. The results, though, were as unquestionable as they had been fifty years earlier. Holcomb described seeing patients revive after the administration of fresh whole blood and characterized it as "a religious experience." Nonetheless, it took the US military more than ten years to transition back to using whole blood. Two key papers (by Holcomb and also by Borgman), both published in 2007, helped persuade the military medical community of the value of shifting back to whole blood.[137] Since then, study after study has demonstrated the efficacy of whole blood for successful resuscitation.[138] The data support what has been visible to doctors in the field since Edward Churchill's campaign in World War II.

In the last fifteen-plus years there has been an ongoing debate about exactly how to take advantage of the benefits of using whole blood amid battle while minimizing the problems. Warm, fresh whole blood implies a walking blood bank. But blood typing in the field inevitably presents challenges, including additional equipment; screening for illness requires even more equipment. A recently proposed solution—one that is also a callback to the Vietnam War[139]—has been to pretest military personnel prior to deployment to see who might be able to serve as low-titer type O whole-blood donors—in other words, type O donors with relatively few antibodies against types A and B blood. The focus on low-titer type O whole-blood donors is now the center of many discussions in the trauma care community.[140] One issue that has been raised recently, and controversially, is potential gender differences in the reception of blood; women—especially those who may be pregnant—could be more likely to react negatively to some "universal" blood types.[141]

While blood loss remains the primary cause of battle deaths deemed "preventable," accounting for 90 percent of preventable prehospital deaths, it is not the only one. The second- and third-most-frequent causes of preventable battle death are airway obstruction and tension pneumothorax (when air is trapped in the pleural cavity around the lungs), both of which compromise breathing. While some innovations have emerged during the United States' most recent counterinsurgency wars to address both issues, they have been limited in comparison to the focus on blood.[142]

Most of these interventions—tourniquet use, initial transfusion, application of tools like a bougie or stylet to address airway obstruction—occur in the prehospital setting. Medics expect that patients who survive will be evacuated further to the rear. Bearing this in mind, they focus on "damage control surgery." In other words, the first surgeon (say, a member of a forward surgical team at a Role 2 facility) does not expect that she will be the last surgeon to operate on a given patient; given this expectation, she does not necessarily close the wound, but instead focuses on debridement (cleaning a wound by removing dead tissue) and immediately necessary surgery. Definitive surgery will come later. Like the return to whole blood, this practice—the avoidance of "primary closure"—echoes Edward Churchill's call from World War II.

The more frequently soldiers are kept alive after being wounded, the more doctors have to focus on managing their pain. Advances in the pharmaceutical industry mean that new anesthetics are available beyond the morphine used in the world wars. While morphine is still in use, in Afghanistan and Iraq, military medical personnel also administered fentanyl citrate and ketamine, alongside more ordinary medicines like acetaminophen. Many analgesics have historically been administered intravenously. The focus on prehospital care has meant advances in other strategies, like the more immediate, albeit temporary, pain relief from intranasal anesthetics.[143]

Advances in treating other, nonfatal injuries speak to the longer-term improvements in military medicine. The fact that more people are surviving major injuries means that more attention can and should be paid to injuries that are not life-threatening. For example, a nontrivial number of casualties in the Afghanistan and Iraq Wars came from burns, especially from IEDs. Burns can be fatal, but more typically are not—especially today. This is in part due to advances in fluid resuscitation practices for burns, as well as dressings treated with the antiseptic silver sulfadiazine to prevent infection.[144] Additionally, researchers have recommended improved PPE for parts of the body—such as hands—that are often vulnerable to burn injury.[145]

That military doctors can train so much attention on nonfatal injuries is a reflection of their success rate in saving lives. At the same time, many military doctors have reservations about their patients' quality of life—especially those on the receiving end of extraordinary measures. Here is where we see a shift in the human costs of war: over time, as more lives are saved, the nature of postwar life changes dramatically in character.

Veterans' Benefits

Veterans' benefits have trended upward since World War II, albeit with some bumps along the way. Between World War II and the end of the draft, benefits periodically grew less generous rather than more; the post-Korea GI Bill, for example, saw a contraction of benefits offered in the 1944 bill, especially with respect to education.[146] Korean War veterans who had been prisoners of war were sometimes denied benefits altogether, due to McCarthyist fears that they had been "turned" communist.[147] And Vietnam veterans, who were famously spurned by the public, lobbied for many years before the VA acknowledged health problems associated with the use of the defoliant Agent Orange. The bumpiness of the trajectory of veterans' benefits eventually smoothed out, becoming a clean upward trend, for two main reasons. First is the shift to the all-volunteer force in 1973, which means that the military has to recruit actively in ways it did not have to during eras of conscription. Second—and related—is the fact that, in an era of remarkably high political polarization in the United States, veterans' benefits has been one of the few issues that receive regular bipartisan support.[148]

The current Department of Veterans Affairs budget is higher than it has ever been, at over $300 billion.[149] Following the Civil War, as we know, more than 40 percent of federal income went to veterans' pensions.[150] Today, the Department of Veterans Affairs accounts for just over 4 percent of the federal budget. But even though it does not compare to the post–Civil War era, today's 4 percent of the federal budget is considerable; VA spending outstrips that of the Departments of Agriculture, Education, and Homeland Security.[151] This ordering of spending reflects a national consensus on spending for veterans as well as dissensus on the federal government's role in other areas, such as education; it is a clear illustration of the effects of political polarization in US politics.

That the United States spends proportionately less today on veterans' benefits may at first appear somewhat at odds with the common claim that veterans' benefits have become sacrosanct in American society.[152] But when a scandal breaks regarding the quality or quantity of veterans' benefits, there tends to be an overwhelming response in support of veterans.[153] For decades, the military has been the most trusted institution in US politics, and this confidence in the military spills over into a commitment to veterans' benefits.[154] In a 2017 survey asking which sections of the budget to increase, decrease, or maintain at current levels, veterans' benefits received the most votes for an increase, at 75 percent; the next-most-popular category was education, where an increase was supported by 67 percent of respondents.[155] The fact that a very small proportion of the US population serves in the military today makes this kind of reaction surprising because, unlike in the post–World War II era, we have many fewer veterans to clamor for benefits. But veterans wield considerable political clout precisely because they are few in number and because, after 1973, they chose to serve. Citizens who opt not to join the military may be especially willing to support the provision of benefits to reward those who do join.

The government's share of spending on veterans' benefits often tracks ongoing or recent wars, as shown in Figure 3.5.[156] For example, spending on

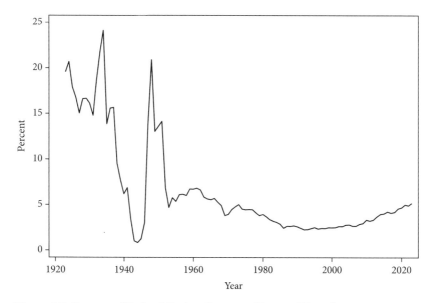

Figure 3.5 Percent of Federal Budget Spent on Veterans' Benefits, 1923–2022

Budget data taken from the St. Louis Federal Reserve website: https://fraser.stlouisfed.org/title/budget-united-states-government-54?browse=1920s#18966. Here, veterans' benefits can be divided into two main categories: pensions and disability compensation, and VA spending (including health insurance, burial benefits, administrative expenses, and more). The St. Louis Federal Reserve is missing data for 1995–1997 and 2014–2022. Internet archives via the Wayback Machine were used to access Office of Management and Budget archives for those years. Historical spending rather than actual spending is used for 1995–1997.

Source: Budget of the United State Government, 1921–2022; St. Louis Federal Reserve.

veterans' benefits accounted for 6.6 percent of the federal budget in 1962, but only 2.3 percent thirty years later, in 1992.

The fact that the VA accounted for a decreasing share of the federal budget in the 1970s and 1980s, however, does not mean that VA spending decreased in absolute terms. Figure 3.6[157] presents a slightly different view, showing an overall increase in VA spending since 1940, with observable peaks during World War II, during the Vietnam War, and concurrent with the United States' most recent wars in Iraq and Afghanistan. It is worth noting that both Figure 3.5 and Figure 3.6 demonstrate an upswing in spending on veterans' benefits starting in the early 2000s. This suggests that the immunity of US veterans' benefits to criticism may be of relatively recent vintage. The Afghanistan and Iraq Wars were the first conflicts to generate sizable cohorts of veterans since the establishment of the AVF. This combination of events is surely part of why—and when—veterans' benefits began to appear untouchable.

To at least some extent, increased spending by the VA in terms of absolute dollars (and perhaps also in terms of the federal budget share) is driven by the aging population of veterans in the last several decades. With advances in medical care, veterans are living longer. Even so, with relatively few surviving

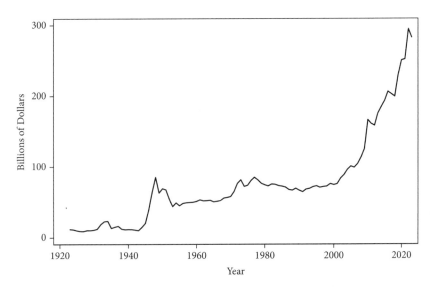

Figure 3.6 Total Spending on Veterans' Benefits in Constant 2022 Dollars, 1923–2022

Source: Budget of the United State Government, 1921–2022. St. Louis Federal Reserve.

World War II veterans today, age alone is not a sufficient explanation for the increase in spending on veterans' benefits. Indeed, starting in 2016, First Gulf War veterans superseded Vietnam War veterans as the plurality of US veterans.[158] As Linda Bilmes notes: "Federal expenditures to care for veterans doubled from . . . 2001 to 2020, even as the total number of living veterans from all US wars declined."[159]

Because citizens are no longer being compelled to join the military in time of war, they must be induced to do so. The promise of benefits is crucial to such inducement. Today's military veterans receive a wide array of benefits beyond the pensions available to those who serve for at least twenty years.[160] In addition to the nonpension benefits set out in the 1944 GI Bill, the so-called Montgomery GI Bill of 1984 increased educational benefits for veterans. The post-9/11 GI Bill, passed in 2008, further expanded benefits to cover housing assistance during postsecondary education; this benefit also can be transferred to a family member and was explicitly designed to help boost recruitment.[161] Even more recently, 2017's Forever GI Bill effectively removed the expiration date from educational benefits, extended certain benefits to family members (especially spouses), and expanded educational benefits to veterans pursuing postgraduate degrees in STEM fields. These benefits are also described in military recruitment materials. The front page of the US Army's recruitment website mentions a possible $40,000 signing bonus for some recruits.[162] The "Benefits" page's first story is titled "Benefits That Last a Lifetime."[163] Additional pages mention benefits such as tax-deferred retirement accounts available to those serving in the Army.[164] The Navy's website has a similar focus, highlighting the ability to retire prior to age forty in some cases, with lifelong benefits.[165] These benefits differ significantly from those offered to, and received by, enlistees prior to 1973.

Veterans of the United States' most recent wars have used their (nonpension) benefits much more so than previous cohorts. Several factors likely contribute to this increase, from more expansive and targeted VA outreach to veterans who served fewer than twenty years possibly using disability payments as a substitute for pensions.[166] Nearly half of today's 20.4 million veterans use the VA healthcare system;[167] similarly, about half of undergraduates who were veterans financed their education via the GI Bill as of the 2011–12 academic year.[168] Significantly, eligibility for healthcare has been relaxed for Afghanistan and Iraq War veterans, who automatically receive at least five years of care from the VA after separating from the military.[169] As Linda Bilmes shows, more than 40 percent of this same cohort of veterans have a disability rating from the VA, compared to 23 percent for veterans of World War II, Korea, and Vietnam. The VA describes a disability rating as measuring the severity of a particular veteran's disability: "We express this rating as a percentage, representing how much your disability decreases your overall health and ability to function."[170] Higher disability ratings translate into higher rates of compensation and care. Over a million post-9/11 veterans have a disability rating of 60 percent or more—qualifying them for more extensive (and expensive) benefits—compared to about 700,000 veterans of previous wars. This comparison is striking given the smaller size of today's military as well as the comparatively lower number of those deployed. According to Bilmes, "The biggest single long-term cost of the post-9/11 wars will be providing benefits and medical care to the men and women who supported the wars in Iraq, Afghanistan, and related theaters since 2001, and their dependents."[171]

There are calls from within the military community to moderate use of the veterans' benefits system. For example, in a 2021 monograph, two retired Army officers warn of abuses of the veterans' disability system. They note an increase in the percentage of soldiers receiving a disability rating of 50 percent or higher, from 2 percent in 1998 to 51 percent in 2017. Some of this increase is surely due to the increasing percentage of soldiers who were wounded but lived, as well as wider acceptance of mental health issues, discussed in the following chapter. The increase also results from military personnel having more and better information available to them as they separate from the military, as well as during their military service. But, the authors caution, there is also a fair amount of manipulation of the system, which they attribute to a sense that veterans are owed whatever compensation they can get, especially in an era when such a small percentage of the population serves in the armed forces.[172] A cottage industry of organizations that assist veterans in demonstrating that their disability is a result of their military service—thereby qualifying them for a higher disability rating—has sprung up; this trend is in part due to the generosity of health- and disability-related benefits today.

Veterans organizations are vigilant in pushing back against any attempts to limit benefits. Groups such as the Grand Army of the Republic were remarkably successful in advocating for veterans' benefits following the Civil War, and the American Legion was similarly successful as a successor.[173] Even though there are many fewer veterans today, as a proportion of the population, than in the past, in absolute terms groups such as the American Legion and Veterans of Foreign Wars have large memberships. The American Legion reports a membership of nearly two million, while the VFW reports a membership of 1.4 million.[174] Newer organizations, such as the Iraq and Afghanistan Veterans of America, are smaller (IAVA has 425,000 members) but extremely active.[175] For comparison, consider that the National Rifle Association (NRA)—whose lobbying prowess is mentioned with great frequency—is estimated to have approximately 5 million members.[176] With that said, of course, a crucial difference is funding. The NRA spent about $250 million in 2020, while the combined net assets of the VFW, the American Legion, and IAVA are less than $100 million.[177]

Nonetheless, veterans' organizations have been especially successful in lobbying for members with conflict-specific illnesses. For example, veterans suffering from Gulf War Disease, which the VA describes as a "medically unexplained illness," are eligible for benefits in part because of lobbying efforts by groups like the American Legion.[178] More recently, veterans organizations—and activists, including comedian Jon Stewart—have argued strenuously in support of the PACT Act, which provides for support for veterans suffering from exposure to toxic burn pits.[179]

In 2017, National Public Radio's Robert Siegel described the Forever GI Bill as unusual because "Congress [was] acting in a bipartisan fashion, sending legislation quickly to the president. He's signing it. This is the exception to the rule in Washington these days."[180] This characterization appears to be part of a longer trend that is unusual in today's domestic politics in the United States. In what has become a remarkably polarized political landscape, both parties—and most US citizens—agreed that military veterans should receive a generous and increasing benefits package.

This consensus may be fraying. Recent debates about supporting veterans exposed to fumes from burn pits suggest that political polarization has spilled over into veterans' issues. The nature of the current polarization is also somewhat surprising, with Republicans—more typically considered the party of the military—opposed to increased veterans' benefits, and Democrats in support. At the same time, there are some calls for reducing veterans' benefits from the center-left, such as a 2023 *Washington Post* editorial arguing for means-testing disability payments.[181] This new political array suggests potential early echoes of the backlash against Civil War pensions.

Conclusion

The United States' wounded-to-killed ratio in the Afghanistan and Iraq Wars was higher than it had ever been previously. In Operation Enduring Freedom, there were more than ten wounded in action for every US military personnel killed; in Operation Iraqi Freedom, the ratio was a bit lower, at just over 9:1. Both numbers represent a stark increase over anything that had come before.

As in past wars, however, there is unevenness among potential beneficiaries of medical care. More women in the military has meant more attention paid to issues around sexual assault. Sexual assault has always been a feature of war—occurring both as invading armies attack local populations but also within all-male military forces. Gender integration in the military reveals blind spots about who the "typical" soldier is and what their medical needs are. Notably, less military medical research focuses on race today than in the past. When I asked military medical personnel why this was so, answers ranged from shrugs to an ironic "It's because the military thinks it's solved its race problem."

US military medical care has not been limited to US forces. Consistent with the Hippocratic oath as well as the 1949 Geneva Conventions, local civilians, allied military personnel, and enemy combatants are also treated in US medical facilities in theater. But when it comes to treating "host nation" casualties, there are two key differences that speak to longer-term medical outcomes. First, those injured or ill among the local population are likely less healthy to start than US military personnel. Therefore, they might be less likely to survive ex ante. Second, while US military personnel were evacuated to higher-level medical facilities—often outside Afghanistan and Iraq—as a matter of course, this kind of evacuation was not typical for Afghan or Iraqi nationals. These patients would be more likely to stay in-country in a combat support hospital longer-term, or to be transferred to an Afghan or Iraqi hospital. While they might have received the best care available to them, they did not receive the best care available.[182]

The dramatic, if unevenly distributed, shift in the United States' wounded-to-killed ratio resulted from a combination of the nature of the wars being fought and the military medical lessons that were learned—and relearned. One hallmark of military medicine in the United States' most recent counterinsurgency wars is the recovery of earlier medical practices, most importantly the use of whole blood for resuscitation. One reason these wars enabled such advances was their length. As opposed to the United States' brief participation in the First World War, the wars following the invasions of Afghanistan and Iraq were so long that they provided space for the development of Critical Casualty Air Transport Teams, the maturation of the Joint Trauma System, and the invention of new devices such as the Combat Application Tourniquet. And a tremendous effort was made to ensure that the injured received appropriate medical care within the first hour after injury, the "golden hour." These developments were significant: according to one study, they account for a reduction of over 44 percent in US battlefield mortality.[183] Those whose lives were saved returned to a newly expanded—and recently controversial—array of veterans' benefits, including for healthcare. The costs of the Afghanistan and Iraq Wars—from deficit financing to veterans' benefits—have been immense.[184] Indeed, they are still being tallied. These wars are also frequently deemed major US foreign policy failures; medical improvements may be one of their few silver linings.

4

Soldiers' Hearts

Reckoning with Psychological Trauma

Missiles and microbes of war do not merely ravage the body. Like physical injury, psychological trauma induced by war is as old as war itself. A key reason soldiers undergo intensive military training is that, in the civilian world, killing is both anathema and illegal. Soldiers, though, must be trained to overcome this taboo and accept killing, as well as the possibility of being killed, as part of their job. Being in the midst of such violence—as a perpetrator, victim, or observer—almost inevitably produces psychological trauma of some sort. How such injuries and illnesses are identified, categorized, treated, and accepted by society has changed dramatically over time. And, not surprisingly, so too have the costs of war-induced psychological trauma.

To underline the long history of psychological trauma caused by war, consider Homer's description of Achilles in *The Iliad*. Distraught over the death of his dear friend Petraklos, Achilles attacks the enemy ruthlessly: "He raged in every direction with his spear."[1] Psychiatrist Jonathan Shay invokes the term "berserk" to describe Homer's analysis of Achilles's behavior, arguing that today a psychiatrist would likely diagnose Achilles with "post-traumatic stress disorder" or even "moral injury."[2] The passage of two millennia of war has only emphasized this dynamic—the recurrent relationship between war and psychological trauma is undeniable. Indeed, prominent scholars of war-induced psychological trauma frequently invoke the ancient Greeks in both their scholarship and practice.[3]

There is no straight line, however, between Achilles's fit of berserk and today's diagnoses of post-traumatic stress disorder. Labels have changed with nearly every war the United States has fought. In the Revolutionary War, military doctors labeled despairing soldiers "nostalgic" or "hysterical."[4] Diagnoses of "soldier's heart" and "irritable heart" were common in the Civil War. World War I was famous for an abundance—some called it an overabundance—of "shell shock." By the Second World War, the official terminology changed again, to "combat exhaustion." Soldiers exhibiting many of the same symptoms that would have generated a "combat exhaustion" designation in World War II were instead discharged during the Vietnam War, often to fall prey to mental illness after their service. After 1980, when "post-traumatic stress disorder" entered the American Psychiatric Association's *Diagnostic and Statistical Manual of Mental Disorders* (*DSM*), PTSD (or PTS, as it is often referred to today) became the dominant diagnosis for war-induced psychological trauma through the United States' most recent wars in Afghanistan and Iraq. And as these wars continued, a new diagnosis—"moral injury"—has emerged, but it remains contested in both research and practice.

Unlike purely physiological conditions, war-induced psychological trauma has changed not only in name but also in symptomatology and treatment. Mumps and malaria appear essentially the same today as they did during the Civil War. But it is hard to even recognize the way we talk about psychological conditions. Whereas soldiers in World War I might have suffered temporary blindness, today's servicemen and -women are more likely to present with symptoms of anger or sleeplessness. During World War II, combat exhaustion cases were treated with sedation, whereas in Vietnam self-medication via drugs or alcohol was more common. While some scholars argue that these changes obscure a common and fairly constant core, others suggest that the nature of war-induced psychological trauma itself changes, alongside advancements in medicine but also shifts in society as a whole.[5] Still others are skeptical of such diagnoses at all. According to one British physician, "Post-traumatic stress disorder is the diagnosis for an age of disenchantment."[6] Either way, the fact that more military personnel are surviving today—due to the many other advances in medicine—translates into an increased incidence of diagnoses that fall under the broad umbrella of war-induced psychological trauma; in other words, more people are diagnosed with illnesses such as post-traumatic stress disorder today simply because they are still alive.

Because the names for and, possibly, causes and symptoms of war-induced psychological trauma have changed so much over time, it is especially difficult to track the changing costs associated with this class of illnesses. Psychiatry and psychology have made considerable strides, developing clearer diagnostic criteria as well as treatment protocols. Illnesses such as PTSD have also become increasingly accepted in the military and society, and this acceptance has translated into a greater willingness to accept the diagnosis and also to increased benefits for veterans with PTSD. If all else were equal over time, we could likely conclude that the long-term costs of war-induced psychological trauma have increased over the past two centuries. As this chapter will make plain, however, all else has not been equal. Thus, while we can certainly document and analyze the *changing* costs of war-induced psychological trauma, it is much more difficult to assess its *net* costs.

Psychological trauma has always bedeviled militaries for at least two reasons. First, mental illness tends to present in early adulthood—a time in life that often overlaps with military service.[7] Like colleges and universities, militaries host populations that are already prone to substance, mood, and impulse-control disorders. This selection bias means that militaries have never been able to escape the issue of psychological trauma, even if their approaches to it have varied dramatically across space and time. And second, this already vulnerable population is deliberately, and regularly, exposed to trauma—they are sent to kill. Thus, we should expect rates of psychological trauma to be especially high in militaries.

At the same time, military medicine has struggled to address psychological trauma. The ostensible purpose of having doctors, nurses, and all the other people who constitute a military's medical corps is to bring more people to the fight; like all other aspects of a military, in other words, military medicine is supposed to make the military more effective. Treating visible wounds is an obvious first step. But "invisible injuries" can be just as debilitating, if not more so. While the *symptoms* of psychological trauma are often visible, ranging from blindness to sleeplessness to angry outbursts, their causes were not visible to doctors in the same way as a mosquito bite inducing malaria or a gunshot causing hemorrhage. Especially in the nineteenth and early twentieth centuries, this inability to observe a direct cause often produced doubt about whether a patient's symptoms were real. Traumatized soldiers were regularly accused of faking their illness. From the Civil War through Vietnam, diagnoses of "soldier's heart" and "shell shock" were often viewed as a source of shame both within and without the military. More sympathetic doctors took patients at their word but struggled to help them. It has only been in recent decades that this set of diagnoses has begun to receive the credibility and sustained attention that those who suffer from psychological trauma have always deserved.

The Civil War: Psychological Trauma in Pre-Psychological Times

However rudimentary their skills and knowledge were by today's standards, doctors and nurses in both the Union and Confederate armies spent a great deal of time, treasure, and blood to determine how to best serve their patients.[8] And almost from the start of fighting, they started to see symptoms they could not explain. Perhaps because the United States had not previously fought a war that required the degree of mobilization seen in the Civil War,[9] they were especially surprised by what appeared to be a new class of illnesses that could not easily be traced to visible physiological injury or disease. The associated symptoms were often attributed to other illnesses, especially gastrointestinal diseases like "entero-colitis," but mostly because doctors initially had no other way to categorize these patients. A Union Army physician who later specialized in mental illness wrote:

> There is yet another very distressing affection which sometimes occurs as a result of this disease, and to which I cannot give a name. To those who have suffered long from entero-colitis, or have been subjected to prison diet, it is most marked. I allude to a state of the mind which may with propriety be called mental incapacity. In this condition a feebleness of purpose, a want of stability and incoherence are exhibited. The derangement may continue for some time after the primary disease has entirely left the patients. When a question is asked they hesitate several minutes, apparently endeavoring to find language for an answer, which when made is in the fewest words. This was observed particularly, among those men who had been several months in southern prisons, suffering from the effects of entero-colitis, with the scorbutic diathesis [being prone to scurvy]. They would sit by the hour, gazing on the ground, paying no attention to what was going on about them. Their movements were slow; they were irritable; nothing would please them. The face wore an expression of complete dementia. . . . From this state some recovered entirely; others did not while they remained in hospital.[10]

Soldiers suffering from such invisible injuries in the Civil War were variously diagnosed with "nostalgia" (sometimes called "melancholia" in Europe), "sunstroke," "irritable heart," or "soldier's heart." Initially, doctors believed that cardiovascular distress—brought on by marching with heavy packs whose straps cut off circulation—was responsible for the exhaustion, breathlessness, heart palpitations, and general cardiac weakness that characterized the diagnosis.[11] As it turned out, however, irritable heart syndrome was also presenting among artillerymen and cavalrymen, who were not wearing these same packs. Thus, concluded Army physician Jacob DaCosta in 1871, there must have been some other cause.[12]

Just as abundant were diagnoses of "nostalgia," which the US government described as follows:

> A temporary feeling of depression frequently pervaded our camps on account of the discomfort, hardships, and exposures, especially when these were recognized or assumed by our volunteer soldiers to be of a preventable or uncalled for nature. During its continuance, the happiness and comforts of home arose to mind, coupled with the desire to again experience them. The natural result of existing discomfort constituted the only nostalgic influence to which our troops as a rule were subject.[13]

The assistant surgeon general of the Union Army described it similarly:

> First, great mental dejection, loss of appetite, indifference to external influences, irregular action of the bowels, and slight hectic fever. As the disease progresses it is attended by hysterical weeping, a dull pain in the head, throbbing of the temporal arteries, anxious expression on the face, watchfulness, incontinence of urine, spermatorrhoea, increased hectic fever, and a general wasting of all the vital powers. The disease may terminate in resolution, or run into cerebral derangement, typhoid fever, or any epidemic prevailing in the immediate vicinity, and frequently with fatal results.[14]

The reported incidence of nostalgia hovered between 2 and 3 percent during the first year of the war, although this statistic is limited to white troops and to the Union Army.[15] To understand the extent of the illness, it is useful to compare it to the incidence of other injuries and illnesses. As Figure 4.1 shows, the incidence of nostalgia and sunstroke for white soldiers in the Army of the Potomac was consistently lower than that of measles, but generally quite similar to the incidence of fractures (which here includes both simple and complex fractures). Indeed, the percentage of soldiers suffering from psychological ailments exceeded those suffering from fractures (and

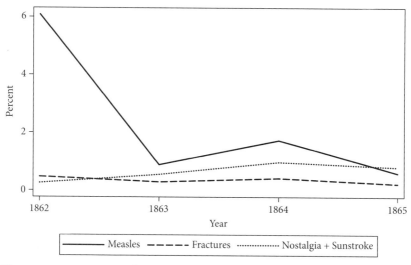

Figure 4.1 Frequencies of Certain Illnesses and Injuries
Source: MSHWR, Vol. I, Part 1, 31–35, 175–79, 324–29, 491–95

even measles) as the war went on; the grind of war took its toll on soldiers' psyches as well as on their bodies.

"Windage" was another condition that surfaced during the Civil War. Windage was frequently associated with paralysis, and was ascribed to the nearby passage of a projectile.[16] In this respect, it may well have been a predecessor of World War I's shell shock, and a sign of a period that saw developments in weaponry like the Napoleon 12-pound howitzer artillery piece and rifles using the minié ball.[17] Like irritable heart and nostalgia, windage accounted for a surprisingly high number of Civil War casualties; Anthony Babington reports that "20.8 out of every 1000 men were discharged from the Union army during the war owing to paralysis of one or more of their limbs" attributed to windage.[18] In his examination of medical records from Civil War veterans in an Indiana mental hospital, historian Eric Dean notes a striking resemblance in their symptoms to those diagnosed with PTSD today, as well as combat exhaustion in World War II. Flashbacks, phobias, and anxiety were common.[19]

Another key characteristic all these illnesses had in common was that doctors lacked the knowledge to treat them.[20] Typically, one of three options was pursued. First, the soldier might be allowed to rest and recover. This treatment was likely to be most effective (in comparison to the others), and it was also adopted in subsequent wars, especially in addressing combat exhaustion in World War II. But it also depended on where the soldier was able to rest. If he was sent to an Army hospital, he might be just as likely to fall ill as he was to recover, especially given that doctors of the time were unaware of the germ theory of disease.

A second treatment option was administrative rather than medical, and sometimes self-administered. That is to say, a soldier exhibiting the symptoms of nostalgia, for example, might be accused of malingering and dishonorably discharged.[21] He might also desert. Both the Union and Confederate armies staged public executions of deserters to deter future cases.[22] Nevertheless, by 1865, nearly one-third of Union soldiers and more than one-half of Confederate soldiers appear to have deserted.[23] A *New York Herald* reporter following the Union Army in Virginia described the causes of desertion in terms that are highly evocative of "nostalgia" or "homesickness," both labels for war-induced psychological trauma in the mid-nineteenth century:

> The soldier who will lead a forlorn hope, face instant and almost certain death, when ordered to do so, under the excitement of battle, becomes the most restless mortal in existence when confined to the daily routine, of eating, sleeping, performing a little fatigue duty and cleaning his arms equipment and clothing, without any apparent compensations. He became morbidly discontented and homesick, commencing perhaps with laziness, sulkiness, and ending in desertion.[24]

In either case, the soldier was less likely to return home than to struggle behind the army and, sometimes, rove the countryside as part of a group of bandits. To a large extent, the tendency to avoid returning home seems to indicate the growing sense, vague but also palpable, that these psychological illnesses, as yet unnamed as such, were emasculating and dishonorable.

The third treatment option, reserved only for particularly severe cases, was hospitalization. Typically, however, these hospitals were outside the structure of the Army, although at least one—St. Elizabeth's in Washington, DC—was meant to serve active-duty soldiers suffering from what we would call today psychiatric illness.[25] Recall that hospitals were rare in mid-nineteenth-century America. With the exception of the indigent, most people who fell ill were cared for at home. This meant that hospitals were for those who were too poor or, often, too mentally ill to be tended by their mothers and wives. These institutions were unwelcoming, to say the least, and certainly were not able to offer appropriate care for soldiers afflicted with war-induced psychological trauma.[26] After the war's end, psychiatrically ill veterans were also frequently jailed.[27]

A major wartime cost of the nature of military medicine in the Civil War was the loss of personnel who fell prey to psychological illnesses but were not treated effectively. With proper treatment, they might well have been able to return to duty. Not surprisingly, the costs of war-induced psychological trauma outlasted the war, although in some respects less so than in future conflicts. Much of what we know about psychological illness can be deduced from the use of benefits (or the lack thereof) in the aftermath of the Civil War. The primary initial benefit to (Union) Civil War veterans came in the form of disability pensions.[28] Until 1890, eligibility for pensions was determined by physicians. The vast majority of qualifying disabilities fell into obvious physiological categories: "gunshot and shell wounds," "chronic diarrhea," or "incised and contused wounds and other injuries."[29] Physicians were typically unsympathetic to diagnoses of "irritable heart" or "nostalgia."[30] While the undefined condition of "nervous prostration" was listed by the Pensions Bureau, along with "sunstroke," as a disability for which Civil War pensions were granted, the number of cases was considerably lower than for other conditions, such as "malarial poisoning." As a result, it was not until the 1879 Arrears Act and, especially, the 1890 Dependent Pensions Act (when pension laws were changed to apply to all veterans, regardless of disability) that soldiers with a primary diagnosis of what we would call today a psychological or psychiatric illness could qualify for a pension.[31] By then, however, many such veterans had died or been unable to navigate the pension application system. And if they had been dishonorably discharged, as many deserters were, they would not have been eligible anyway.[32]

Psychologically ill veterans who were able to navigate the veterans' benefits system also would have been eligible to claim land in the West via the Homestead Act of 1862 and residency in veterans' homes (again, unless they had been dishonorably discharged).[33] The Homestead Act required that claimants live on and cultivate the land for five years; Union soldiers could deduct their time in service from this requirement (recall that Confederate Army veterans were ineligible for benefits of any kind from the federal government). Demonstrating this eligibility was challenging even for nondisabled veterans, which may explain the relatively low rate of veterans taking advantage of this benefit.[34] Like the pension system, access to veterans' homes for the disabled required demonstration of a service-connected disability in the immediate aftermath of the Civil War, although this restriction was later liberalized.[35]

Prejudice against invisible injuries and general bewilderment about war-induced psychological trauma combined to keep the long-term financial costs of this set of illnesses low—for the government, anyway—after the Civil War. Add to these factors generally poor medical care, which meant a relatively low wounded-to-killed ratio. Put bluntly, hundreds of thousands of soldiers on both sides died before they could fall prey to war-induced psychological trauma, although the magnitude of the conflict may have made such trauma more severe or widespread among survivors. And while the veterans' benefits system put in place after the Civil War and then subsequently expanded was notoriously generous, even to the point of corruption, soldiers suffering from war-induced psychological trauma were among the least likely to receive these benefits.

World War I: The Mysteries of Shell Shock

Soon after World War I began in 1914, British soldiers began to exhibit a wide array of seemingly unrelated symptoms—impairment of sight and hearing, tremors, and nightmares. Military physicians were perplexed. These soldiers did not appear to have been directly injured, whether from bullets or artillery shells, nor were they suffering from common illnesses, such as tuberculosis and typhus. Not knowing how to treat these soldiers, who appeared useless to the fight, they tended to send them back to the United Kingdom, where they were often placed in insane asylums. This was not an effective solution, both because these soldiers tended not to recover and because it led to significant force depletion. Addressing this amorphous condition—which would eventually be called "shell shock"—became the primary task of Allied psychiatrists in the Great War.

Months after Britain entered the war, British psychiatrist Charles Myers began to see the kinds of patients described above; in 1915, he coined the term "shell shock" for the condition. Myers could not explain the symptoms he observed, but he noted that all his subjects timed the beginning of their symptoms to a nearby explosion and that "the close relation of these cases to those of 'hysteria' appears fairly certain."[36] Legitimizing shell shock as an actual disease was crucial in the British armed forces, which had been so intent on maintaining discipline that many soldiers exhibiting symptoms of what would ultimately be understood as shell shock were court-martialed for cowardice or desertion, and hundreds were executed.[37]

By the time the United States entered World War I, its military medicine had, of course, evolved significantly from the days of the Civil War. In addition, the US military had been keeping a close eye on its counterpart in Britain, modeling the US military medical corps on the British, and was especially concerned about shell shock, as well as neurasthenia, hysteria, and "disordered action of the heart." In preparation for a potential onslaught of cases, the US military recruited a new category of doctor, neuropsychiatrists—one of which was assigned to each combat division—and built a Hospital for War Neuroses (Base Hospital No. 117) in France.[38] At the time, the prevailing view was that biological—rather than psychological—causes were behind most psychiatric illnesses.[39] Indeed, Thomas Salmon, chief of Army psychiatry for the American Expeditionary Force during the First World War, argued for a psychological rather than physiological explanation for shell shock only after the war ended.[40]

While US neuropsychiatrists entered the war convinced of the legitimacy of shell shock as an illness, US military physicians more broadly (i.e., nonpsychiatrists) were often skeptical of the diagnosis, especially amid concerns over malingering. It was hard to understand, and discomfiting to realize, that not all "malingering" was intentional; feigning an illness could actually be a symptom of psychological trauma. As Dr. Harry Solomon, a US psychiatrist who served with the AEF in World War I, put it, "Malingering is a nasty word—[because it could obscure] conscious or unconscious appearance of symptoms."[41] For soldiers who did experience shell shock, there may have been incentives for some to make their symptoms appear worse than they were. In this sense, the possibility of malingering had to be considered on a spectrum rather than as a binary condition.

Military leaders were also concerned about a rash of shell shock diagnoses eroding morale.[42] A neuropsychiatric report issued during the war suggested that the AEF should "check the development of neurosis by denying its existence at the start."[43] Ambivalence regarding shell shock was similarly reflected in a World War I circular to the AEF from the Office of the Chief Surgeon. Military psychiatrists were directed as follows:

> It is essential for such officers to bear in mind the prime necessity of preserving, or restoring for military duty, as many as possible of the officers and enlisted men who may be brought to their attention. On the other

hand, they should recommend the evacuation, with the least practicable delay, of all persons likely to continue ineffective or to endanger the morale of the organizations of which they are a part. This is particularly true in the case of the functional nervous disorders loosely grouped under the term "shell shock."[44]

In response to these pressures, one strategy used with great frequency to limit the designation of shell shock was to label patients as "Not Yet Diagnosed—Nervous," at least initially.[45] This deferred diagnosis, however, was merely a stalling tactic. Patients still needed to be treated and returned to duty to win the war.

How best to treat shell-shocked patients was a hotly debated topic through World War I, especially once the diagnosis gained at least some acceptance in military as well as medical circles. A key question was *where* patients should be treated. Removing the patient from the source of the trauma—the war—at first seemed logical. But distance from the front appeared to impair recovery, especially in less severe cases. According to some physicians, evacuated shell-shocked World War I soldiers who preferred not to return to the front were incentivized against recovering, consciously or subconsciously.

Early examples of forward psychiatry argued for treatment closer to the front. The psychiatrist assigned to the 4th Division of the AEF, for instance, was positioned with triage units, "and having set aside a field hospital about 6 miles farther to the rear, was able to divert from the evacuation hospitals a large number of men suffering from conditions likely to result in war neuroses, and to return many of them to the front."[46] Some psychiatrists also argued that psychologically traumatized military personnel would be more likely to recover quickly if they remained with, or close to, their unit, in part because of the personal bonds they forged with their fellow soldiers. Partly as a result of this type of analysis, military psychiatrists developed the "PIE" method to treat psychological trauma: shell-shocked patients were treated in *proximity* to the front, as quickly (*immediately*) as possible, and with the *expectation* that they would return to duty.[47]

A key logistical constraint, of course, was the availability of appropriate medical facilities. Having observed the British response to the influx of shell shock cases—they "provided facilities for little more than convalescence with limited psychiatric input"—the American Expeditionary Force arrived in

France with a plan to set up Base Hospital 117 before major deployments of US troops.[48] The hospital, near the French village of La Fauche, was meant to isolate neurasthenic troops from the rest of the AEF, but also to provide an environment conducive to recovery.[49] Even with a hospital dedicated to neurasthenic illness, the evacuation system was imperfect. In part, these imperfections were due to the state of evacuation at the time—despite the fact that faster motorized ambulances were now available.[50] What is more, neuropsychiatric patients were given lower priority for evacuation than those who were visibly injured.

In the midst of war, military psychiatrists had to be at least as concerned with the overall health of fighting units as with the health of individual military personnel, and this concern sometimes affected treatment of psychologically traumatized patients. Even if it might have benefited the mental health of such patients to be returned to their units quickly, nonmedical officers sometimes opposed this practice. There was widespread concern that soldiers with a shell shock diagnosis could not be relied upon in battle. Officers also worried that shell shock might be contagious. Returning shell-shocked troops to their unit after treatment had the benefit of normalizing the illness to some extent, but this benefit was often perceived to come with a military cost. Soldiers might become less reticent about requesting treatment, or, from a more cynical perspective, malingering might increase if a shell shock diagnosis was expected to lead to a few weeks of rest and relaxation (R&R). On the other hand, a quick return to duty was also viewed as having "a very favorable effect in lessening the incidence among their comrades . . . [if] a large proportion of these patients are evacuated indiscriminately to hospitals in the S.O.S. [Services of Supply, at the rear] or to home territory, the effect will be to increase the incidence."[51]

The most common solution to this dilemma—of what served patients and fighting units best, particularly as shell shock diagnoses became increasingly frequent—appears to have been to return soldiers to duty, but to a less dangerous assignment. Soldiers who had previously fought in the trenches would instead be assigned to duty farther to the rear. For example, a twenty-year-old Massachusetts man serving in the 30th Infantry who had served on the front lines in France from May to June 1918 and who had been "digging in" to the trenches lost consciousness during battle. Upon waking in the hospital, he described experiencing headaches, dizziness, and getting "winded quick." A physician noted: "Not much energy—neurasthenic type?" The private was returned to duty but reassigned to the line of communications that connected the front to military bases, rather than returned to the trenches.[52]

At the close of the First World War, psychiatrists believed that shell-shocked patients could be cured with a few months of treatment.[53] This belief dovetailed nicely with the federal government's shift to rehabilitation, and away from the Civil War pensions that had threatened the nation's financial health.[54] But the treatment regimens evinced skepticism of the legitimacy of the condition itself. Dr. Harry Solomon reminisced about the "Mitchell rest cure," in which shell-shocked officers sent to a neuropsychiatric hospital in Cape May, New Jersey, were brought to a farm to hoe corn. They refused, claiming illness and military heroism. According to Solomon, who was serving at the hospital:

> McCarthy [a neurologist and lieutenant colonel] said, "All right, get back into the truck. We'll go back to the hospital and go to bed now." He took the clothes away from them. "No privileges. Can't get out of bed. No cigarettes. You're sick." . . . Within two days they capitulated and asked if they might go out and hoe some corn.[55]

Nearly ten years after the end of the war, it became clear that these initial expectations of a quick recovery were unfounded: "A survey taken in February 1927 revealed that ex-service men with neuropsychiatric disabilities constituted 46.7 per cent of all patients receiving hospital treatment as beneficiaries of the United States Veterans' Bureau."[56] John Kinder reports that "more than 25,000 mentally traumatized veterans were under the permanent guardianship of the state" in the early 1930s, a number that threatened "to swamp the facilities."[57] Dr. Thomas Salmon, a major figure in early twentieth-century American psychiatry who had served as chief psychiatric consultant to the AEF, further argued that this treatment was subpar in that shell-shocked veterans had been "discarded" in general hospitals (rather than specialized psychiatric hospitals) that were not conducive to their recovery.[58]

A key issue for veterans seeking benefits for war-induced psychological trauma was demonstrating that this trauma was connected to their military service. For those World War I veterans discharged from the hospital, applications for pensions were often unsuccessful, in part because of the difficulty of getting a physician to certify that a veteran's psychological trauma was war-related.[59] This difficulty was equally present for veterans making claims that their psychiatric condition made them eligible for health benefits. The changing bureaucratic landscape around veterans' benefits in the interwar period made these attempts especially challenging. Recall that two organizations—the Bureau of War Risk Insurance and the United States Public Health Service—were tasked with managing financial and health benefits for veterans after World War I. But the relatively young BWRI had no experience delivering healthcare, and the USPHS had limited experience with military or veteran populations. As the two agencies competed both to gain power and, at times, to evade certain responsibilities, the failings of the veterans' benefits system came into sharp relief. As we know, the Veterans Bureau (a precursor to today's Department of Veterans Affairs) was created in 1921. As part of the creation of the Veterans Bureau, Congress determined the conditions under which veterans were eligible to receive specific benefits. As Jessica Adler reports, Congress concluded that veterans with neuropsychiatric disease should be treated more leniently with respect to the determination of their benefits. Lenience was appropriate because of the extreme difficulty of proving that neuropsychiatric illness was a result of military service. Veterans with neuropsychiatric illnesses contracted within two years of discharge were given the benefit of the doubt when it came to the question of whether the illness was connected to their military service and, by extension, whether they were eligible for benefits.[60]

Compared to the Civil War, the long-term costs of war-induced psychological trauma rose modestly in World War I. There are good reasons for this increase in cost, which reflect investments in medicine and veterans benefits. Having psychiatrists on staff in the Army meant that there were doctors trained to diagnose and treat illnesses such as shell shock.[61] The combination of better overall medicine and the practice of returning shell-shocked patients to less dangerous duty also meant that more military personnel survived to endure psychological trauma. And while veterans seeking benefits based on their psychological state initially confronted roadblocks, these barriers were eventually removed. At the same time, however, the nature of benefits had changed, from pensions to healthcare. Healthcare for veterans was certainly expensive, but it accounted for a much lower percentage of the federal budget than did Civil War pensions at their peak. But greater acceptance of these illnesses in society and in the military meant that more veterans were likely to qualify for benefits.

"Combat Exhaustion": World War II's Diagnosis

One of the legacies of treating large numbers of shell-shocked veterans of World War I was the subsequent anticipation, at the start of the Second World War, of an impending influx of psychologically traumatized soldiers.[62] This concern emerged from the dual frustration of not having been able to treat shell-shocked veterans effectively and a sense that they represented a significant financial burden on the government at a time of great economic stress.

By the time the Second World War began, US military psychiatry had moved from attributing shell shock to a particular traumatic experience toward a belief that certain people were predisposed to this class of psychological illnesses. This belief led to an extensive psychological screening process during the recruitment period for World War II.[63] Among other concerns, the US Public Health Service anticipated higher numbers of "mental disorders" in a second world war due to the additional "terrors" associated with aerial and naval warfare. But amid these challenges there was optimism. An August 1940 confidential report to the Federal Board of Hospitalization argued that the US medical community was much better equipped for screening in 1940 than it had been in 1918. "Psychiatry has made marked strides during the past twenty years and ... well-trained men would be available for an emergency. ... In 1918 psychiatric nurses were decidedly scarce. Since that time there has been marked development in the training schools and a large body of well-trained psychiatric nurses, both male and female, are available."[64]

In addition to the culling of unsuitable candidates, another aim of the screening process was to limit the financial liability of the Veterans Bureau for psychiatric cases after the war. In the same memo, the USPHS noted:

> If the very generous presumption of service connection which is now provided by law in the case of neuropsychiatric patients obtains in the future, as is likely, a progressive increase of hospital beds will be called for on account of this group of patients.... In 1922 approximately one-half of one per cent, or 500 per 100,000, of all living veterans were receiving compensation from the Government while seventeen years later about two and two-tenths per cent of the living veterans were receiving monetary aid from the government by reason of "neuropsychiatric" disorder. The cost to the Government on account of these disorders is little short of staggering.[65]

In the end, however, the screening process was counterproductive, in part because of lack of training for psychiatrists (despite the USPHS's optimism), and in part because even well-trained psychiatrists simply could not have identified this imagined predisposition.[66] According to one retrospective of the World War II screening process:

> Because psychiatrists were used in large numbers to help assess the suitability of volunteers and draftees for army service as well as to decide whether large numbers of ineffective soldiers should be retained in the military or should be released prematurely back to civilian life, the Army early on engaged in a large-scale retraining program to convert general practitioners into "psychiatrists," who were known in the Army as "90-Day Wonders," such being the length of their training. Considering the facts that close to 1.5 million draft-eligible men were rejected for military service because they were diagnosed as being mentally or emotionally unfit and that about 750,000 enlistees and draftees were prematurely discharged from the service because of supposed psychiatric or other similar conditions or behaviors, the "90-Day Wonders" may have done more harm than good.[67]

The psychiatric screening process was ultimately deemed excessive. Even during the war, military higher-ups protested that too many potential recruits were turned away. The belief that psychiatric symptoms were disqualifying extended to those who presented with such symptoms after passing the initial screening and being inducted into the military—these men were quickly discharged rather than treated. Indeed, by 1943, the number of psychiatric discharges was greater than the number of new enlistments.[68]

Amid the growing debate around, and increasingly clear ineffectiveness of, screening soldiers, as World War II lumbered on there was also a shift in the very terms used to describe psychological trauma. At the start of the war, "shell shock" was still the most common description. The United States then traded one broad term for another. "Psychoneurosis" replaced "shell shock," and (not very usefully) covered "all types and severity of neurotic disorders."[69] "Psychoneurosis," however, was objectionable not just because of its breadth and vagueness but also because it carried negative connotations. Soldiers in particular did not distinguish between "psychoneurosis" and "psychosis," a confusion that quickly tarred anyone with a psychoneurosis diagnosis as "psycho." Thus, by 1943, yet another term emerged: "combat exhaustion."[70]

The relabeling of shell shock as "combat exhaustion" or "battle fatigue" in World War II is evidence of the US military psychiatric community's pendulum shift from the idea that certain people were predisposed to suffer from war-induced psychological trauma back to the notion that most people had a breaking point, and that enough time in intense warfare would hasten the journey to that point.[71] Symptoms of combat exhaustion included slowness, indifference, fearfulness, irritability, disorientation, and gastrointestinal distress.[72] In this case, the renaming itself may have been a strategic decision that blunted some of the dilemmas of diagnosis. Soldiers—both patients and commanders—were more willing to accept a diagnosis of exhaustion than of the much more nebulous "psychoneurosis." And doctors could feel reassured that they were not stigmatizing a patient for life, or even for the duration of the war.[73] Returning to duty after a diagnosis of combat exhaustion was, even though some stigma still remained, psychologically and socially easier for all involved.[74]

It was also easier on the military. The diagnosis of combat exhaustion was explicitly selected to replace shell shock and psychoneurosis as part of a campaign to instill in soldiers the belief that their symptoms were temporary and could be relieved with a short period of rest, typically in a hospital setting.[75] This new diagnosis had the salutary effect of making it socially easier to return soldiers to their unit after treatment—they were not "psychos" but rather had just reached their limit and only needed some time to recover. But the "combat exhaustion" label also had the perceived downside of possibly increasing malingering, especially given high rates of psychiatric illness. According to a psychiatric report conducted toward the end of operations in Europe, "It has been said that as tuberculosis accounted for the highest percentage of medical casualties in the First World War, so psychiatric problems have proved to be the largest single category of disability discharges in World War II."[76] Concern regarding the possibility of malingering prompted the army to try to make examples of specific soldiers, although fewer than fifty US military personnel were actually convicted for malingering in the US armed forces during World War II.[77]

Treatment for combat exhaustion typically included rest and relaxation, but also psychotherapy and some pharmacology (usually sedatives).[78] As in World War I, the PIE method—particularly, the notion that psychiatric casualties ought to be treated close to the front and, ideally, be returned to their units quickly—dominated. By some measures, this treatment regimen was extremely successful. According to one study, "About 60% of the soldiers who became neuropsychiatric casualties were returned to duty within 2–5 days. The highest success rates were found in forward combat units; the lowest at rear-echelon hospitals."[79] But military doctors were often unsure of treatment practices, and felt overwhelmed by psychiatric cases.[80] As in the First World War, command officers during World War II began to express concern that returning psychiatric patients to a lesser duty was depleting the front-line force too greatly. Along these lines, a July 1944 memo from the Office of the Surgeon stated: "Too lenient an attitude is being taken in regard to psychoneurotics. Not enough cases are being returned to duty. Many cases are being evacuated to Base 'B' which . . . could have been sent to duty."[81]

Decisions regarding whom to return to duty and when changed as the war went on; namely, the standards to qualify for evacuation rose.[82] This change could be attributed to changing medical practices, such as the determination that it was better to treat neuropsychiatric patients closer to the front. But military necessity also mattered, with the demands of war becoming more desperate either because the Allies felt they were in danger of losing or because there was a perception that they were close to winning. Either way, every man was needed at the front.

Standards for evacuation also may have risen because the incidence of war-induced psychological trauma is correlated with the duration of war. If longer deployments lead to more trauma but also are indicative of more dire military straits, the imperatives of patient care and military obligation run, as in most conflicts (especially lengthy ones), in opposite directions for military psychiatrists. As a conflict becomes more acute, force depletion is increasingly militarily unacceptable. One solution adopted in World War II was to try to prevent combat exhaustion from emerging in the first place. R&R time in cities such as Paris was built into soldiers' schedules, and the duration and number of deployments were limited for each soldier.

But R&R could not prevent all cases of combat exhaustion or, for that matter, other psychiatric illnesses. Like all doctors in war, military psychiatrists must wrestle with two imperatives that are often in tension: providing the best healthcare possible for their patients, and ensuring that the military has as many troops as possible available for the fight. Military psychiatrists have consistently pushed back against pressures they felt ill-served their patients, even knowing they could be punished for taking too many troops out of action. World War II psychiatrist Sanford Gifford protested in writing when he learned that his patients had not been transferred to general hospitals, as he had recommended, but instead had been sent to smaller hospitals closer to the front where staff members tried to persuade them that their symptoms were psychosomatic. In Gifford's own words: "I cannot repress a desire to comment on the disposition of these cases. If it has taken the field of psychiatry 60 years to demonstrate the fact that functional and neurotic symptoms constitute disease-entities as serious and disabling as any other type of illness, I believe that to treat these patients as if their symptoms did not exist, simply because they are not organic, is to return to the most primitive days of psychiatric knowledge."[83]

As US troops returned home from World War II, the understanding of psychological trauma had advanced only slightly from where it had been at the war's outset. On one hand, it was now clear that war produced psychological trauma. Thus, screening was of limited use at best. On the other hand, treatment for such psychological trauma remained rudimentary, both during war and in its aftermath. Soldiers could be treated at, or near, the front. But these temporary measures were often insufficient to resolve their trauma.

That such a high proportion of World War I veterans suffered from what military psychiatrists referred to as neuropsychiatric illness ensured that the war-ravaged mind would return after World War II. The mass mobilization of the Second World War translated into hundreds of thousands more cases of war-induced psychological trauma. This surge put enormous pressure on the VA's resources. Concerned doctors protested against the notion that the VA ought to be responsible for non-service-connected mental illness.[84] According to historian Ben Shephard, more than 475,000 veterans were receiving pensions from the VA two years after the war ended for psychiatric illness.[85] The need for beds for neuropsychiatric veterans continued many years after the fallout of World War II, with a 1955 VA review stating that "over 80% of the nation-wide total number of veterans on hospital waiting lists are psychiatric or neurologic patients."[86] Efforts to screen out recruits prone to war-induced psychological trauma had clearly failed.

Some observers were concerned that the presence of psychologically traumatized veterans undermined the traditional fabric of American society. Hans Pols, for example, argues that shell shock was viewed as an emasculating illness that threatened the structure of the American family.[87] Similarly, Adam Montgomery notes in his history of how Canada has dealt with its psychologically traumatized military personnel that "nervousness, exemplified in the shell-shocked veteran, was deemed the behaviour of 'weak and womanly men' and viewed as a threat to society."[88] The issue was complicated by the fact that there had been a blackout on public information regarding US psychiatric casualties during much of the war.[89] Along these lines, Mark De Rond notes that medical records of officers suffering from psychological illness were, after 1945, "systematically destroyed to protect the patient's identity."[90]

We cannot know for certain whether a soldier diagnosed with shell shock in World War I would have been diagnosed with combat exhaustion in World War II, perhaps especially given the differing circumstances of these wars, including the longer duration of the United States' participation in the latter. We do know that a diagnosis of combat exhaustion would not necessarily have led to the kind of long-term treatment that a shell-shocked soldier received. In this respect, the construction of war-induced psychological trauma in World War II could have decreased the long-term costs of war. At the same time, though, improvements in military medicine more broadly—including and especially the use of whole blood, forward surgery, and better evacuation—meant that more military personnel survived. There were, in other words, more bodies alive to develop such trauma. And as we've seen, unlike in previous wars, the GI Bill applied to all veterans, regardless of physical or mental status. Thus, any social undesirability of war-induced psychological trauma would not in itself have impeded the ability of World War II veterans to receive support to attend university or obtain a home loan.

The combination of the perceived temporary nature of war trauma, more survivors, and a veterans' benefits package that was contingent only upon service—rather than disability—makes it difficult to establish whether there were any increased costs of war-induced psychological trauma from one world war to the next. Certainly, psychologically traumatized patients were viewed as a lingering issue in the VA health system. But many traumatized soldiers would have returned fully to civilian life, buying homes and going to college on the GI Bill and receiving treatment for nonpsychiatric conditions from the VA. Here, the main increase in cost may have been highly personal, with veterans who likely should have received psychological and psychiatric care internalizing their trauma in an era when seeking such care would have been highly stigmatized. Thus, many of the costs were acutely human, borne directly by veterans and their families.

Counterinsurgency and PTSD

Changes in both psychiatry and warfighting have governed how war-induced psychological trauma and associated costs have been viewed in the decades since World War II. Psychiatrists agreed—eventually, slowly, and after a highly politicized fight—on a new diagnosis, based on symptomatology rather than biology. The influence of politics on these changing costs is also visible in decisions around screening, diagnosis, treatment, and benefits, as well as the nature of wars the United States has fought since 1945.

With the continued professionalization of psychiatry after World War II came the first edition of the American Psychiatric Association's foundational publication: the *Diagnostic and Statistical Manual of Mental Disorders*. The first edition of the *DSM*, published in 1952, documented a shift in psychiatry, from a focus on physiological to psychological causes of psychiatric illness.[91] Written primarily by military psychiatrists (whose stature had risen as a result of the war),[92] the *DSM* did not include combat exhaustion but instead contained a section on "gross stress reaction," described as follows:

> Under conditions of great or unusual stress, a normal personality may utilize established patterns of reaction to deal with overwhelming fear. The patterns of such reactions differ from those of neurosis or psychosis chiefly with respect to clinical history, reversibility of reaction, and its transient character. When promptly and adequately treated, the condition may clear rapidly. It is also possible that the condition may progress to one of the neurotic reactions. If the reaction persists, this term is to be regarded as a temporary diagnosis to be used only until a more definitive diagnosis is established.
>
> This diagnosis is justified only in situations in which the individual has been exposed to severe physical demands or extreme emotional stress, such as in combat or in civilian catastrophe (fire, earthquake, explosion, etc.). In many instances this diagnosis applies to previously more or less "normal" persons who have experienced intolerable stress.
>
> The particular stress involved will be specified as (1) combat or (2) civilian catastrophe.[93]

Both the focus on combat as a cause of gross stress reaction and the view that it was, by definition, temporary meant that it was, in effect, very similar to understandings of combat exhaustion in World War II. Gross stress reaction was dropped from the second edition of the *DSM*, published in 1968;[94] instead, the authors included a new diagnosis—"adjustment reaction to adult life"—that could be caused by "fear linked to military combat."[95]

The Vietnam War, of course, drew renewed attention to the issue of war-induced psychological trauma. During Vietnam, military psychiatrists reverted to the diagnostic categories of combat exhaustion and battle fatigue. Bernard Rostker quotes the Army surgeon general's chief of psychiatry's assessment of psychiatric illness in the Vietnam War: "The absence of 'combat exhaustion' may have to do with seasoned and motivated troops; if this is true, we might expect a change if 'greener' and less motivated troops replace those who have completed their tours."[96] In general, psychiatrists congratulated themselves for low rates of psychiatric discharge. But after the war, there was an extremely high prevalence of psychiatric illness among Vietnam veterans.[97] Post-Vietnam, psychiatry shifted from a Freudian focus on psychoanalysis that required understanding of the deep causes of mental illness to "descriptive psychiatry," focused on diagnosis and treatment based on current symptoms, rather than assuming pre-existing dispositions often rooted in childhood trauma or fantasies.[98] When it came to war-induced psychological trauma, an emerging diagnosis moved away from concluding that affected military personnel had failed to adapt to their environment (per the *DSM-II*'s "adjustment reaction to adult life" diagnosis) and toward a diagnosis that could be rendered based on the expression of a collection of symptoms.

In the years after the war (and after war-induced trauma was dropped from *DSM-II*), Vietnam veterans, along with a group of psychiatrists, lobbied for the (re)inclusion of war-induced trauma in the new edition of the *DSM*. They based their campaign on that of gay rights activists, who had blazed the trail for successful lobbying of the American Psychiatric Association by arguing that homosexuality ought not be classified as a disorder in the *DSM*.[99] The scale of the problem—which was in evidence more so after the war than during—eventually led to the emergence of "post-traumatic stress disorder," which was included in *DSM-III* in 1980. Following the success of veterans' advocates, attention to PTSD increased dramatically. A 1990 congressionally commissioned report found that at least 480,000 Vietnam veterans (approximately 15 percent of those who had served) were still suffering from PTSD and that an even larger percentage of Vietnam veterans had suffered at some point from the condition.[100] Additional reports suggest that over 250,000 Vietnam War veterans likely still suffer from PTSD today.[101] Notably, Vietnam veterans originally returned home to a public frequently unsympathetic to their service as well as to this specific illness, a combination that may have made getting treatment and benefits for PTSD more difficult.[102]

By contrast, today the validity of a PTSD diagnosis is widely accepted, thanks in part to the work of veterans' groups, military medical personnel, and the Department of Veterans Affairs. The VA's National Center for PTSD offers the following definition: "PTSD (posttraumatic stress disorder) is a mental health problem. PTSD can only develop after you go through or see a life-threatening event."[103] Ongoing research continues to delve into various dimensions of war-induced psychological trauma. The diagnostic criteria for PTSD listed in the most recent version of the DSM (*DSM-5*) expand on those included in the third and fourth editions, and include "the exposure to actual or threatened death, serious injury, or sexual violence"; the presence of "distressing memories," "dreams," or "flashbacks" associated with exposure to traumatic events; "avoidance of stimuli" associated with the traumatic events; "negative alterations in cognitions or mood associated with the traumatic event(s)"; and behavioral changes such as unprovoked "angry outbursts" or "hypervigiliance."[104] Conflict-specific illnesses, such as Gulf War Syndrome, appear to have some overlap with PTSD symptoms, raising questions about how to delineate the boundaries between different conditions. Also still debated is whether these syndromes have physiological or psychological roots.[105]

In addition to evolving criteria for diagnosing war-induced psychological trauma, military screening practices have changed. To some extent, the shift in these practices reflects a change in beliefs about the causes of PTSD. The dominant understanding today is that everyone is potentially vulnerable to PTSD (although the pendulum may be swinging back in the biological direction). During today's Military Entrance Processing Station (MEPS) examination, potential recruits are asked to self-report any psychological or psychiatric conditions; they are not subject to a psychiatric examination, as they would have been in the 1940s. There is no genetic testing for a predisposition for psychological trauma, nor is there an examination of a potential recruit's own history of such trauma.[106] The National Defense Reauthorization Act for fiscal year 2016 requested information about the possibility of more extensive health screening.[107] The Defense Department's response, echoing a conclusion first reached by the end of World War II, was that an accurate procedure was not currently available.[108]

One explanation for this change in screening practices is the evolution of our understanding of war-induced psychological trauma. Another is the changing structure of the military. With the shift to an all-volunteer force in 1973, and a considerably smaller force at that, the military may be reluctant to turn away potential recruits. Such reluctance may be particularly evident today, when so many Americans cannot meet the military's basic physical fitness requirements.[109] Thus, screening for PTSD generally occurs only after enlistment; that said, the same screening is mandatory once a soldier returns from deployment, a clear example of Vietnam's long shadow.[110]

Two reasons for mandatory postdeployment mental health screenings for US military personnel are the increasing frequency of deployment and the changing nature of warfare. Even though it has a smaller military than in previous eras, the United States has deployed its armed forces to more than fifty theaters over the past four decades.[111] As we know, these deployments have increasingly entailed counterinsurgency operations. Two key features of such operations are the challenges of distinguishing civilians from combatants and the importance of relying on local populations for the purposes of information-gathering and, especially in recent conflicts, nation-building. The types of psychological stressors associated with COIN operations are not necessarily greater or lesser than those associated with the trench warfare of World War I or the front-line combat of World War II, but they are different. As Shephard notes, the difficulty of distinguishing combatants from civilians has led to the dehumanization of the enemy; perhaps especially in Vietnam, junior officers shouldered an unusual amount of responsibility for making hard choices with regard to targeting, even though their lack of seniority made maintaining discipline challenging.[112] And one of the most robust (albeit unsurprising) findings from research studies of PTSD onset is correlation with combat deployment, although estimates of how many deployed military personnel develop PTSD vary significantly, from less than 1 percent to more than 30 percent.[113]

Another change that bears on the incidence of PTSD today refers back to the all-volunteer nature of the military. The combination of fewer people and long wars means that the same person is more likely to be deployed again and again. Frequent redeployments of US military personnel in the "global war on terror" have been indicated as a risk factor for PTSD among troops today.[114] This finding is consistent with data from earlier wars that suggest a higher incidence of war-induced psychological trauma as the war wore on (although it could also be that data collection improved as the war went on).

Changing weaponry also plays a role, with IEDs replacing artillery as the most common cause of US war casualties. With the associated blast injuries has come another frequent diagnosis: traumatic brain injury. Along with PTSD, TBI has been named a "signature injury" of the wars in Afghanistan and Iraq. Mild TBI, which is the most common form, is characterized by an impact to the head, generally followed by loss of consciousness, memory, or altered mental state for no longer than thirty minutes.[115]

One striking—but also puzzling—feature of TBI is its comorbidity with PTSD.[116] As Murray Stein and Thomas McAllister show, the list of symptoms identifying these two conditions overlaps significantly.[117] And while there is reason to think that a traumatic event that could cause TBI could, in turn, lead to PTSD, the fact that mild TBI is defined by loss of consciousness during the traumatic event means that victims cannot necessarily recall the event that would be foundational to a PTSD diagnosis.[118] The role of memory of the traumatic event is central to the debate over the relationship between mild TBI and PTSD. Studies that do find a relationship between the two illnesses suggest that it is the "trauma of the trauma"—recollections of being in the hospital and the challenges of recovery—that produce PTSD in mild TBI patients, and/or that the form of PTSD experienced by mild TBI patients differs slightly from "standard" PTSD.[119]

Along with changed weaponry in COIN wars has come the introduction of the concept of moral injury, the notion that "psychological injury can result from transgressions of deeply held moral and ethical beliefs."[120] Medical anthropologist Allan Young's suggestion that PTSD's diagnostic basis lies in guilt and shame may have set the stage for this new diagnosis.[121] Psychologists argue that military personnel are more likely to confront especially morally hazardous situations in COIN operations, with their persistent challenge of distinguishing civilians from combatants.[122] As a result, wartime atrocities, both accidental and intentional, are more likely. While moral injury is distinct from PTSD, researchers are investigating possible relationships between the two conditions, albeit in an atmosphere of skepticism about moral injury (that is not dissimilar from skepticism in earlier eras about other manifestations of war-induced psychological trauma). As with PTSD and TBI, there appears to be significant overlap in the causes and diagnosis of PTSD and moral injury.[123]

Today's military medical community has developed standardized practices for treating PTSD among active-duty personnel. Early in the Afghanistan and Iraq Wars, doctors found a correlation between combat exposure and

PTSD onset. They also found, however, that affected military personnel were unlikely to seek care for mental health issues; even at the start of the twenty-first century, soldiers feared being ostracized by their peers if they were to receive a diagnosis of, and care for, a mental health condition such as PTSD.[124] Partially as a result of these findings, the military began to devote more resources to embedding mental health professionals in deployed units, although the efficacy of this practice remains somewhat unclear.[125] In addition, the military now offers intensive outpatient treatment programs at Warrior Resilience Centers. Treatment includes talk therapy, meditation, and acupuncture, as well as pharmacology. Researchers have also highlighted the importance of long-term screening for PTSD, having found that initial post-deployment screenings often miss cases that are found in subsequent tests.[126]

Back in the 1970s the VA was opposed to including PTSD in the *DSM* because of concerns about the financial burdens of caring for and compensating veterans with the diagnosis.[127] Today, treatment for military personnel diagnosed with PTSD and benefits for veterans with PTSD have become normalized—both are more generous and more widely available. Upon separating from the military, a new veteran diagnosed with PTSD would qualify for at least 10 percent disability, and possibly up to 100 percent.[128] For reference, in 2023 a single veteran with one child and a 10 percent disability rating would receive $165.92 per month; the same veteran with a 100 percent disability rating would receive $3,757.00/month. The amount received increases with the number of dependents.[129] One of the most challenging aspects of providing benefits to veterans with a PTSD diagnosis has been the persistence of the illness. Vet Centers, to treat traumatized veterans, were originally established in 1979 with the idea that they were temporary and would be eliminated once veterans suffering from psychological trauma were successfully treated. Instead, the Vet Center system has only expanded over time; today there are over 300 centers.[130] The financial costs of PTSD for the VA have been on the rise, with a nearly 80 percent increase in veterans receiving benefits for PTSD from 1999 to 2004.[131] Linda Bilmes attributes a significant portion of the rising costs of the Afghanistan and Iraq Wars precisely to the rise in PTSD cases, and subsequent increase in VA spending on patients with this diagnosis.[132] The financial costs have become so high there is some evidence that military and VA physicians have been discouraged from giving PTSD diagnoses to avoid adding to the government's bill.[133]

While PTSD is much more accepted today, the diagnosis—and attendant benefits—remain politically fraught. For example, both as a candidate and as president, Donald J. Trump expressed ambivalence about PTSD. In October 2016, he suggested that military personnel and veterans diagnosed with PTSD were unusually weak and "couldn't handle" the horrors of war. In 2018, while president, he presumed that a veteran who committed a mass shooting in California had a PTSD diagnosis.[134] Trump's comments harken back to an era when psychological trauma—and, especially, admitting to suffering from mental illness—was viewed as effeminate and, therefore, bad. But there is a strange juxtaposition in that the same people who are skeptical of diagnoses like PTSD are often quite supportive of the military in general—even as the military itself has become much more accepting of PTSD.

Veterans are also sometimes accused of taking advantage of the current VA benefits system by "chasing" a PTSD diagnosis. A Google search of "PTSD qualifying for VA benefits" generates a large number of hits, principally for organizations offering to coach veterans on how to present, for example, "a strong VA PTSD claim."[135] Skeptics point to pamphlets such as one titled *Posttraumatic Stress Disorder: How to Apply for 100% Total Disability* as justification for pulling back on providing benefits for veterans claiming a PTSD diagnosis.[136]

There is also ambivalence in the military community. Some veterans have expressed concern that the civilian population views all veterans as suffering from PTSD, especially following the release of films such as *Thank You for Your Service*. Active-duty personnel confront a slightly different set of issues. There is a common belief that a diagnosis of PTSD or another mental illness might mean denial of promotion or even dismissal from the military. Alternatively, treatment for PTSD could mean the extension of a deployment. But there are also incentives to receive a PTSD diagnosis while serving in the military: being diagnosed with PTSD prior to separating from the military makes qualifying for PTSD-based disability much easier upon separation. How service members, veterans, healthcare providers, and policymakers ought to weigh these costs and benefits is unclear, as it is inherently difficult for researchers to gather reliable data on these phenomena.

Despite these issues, the validity of a PTSD diagnosis is widely accepted among the public. One consequence of the social acceptance of PTSD, in combination with the currently high levels of popularity and trust enjoyed by the US military,[137] is that there is currently little to no resistance to the notion that veterans with a PTSD diagnosis ought to receive benefits. In contrast to the challenges faced by psychologically traumatized veterans in previous wars, today's veterans are trained to apply for benefits if they receive a PTSD diagnosis. But such benefits, while welcome in many respects, may raise a new set of dilemmas relating to the course of PTSD as an illness and the most effective treatment plans. PTSD has been shown to have significant comorbidity with alcohol and drug abuse. In his telling history of how the Canadian military has dealt with war-induced psychological trauma, for example, Adam Montgomery shows that lump-sum payments to veterans with PTSD have sometimes been used in ways that exacerbate some of the more troubling symptoms of the disease.[138]

Among these is a rise in suicide among military personnel and veterans.[139] The active-duty suicide rate has increased every year since 2011, with the exception of a small drop in 2021.[140] From 2006 through 2021, more active-duty military personnel died by suicide than were killed in action or died from wounds.[141] Veterans likewise suffer from an unusually high suicide rate. One question is whether increased suicide rates are related to the nature of recent counterinsurgency wars. Here the science is somewhat mixed. While acknowledging the high rates of suicide among military personnel in the post-9/11 era, one study found no effect of deployment to Afghanistan or Iraq on suicide rates.[142] Other studies, in contrast, have shown a correlation between deployment and suicide risk.[143] Studies of Israeli military personnel have investigated the relationship between moral injury sustained in recent military actions and suicide risk, and found that combat veterans suffering from moral injury were at an elevated risk of suicide.[144] Suicide is challenging to study. Analyses are observational and retrospective. Additionally, increased attention to and documentation of both PTSD and suicide rates among military and veteran populations make it difficult to disentangle possible time trends. The science will carry on. But, as David Finkel writes, "the after-war continues, as eternally as war itself."[145]

All signs point to increases in the cost of war-induced psychological trauma in the era of modern US counterinsurgency war. While the military is smaller than in previous eras, a greater proportion of active-duty military personnel as well as veterans receive a PTSD diagnosis and attendant veterans' benefits than in the past. Diagnosis has become almost normal, in both the military and civilian spheres. The diagnostic category of PTSD has expanded over time, as has the pool of potential PTSD patients, because the dramatic improvements in military medicine mean that more people are surviving war. The nature of counterinsurgency warfare—especially as waged by the United States, and given multiple deployments—may be correlated with higher levels of PTSD onset. And high levels of public support for spending on veterans' benefits have translated into nearly automatic benefits for veterans with a PTSD diagnosis, in contrast to the struggles of veterans of earlier wars.

Conclusion

Mental illness has always been plagued by questions of veracity in a way that no other branch of medicine has. No one doubts the seriousness of a broken arm or a gunshot wound. And yet, the treatment of psychological trauma is inextricably colored by whether you believe that such trauma is real. I do. My own understanding of the history of this type of trauma also leaves room for its social construction. That is to say, both the expression and understanding of the symptoms of war-induced psychological trauma can change over time; nineteenth-century labels such as "sunstroke" and "nostalgia," for example, were used because they lay within the realm of conceptual possibility for their time. Similarly for the transition from "shell shock" to "combat exhaustion," where doctors actively tried to reconstruct understanding of war-induced psychological trauma. Generally speaking, such social constructions of illness come as much from doctors as from soldiers or from society writ large.[146] After all, most studies (including this one) of the history of psychological trauma rely heavily on doctors' reports. Indeed, that reliance is one of the few historical constants in analyses of past views of trauma. And it is clear that the medicine has changed. Doctors began with the belief that war-induced psychological trauma was caused by personal weakness ("nostalgia"), then turned to physical causes ("shell shock") and next to traumatic memories (PTSD). Today, the pendulum seems to be swinging back to a more biological view of the causes of PTSD.[147]

The medical debate over the sources of war-induced psychological trauma is likely to endure. So are its long-term costs. Four factors have translated into the steady—and sometimes sharp—increase in the costs of war-induced psychological trauma since the Civil War. First, better overall medicine means that a much higher percentage of military personnel survive to experience psychological trauma. Second, as diagnostic categories have become more established over time, patients are more likely to be treated for such illnesses. Third, even while some stigma remains, illnesses like PTSD are much more accepted—both in the military and in society at large—than they were in the past. And fourth, this acceptance means that it is much easier, even expected, to count illnesses such as PTSD today as a standard disability category for veterans' benefits.

Nonetheless, because of the significantly smaller size of today's military, it seems plausible that even though costs associated with psychological trauma are increasing on a per capita basis, there is no overall net increase in costs. But today's relative ease of receiving a large disability payment as well as the high incidence of PTSD in the United States' counterinsurgency military push back at least somewhat against this conclusion. We must also remember that public support for the military—and, by extension, veterans—has been extremely high in recent decades (despite the recent hints of resistance from Republicans) and especially compared to other institutions in the United States. And the difficulty of recruitment—which accounted in part for the frequent redeployments that have characterized the United States' most recent counterinsurgency wars, and contributed to rising incidence of PTSD among military personnel—is likely to endure, deepening incentives to provide benefits (including for mental health) for future veterans. From Achilles to Afghanistan, mental illness has always been a symptom of war. While we cannot predict the precise nature of psychological trauma caused by future wars, we can be assured of its inevitable power and presence.

Conclusion

Unraveling the Costs of War

The costs of our recent wars are mounting. By the time you read this, the United States will have spent more than $8 trillion on its post-9/11 military deployments, according to Brown University's Costs of War Project.[1] Given that these wars were financed primarily via debt, it will take decades to pay them off.[2] For context, consider that the US national debt is today greater than the US gross domestic product; it has increased dramatically since the start of—and because of—the Afghanistan and Iraq Wars. And these numbers do not include the nonmonetary, very personal costs—to war victims abroad, to veterans living with injuries and mental illness, and to the families of both—that will last generations. These rising costs of war signify a trade-off, but also a crossroads, between our debt to the past and what we owe the future.

War is, of course, always costly. And the costs have a long tail, seemingly always longer than we anticipate. In the United States, that tail has been lengthened—for military veterans, for their families, for the US government, and for the citizenry of the United States—by two unabashedly good historical trends: improvement in military medicine and the expansion of veterans' benefits. This arc has offered huge value—literally, the difference between life and death, and then an ongoing means of living better lives—for countless members of the armed forces. However, the trouble is that in planning for and executing wars, these costs have too often gone unnoticed. The United States, in other words, has been systematically underestimating the costs of war.

The stakes of getting the costs of war wrong—and, especially, of consistently underestimating these costs—are high. Major policy decisions are often framed in cost-benefit terms. Underestimating the costs of war makes it easier to go to war. Even if war still occurs, a more accurate understanding of its costs could shape how a war is fought—for example, by encouraging a more limited conflict with clear, achievable aims. US decision-makers underestimated the costs of every single one of the wars discussed in this book, often wildly so. The persistence of our underestimations becomes even more concerning when we consider that with each new potential war, those decision-makers have more and more previous data to rely on; in theory, our estimating capacity should be getting better over the course of our nation's history. But it is not.

Whenever human life is in the balance, costs and benefits ought to be weighed carefully. But this principle is especially crucial in wars of choice—a description that characterizes virtually all of the United States' wars since the close of World War II, as well as numerous wars prior to 1945. To take the most obvious recent example, the United States did not face a clear security imperative to invade Iraq in 2003—a war that cost 4,431 US lives, another 31,994 US wounded, over 17,000 Iraqis killed by US forces, hundreds of thousands killed in the war as a whole, and untold Iraqi wounded—not to mention the tarnishing of the United States' reputation abroad.[3] Given that US policy objectives were not only based on faulty intelligence but also ultimately unmet, the costs were certainly not worth it. If we had had a clearer sense of the scale of costs ahead of time, perhaps the fact that going to war was a mistake also would have been clearer. A major course correction is therefore in order. We need to alter the way we think about war. We need to more effectively reckon with the costs of war before human lives on both sides, and the financial health of our country, are put at risk.

Why are we so bad at estimating the costs of war beforehand? One reason is that costing out war is hard. And this challenge is compounded by the inherent unpredictability of war. We cannot know at its start how any given war will end. But rich countries like the United States—and, let us note, mispredictions of the costs of war are certainly not a uniquely American failing—are constantly preparing for war. They are better equipped than most to develop tools, from wargaming to casualty prediction models, that allow them to at least improve their estimates of what a conflict might cost. But even if such tools are available, there is another, more cynical logic behind poor estimations of the costs of war. Political leaders often seek to avoid exposing these costs because they know, or at least fear, that the public will be unwilling to pay. US presidents fear the "Dover effect"—the idea that when images of flag-draped coffins being unloaded at Dover Air Force Base are publicized, public support for war goes down. A similarly poignant and politically potent phenomenon—what I call the "Walter Reed effect"—occurs when images of severely wounded soldiers are publicized. Leaders also obscure the costs of war in how they pay for conflicts. The US public has not paid a direct war tax since World War II; instead, we finance our wars today by borrowing money—incurring debt whose payments are more distant from the general public than a tax. As Sarah Kreps eloquently explains, this obfuscation of the costs of war not only enables our belligerency but also damages our democracy: "Bearing the burden in both blood and treasure is part and parcel of democratic accountability in war, and conversely, the absence of those visible costs is the reason we end up ... with limitless, unaccountable war."[4]

But there is another, less sinister reason we continue to underestimate the costs of war: we keep falling back on old categories of "cost." We still tend to think about the human costs of war principally, if not exclusively, in terms of fatalities. As we have seen, major medical advances belie this traditional view. To reckon with what war really costs us, we must therefore recognize the effects of military medicine and update our conception of what these costs entail today compared to the past.

While our estimating skills have time and again been proved lacking, the corollary issue here is that assessing the future and estimating its price tag are tricky endeavors. As we've seen throughout this book, tracking increases in the costs of war is itself challenging because of inconsistent data collection practices, changes over time in the bureaucracies that govern veterans' benefits, and key differences between wars. The wounded-to-killed ratio is the best measure we have to assess historical changes in military medicine. This ratio, as we know, has gone up enormously between the Civil War and today. The one exception is the noticeable dip in World War II compared to the First World War; the reason for this dip, however, is not a reversal in military medical advances, but instead changes in weaponry that increased the numbers of those killed very quickly. (Another statistic, the case fatality rate, confirms this claim: though it is much harder to calculate for the Civil War, we see a clear improvement in World War II over World War I.) The bottom line is that injured military personnel who receive medical attention are, with each war, increasingly likely to survive their injuries, and today are vastly more likely to survive than they would have been at any point in the past.

Comparing veterans' benefits across wars is similarly challenging. What is more, the trajectory of veterans' benefits in the United States has not been as uniform as the trajectory of military medicine. As we know, veterans' benefits were extremely generous for Civil War veterans, contracted after World War I, started increasing again after World War II, and have been on a nearly uninterrupted upswing since. Here, it is especially useful to examine the array of benefits. Since World War II's groundbreaking GI bill, the very concept of veterans' benefits has grown far beyond pensions, and today includes education subsidies, mortgage assistance, and unemployment payments. Additionally, healthcare for veterans is a (relative) constant. From soldiers' homes after the Civil War, to the intense rehabilitation movement following World War I and the extensive veterans' hospital system today, veterans have received free medical care for decades. And the rising cost of veterans' healthcare today is largely attributable to the increasing eligibility of what injuries (physical and mental) are covered, as well as the fact it that has become bureaucratically easier for veterans to connect any disabilities to their time in the military.[5]

That US military medicine has made great strides, that veterans' benefits have been on an upward trajectory, and that these two trends have combined to increase the long-term costs of war, should be evident at this point. But past is not necessarily prologue. With an eye to the future, let us consider what comes next. What might the futures of war, military medicine, and veterans' benefits look like for the United States? What lessons should we learn from past developments in military medicine and veterans' benefits? And, most important, what changes should we enact to increase the odds that we get estimations of the costs of war right in any future conflicts?

Looking Ahead

For the past thirty years—since the end of the Cold War—the United States has been the world's hegemon. It was, in the words of William Wohlforth, "the unipolar state."[6] While the United States has deployed its military around the globe during this time—from Bosnia to Djibouti to Colombia to South Korea—it has not experienced an attack on its territory from another state since December 1941. Of course, the so-called global war on terror was a response to the shocking attacks of September 11, 2001—in New York, in Washington, DC, and midair over Pennsylvania. But the nature of the threat posed by groups like al Qaeda and the Islamic State was necessarily and qualitatively distinct from that posed by another internationally recognized state seeking to displace the United States as the world's most powerful country.

Today, circumstances are different. After twenty years in Afghanistan and Iraq, the United States appears to have little taste for any future counterinsurgencies. Over this same period, China's power in the international system has increased substantially. US policymakers have pivoted east and are now increasingly concerned about the possibility of war with China. Simultaneously, Russian revanchism has resurfaced, with Russia's February 2022 invasion of Ukraine raising the specter of a reprise of the major European land wars of the twentieth century.

In other words, what international security experts refer to as "peer/near-peer competition" may be back. China and Russia are much closer military peers to the United States than al Qaeda and the Islamic State were. And wars against China and Russia would look very different from the wars in Afghanistan and Iraq. A 2022 wargame hosted at the Center for Strategic and International Studies showed that tens of thousands of US lives could be lost, as well as up to 10 percent of the carrier fleet, in an air-sea war against China.[7] And while the United States is much more powerful than Ukraine, the ongoing conflict there provides an unfortunate preview of what a war with Russia could look like.

How such a conflict—whether with a military "peer" or with a "near-peer"—might play out is very much up for grabs. Even the nature of the battlefield is in question. Would these wars mostly be fought in cyberspace, where electrical grids and security systems would be most at risk? Would particularly devastating weapons—what the military refers to as CBRN (chemical, biological, radiological, and nuclear) weapons—be used? Would the battlefield be primarily automated, capitalizing on the use of drones and AI to help direct payloads? Or will any such wars of the future more closely resemble those of the past? All of these questions have important implications for the medicine needed, and practiced, in any such future conflict. History has shown that military medicine advances regardless of the enemy. But the particular advances depend heavily on the weapons used and injuries sustained. Stemming blood loss will remain paramount in any conflict with boots on the ground. While bombs dropped by drones are just as devastating to people living in the targeted area as those dropped by aircraft with pilots sitting in a cockpit, any injuries to the attacker are more likely to be psychological than physiological. And a war with CBRN weapons would require new, and perhaps as yet undeveloped, types of treatments, as seen in the response to gas warfare in World War I.

The Future of Military Medicine

At the 2022 Special Operations Medical Association Annual Meeting, Britain's Col. Paul Parker gave a presentation titled "UK Field Medical Care 2032: One Military Vision." A high-production-value video took the audience through a drone dropping medical supplies into an austere environment, a robot conducting damage control surgery, and ultimately a self-flying ambulance that evacuated an injured military casualty to the rear.[8]

While these technological innovations are possible—and others, like telemedicine, exist already—most are decades away. Given current capabilities, the primary focus of the military medical community is the same as it has been for the last twenty years: how to better get blood to injured soldiers, especially in the prehospital setting. Innovations focusing on this issue, such as tourniquets that include sensors for fit and oxygenation, are much closer to market today than AI-driven ambulances, as are new drugs to treat hypoxia or arrest shock induced by blood loss.

But there would be important differences between war in the Middle East, fought against conventionally weaker foes, and a war with Russia or China. One key difference pertains to air evacuation. The ongoing war between Russia and Ukraine trains a spotlight on some of these challenges. The Russians, in particular, seem to be suffering from casualty numbers similar to those of the world wars when it comes to their wounded-to-killed ratio.[9] While Ukraine has been (unsurprisingly) reluctant to release its own numbers, and while Ukrainian military medicine is better than Russian military medicine, the difficulties of evacuation very much compromise both sides' ability to abide by anything close to the "golden hour" rule, let alone the "platinum fifteen minutes."

Because neither side has air superiority, successful aeromedical evacuation from the front is all but impossible. The expectation is that the same would be true if the United States went to war with Russia or China. As former US Air Force Surgeon-General P. K. Carlton Jr. told me: "The biggest challenge is the lack of air dominance."[10] During a tabletop exercise I sat in on at Air University in 2017, we considered the medical consequences of a North Korean air or artillery attack on a US airbase in South Korea. In one scenario, the runway had been damaged, planes had been hit, and pilots had been injured. The participating medical personnel in the room had to decide how to respond without relying on the air evacuation to which they had become accustomed over the last several decades. In harried conversations around the table, they scrambled for supplies, tried to get equipment and drugs from local dentists and veterinarians, and debated about how to incorporate indigenous medicinal plants. They were preparing for what is called "prolonged field care"—the idea that they would have to provide medical care in the absence of reinforcement of supply or personnel. Prolonged field care has rightly become a focus of many future-looking military medical personnel; there is even a podcast about it.[11]

The nature of medical care, not surprisingly, is shaped by the constraints of the mission. One of the few nonmedical personnel in our simulation room was a colonel who was playing the role of base commander. His priority was getting planes back up in the air, which meant that those personnel who could repair the runway and maintain and fly the planes would have to be prioritized for medical treatment—even if they were not the most severely injured. This kind of "reverse triage protocol" is starkly different from the norms of the twenty-first-century counterinsurgency wars, where enormous resources were regularly brought to bear on even a single casualty at risk of dying. But on our simulated base in South Korea, stretched medical assets would be directed to those deemed "mission-essential" rather than the most emergent cases.

Another key difference, with significant medical implications, for a future peer/near-peer conflict—especially with China—is the battle domain. A war with China would be a war much more at sea and in the air compared to a war with Russia, and certainly compared to the United States' recent wars in Afghanistan and Iraq. The United States has not fought a major maritime war since World War II. This fact raises questions around advancements in naval medicine in particular. Historically, there has not been much to do: the catastrophic loss of a ship meant that much, if not all, of the crew was also lost. While the Navy's traditional culture indoctrinates sailors to "save the ship," there have been several changes that may have implications for future naval casualties. First, the last two decades of advances in burn treatment are particularly important here, because burns are a frequent shipboard injury given the risk of fire aboard ships. Improvements in fluid resuscitation therapy mean that burn victims are much more likely to survive even very severe injuries today compared to the past. Second, ships are constructed quite differently today than in the mid-twentieth century. A ship's compartments can be more easily siloed from each other, which means that the ship as a whole is less vulnerable to flooding and, therefore, sinking. And third, at least one view suggests that China's strategy would be to disable rather than sink US ships, in part because US ships are built in such a way that their weapons systems are quite vulnerable to attack. If this is the case, then the catastrophic loss of a ship is much less likely today, but the need for new medical practices relevant to treating crewmembers aboard disabled ships is much more necessary.[12]

These advances in ship technology notwithstanding, there will be more wounded sailors in a twenty-first-century Pacific war than in the Afghanistan and Iraq Wars. How current guidelines and practices for treating the wounded (which were developed in land wars in Afghanistan and Iraq) would be applied to a twenty-first-century war at sea is very much an open question. On one hand, the constancy of human physiology means that the basic principles of the TCCC guidelines should apply—hemorrhage should be controlled, airways should be unblocked, and tension pneumothorax should be relieved, all in a prehospital setting. On the other hand, evacuation is again likely to be a major challenge. To my knowledge, the US Navy has not focused on this issue; they, too, are anticipating the maritime version of prolonged field care (called "prolonged casualty care"), where casualties would be evacuated onto ships with more medical capabilities. Even so, both the ability for ship-to-ship transfer of an injured sailor and the care possible on most ships are currently sorely limited.[13]

As mentioned above, there are also live questions about how technological developments—medical and military—could affect casualty care. The greatest unknown is the possible use of chemical, biological, radiological, or nuclear weapons against US forces. Because military medicine evolves in response to battlefield developments, and because CBRN weapons have not been used against US forces since the First World War, current knowledge about how to respond to such attacks is mostly theoretical. For example, the *Emergency War Surgery* handbook offers advice on triage and decontamination, but the grim expectation is that the best that can be done—and only if it is safe for medical personnel—is to relieve suffering.[14]

Also theoretically, and as Col. Parker previewed, remotely controlled or AI-driven vehicles could assist with evacuation or even treatment of casualties. As discussed above, most of these capabilities are currently in development, although some are in use already. For example, drones are being used to drop medical supplies to the front in Ukraine.[15] Whether a war will erupt between the United States and either China or Russia is just as unknown as when that would happen or how long such a war would last. Even if there was sufficient time to develop these kinds of automated capabilities more fully, there would inevitably be growing pains as they started to be used in the field.

What, then, might a peer/near-peer conflict mean in terms of casualty counts? Would there be a reversion to the wounded-to-killed ratios of the world wars—similar to what we are observing today in the conflict between Russia and Ukraine? Or would the United States be able to maintain the high level of medical care it provided to ill and injured troops in Afghanistan and Iraq?

The answer likely lies somewhere in between. A war with China or Russia would generate many more casualties than war in Afghanistan and Iraq; switching to conditions where medical staff have to treat hundreds, rather than tens (or fewer), of casualties all at once already means that fewer lives are likely to be saved. But if history is any guide, US military medical personnel will adapt quickly, and if the war is a long one, we should expect military medicine to catch up to military conditions in ways that improve upon past outcomes in similar scenarios. In other words, while fewer lives would be saved as a percentage of those deployed, many more lives—in absolute numbers—would likely be saved in future conflicts than in past comparable wars. Thus, the long tail of the costs of war remains highly relevant even in a peer/near-peer conflict.

The Future of Veterans' Benefits

Three main questions offer a window into the future of veterans' benefits in the United States and, at the same time, the relationship between those benefits and the long-term costs of war. First, how many people might serve in a future military—especially one that goes to war? Second, in what ways might today's fraught debates about US healthcare policy spill over into veterans' benefits programs? And third, will the high levels of trust in the military—and, by extension, support for veterans—continue even as political polarization in the United States shows no sign of slowing down?

At the start of 2023, there were 1.38 million active-duty members of the US military. The National Guard and military reserves added up to another 450,000. This number is dramatically lower than the 16 million who served during World War II, as well as the 3.5 million at the height of the Vietnam War.

So what would military recruitment look like in the event of a peer/near-peer conflict? As Jonathan Caverley points out, the United States has a capital-intensive military today; fewer people are needed to complete the same tasks as in previous wars.[16] But this does not mean that the battlefield will be empty of people. A larger conventional conflict would likely require a larger military than was fielded to Afghanistan and Iraq.

There are two main strategies for increasing the size of the military. The first would be a return to the draft. While resurrecting the draft has been floated many times over the years, and for many reasons, it is likely to be highly unpopular.[17] One exception might be if a draft is instituted in response to a conventional or nuclear attack by China or Russia, especially on the continental United States. Such an attack could also produce a bump in voluntary enlistments, as after 9/11 (though even that bump was not particularly large).[18]

Another, more likely strategy is to increase veterans' benefits as an incentive for recruitment.[19] A 2019 RAND report, for example, highlights the importance of educational benefits for military recruiting and notes the ways in which services compete against each other for recruits as they stand up new educational benefits programs.[20] Even if military medicine in such a war did not save as high a percentage of soldiers as in Afghanistan and Iraq, enhanced veterans' benefits would likely mean a continued increase in war's expensive long tail.

The possibility of future war is not the only predictor of future veterans' benefits. We know that, since World War II, veterans' benefits have been increasing, albeit in fits and starts. Each new set of conflicts has brought amendments to the basic contours of the GI Bill. Although some have been more generous than others, there has been a clear upward trend over the past decades. A key reason for this increase is bipartisanship; veterans' benefits have been one of the few issues to receive support across the partisan aisle over the past half century. As Iraq War veteran and celebrated author Phil Klay writes, there has been a national wave of "patriotic correctness."[21] But we are now seeing a fraying of this consensus. Starting with the 113th Congress, debates about veterans' benefits, and the Veterans Health Administration (which includes VA medical centers and is responsible for providing healthcare to veterans) in particular, became much more fraught. Jeff Miller (R-FL), chairman of the House Veterans Affairs Committee, summed the issue up bluntly in 2014 when he said that the "VA can no longer be considered a sacred cow."[22]

Increased political polarization is one reason for the potential loss of future support for expanding veterans' benefits. Another is the declining veteran population, as World War II, Korean War, and Vietnam War veterans get older and pass away, which translates into declining influence for organizations like the American Legion and Veterans of Foreign Wars. And while there are a number of new, very active veterans' service organizations—such as the Iraq and Afghanistan Veterans of America and the Wounded Warrior Project—the declining overall population of veterans has put these groups in competition with each other in ways that may limit their collective influence.[23]

As mentioned in Chapter 3, recent debates about the PACT Act, which provides benefits for veterans exposed to burn pits, have revealed a shift in traditional political positions. Democrats advocated strongly for this expansion of veterans' benefits, while Republicans opposed it. It is too early to know whether this one case is a harbinger of change. Even if the political landscape around veterans' benefits is altered such that this issue no longer enjoys bipartisan support, it is more likely that future benefits will not be expanded than that past benefits will be eroded. A key issue is likely to be the extent to which veterans' healthcare is privatized; even if it is, the United States will still maintain its commitment to provide healthcare to veterans. Thus, again, the long tail of the costs of war remains even if its trajectory decelerates.

This is not to say that veterans' benefits as a whole are deemed unproblematic by Democrats—even if they rallied around the PACT Act. A prevailing concern, one that comes through clearly in multiple works on "veteranology," has been that veterans' benefits create a special class of US citizens.[24] The disarray and inequalities endemic to the US healthcare system—especially as evidenced by the COVID-19 pandemic—underline this point. But those objecting to the veterans' benefits system on these grounds tend to argue more for its expansion to all US citizens—in the form of universal health insurance—than for the dismantling of veterans' benefits.[25]

The continued commitment to veterans—and to wounded warriors more specifically—is seen clearly in the near-universal response to exposés of failures of the Veterans Administration and stateside care for injured military personnel. For instance, a series of *Washington Post* stories in 2007 about substandard care at Walter Reed led to congressional hearings, followed by firings, hirings, and the creation of new systems to deliver better care to the wounded.[26] Seven years later, another scandal broke about extensive wait times at VA hospitals in Phoenix, prompting an official investigation and the resignation of VA secretary Eric Shinseki.[27] Support for veterans remains alive and well among US citizens and politicians, despite some recent pushback, and is unlikely to diminish anytime soon.

Lessons Learned

We cannot know what the future holds. But in studying the history of US military medicine and veterans' benefits, we can learn from the past. This history has repeatedly revealed the tenacity of military doctors, nurses, and medical staff more generally—their commitment to their patients and their ability to find solutions to problems old and new—often in the face of grim odds and seemingly obstructionist bureaucracy. It is a history that is at once inspiring and depressing. But here, aside from these broader points, I want to explore two very specific lessons, each of which has significant ramifications. They are about what is forgotten between wars and the interplay between civilian and military medicine.

With the end of the Afghanistan and Iraq wars, concern about the "Walker Dip"—the notion that military medical skills erode to unacceptably low levels during interwar periods—is frequently voiced in the halls of military medical symposia. That worry may well be justified. But what this book demonstrates is not so much that skills become rusty as that knowledge is often lost—and in ways that can have fatal consequences.

Let us return to the crucial role that hemorrhage—and hemorrhage control—plays in preventable battle death. While systematic studies demonstrating the critical importance of stemming blood loss are relatively recent,[28] doctors in battle have, on some level, always understood this issue. This is why tourniquets were historically part of battlefield medical kits, and why whole blood for transfusion became the standard of care back in World War II.

Something, though, occurred "in between." Tourniquets had been used in war for centuries. But from the end of World War I until the early 2000s, doctors increasingly viewed them with skepticism and even disdain.[29] Doctors said they were often misapplied—with too much or too little pressure—and that it was far too easy to leave them on for longer than they should be, thus posing increased risk to the affected limb. The implication was that tourniquets increased the risk of amputation. That fear, however, overshadowed a more important reality: tourniquets also increased the possibility of survival. It was only the emergence of systematic data, during the Iraq and Afghanistan Wars, that reminded the medical community of what it had already known long ago, and inaugurated the "return" of the tourniquet.

A similar story holds for whole blood. As recounted in Chapter 2, Edward Churchill crusaded for the use of whole blood for transfusion in World War II. After the Vietnam War, however, the military (as well as the stateside civilian trauma system) switched to crystalloids and blood components for transfusion. The reasons for this change are somewhat hazy but appear to be related at least in part to the politics of blood banking in the United States and the close relationship between civilian and military trauma specialists. Screening and typing blood is bureaucratically challenging. And as medicine evolved generally, civilian doctors sought to promote blood components for patients suffering from critical illnesses such as cancer. The theory behind switching to crystalloids (such as saline) was that they would bring up blood pressure sufficiently. They did, but the effects were temporary (and pumping that much saline into trauma victims caused other problems, such as compartment syndrome). Because so many military medical personnel came from the civilian trauma care world, they brought their training with them. It was not until a series of studies was published in the 1990s and 2000s that it became clear that not only was whole blood superior to crystalloids and components but also that crystalloid transfusion might be causing significant problems in patients.[30]

The lesson drawn from both these cases tracks the change in data collection practices documented in this book. With widespread knowledge of the scientific method and the existence of a trauma system that includes a large registry of patients, major medical shifts should be based on systematic data collection and analysis. Scientific debate is both inevitable and welcome—indeed, a recent British study questions the value of blood components over crystalloids—and does not mean that past decisions won't be reversed.[31] But basing those decisions on science, rather than anecdotal evidence—or worse, bureaucratic politics—is crucial to military medicine's ability to continue to save lives. In between wars, it is all too easy for bureaucratic and professional inertia to paper over hard-won lessons from the past.

The second lesson is related to the first, in that it speaks to the relationship between civilian and military medicine. One potential solution to the Walker Dip is to emplace military medical personnel specializing in trauma with major urban trauma centers to keep their skills sharp. But how is that urban trauma center to be staffed when and if war breaks out and the military medical personnel are called to the front? This tension between civilian and military medical needs is not new. During the world wars, for example, something close to entire hospitals decamped to Europe. There was significant concern about staffing hospitals on the home front.[32] Medical schools, short of students, started admitting women (obviously a positive step, but one that was not universally welcomed, to say the least). A similar dynamic emerged during the COVID-19 pandemic, when medical reservists were called away from their local hospitals to medical facilities across the country—leaving their home facilities understaffed and local populations concerned about the health of their communities.

The lesson here is that the military medical community cannot assume that its needs are more important than those of civilian healthcare. The broader lesson is one for the nation: we need more healthcare workers (as evidenced, again, by the COVID-19 pandemic). Like the military as a whole, the military medical community has a recruitment problem. Historically, doctors either were drafted into service or joined because the military funded their medical education. Today, that funding is tied to a much longer time in service after graduation—typically ten to fifteen years—which likely gives some medical students pause and could lead them to turn to alternative sources of funding for their medical training. Some analysts are especially troubled by the fact that doctors of osteopathy (DOs) currently outnumber medical doctors (MDs) in the military medical training pipeline.[33] Maintaining a healthy population requires a top-notch medical system. And, as Pedro Accorsi and I have shown in related research, countries with more physicians per capita are both more likely to be healthier and more likely to enjoy a "medical advantage" that may help them win their wars.[34]

Policy Recommendations

We know that developments in military medicine and veterans' benefits have increased the long-term, downstream costs of war. As we identify the individual elements that increase the cost of war, it is easy to assume that the solution is to reduce or eliminate those elements. But that is not the answer here. We should not roll back advances in military medicine. Nor am I arguing that we should reduce veterans' benefits. Instead, I argue that we must develop a much keener sense and analysis of the costs of war *before a war starts*—rather than address surprising and often costly consequences as it endures, and long after it ends.

#1. Commit to Assessing Costs Before War

Toward the start of each of this book's chapters on the Civil War, the world wars, and the twenty-first-century counterinsurgency wars is a brief section on "prewar assessments of the costs of war." Here, my original intent was to get a sense of how policymakers' ex ante estimates of the costs of war lined up with the actual costs of war. It quickly became evident that assessments of the costs of war have often been slapdash at best, if they happen at all. For example, combing through the *Congressional Record* yielded zero systematic estimates of the costs of war prior to World War I—even though the United States was late to enter the war. In some wars, such as the 2001 invasion of Afghanistan, time was at a premium, so perhaps it is no surprise that cost assessments happened quickly, if at all. But others, such as the 2003 invasion of Iraq, are based on much more deliberate decision-making. Organizations like the Cost Assessment and Program Evaluation (CAPE—established in 2009, but as a new incarnation of a DoD office that has been in existence since the 1960s) in DoD are tasked with assessing costs, but they focus primarily on procurement and financial costs of war. CAPE, in other words, does not include personnel costs, such as how many military survivors will access veterans' benefits, including healthcare for any illnesses or injuries. Indeed, my sense from conversations with staffers at the Department of Defense, as well as members of the military, is that cost projections are extremely disaggregated. On one hand, this kind of disaggregation is the inevitable consequence of bureaucratic specialization—and specialization is essential, especially in large organizations like the Pentagon. On the other hand, it is all too easy to lose sight of the big picture given these circumstances. We have seen, both for Iraq and earlier, that a critical part of the picture was missing. As far as I can tell, the wounded did not seem to figure into decision-making about the potential costs of the Iraq War, even though they were already in evidence given the ongoing war in Afghanistan.

My point here is not (just) that the wounded ought to be included in prewar cost assessments. Instead, I am taking one step further back to argue that careful prewar cost assessments ought to be essential to the decision to go to war. The history of US warmaking makes clear that they have not been. Current cost assessment capabilities are scattered—not just within

DoD, but also across various offices in the executive and legislative branches. Centralizing these capabilities could undermine the separation of powers; we want the two branches to have independent sources of information so that they can check each other. But a simple first step could be to hold meetings to discuss what the main categories of costs *are*—even if there is disagreement on this question—among the community of staffers who assess the costs of war. Such meetings would be a first step in rectifying the United States' systematic underestimation of the costs of war.

#2. Get the Costs Right

How do we know the costs of war ahead of time? Policymakers rely on government analysts such as those who staff the Congressional Research Service, Congressional Budget Office, and of course the Department of Defense. But reports from these organizations are based on out-of-date assumptions regarding the quality of military medicine and, by extension, the long-term costs of war.

Organizations providing cost estimates of war—such as the ones just mentioned—should provide analysis based on the expected number of wounded as well as fatalities. Moreover, they should justify their projections of fatal and nonfatal casualties based on a combination of the current status of military medicine and expectations of the nature of the conflict. Because the wounded may transition to veteran status within a relatively short period, new outlays of veterans' benefits also should be taken into account.

In some ways, this is a big ask. It is not easy to produce a useful casualty estimate for a war that has not yet happened. But the Defense Department has been doing this for years—just not with a focus on the wounded. DoD software, such as the Medical Planners Tool Kit, enables military planners to project casualties (these projections, of course, depend greatly on assumptions keyed into the model). But these projections appear to be in greater use in the heat of war than prior to a conflict. Part of the reason for this limitation is that the software available was trained on and, therefore, designed for, more granular analysis; in other words, the smaller the military unit, the better it works.[35] To be more useful, tools such as the Medical Planners Tool Kit will have to be aggregated up. But solving the aggregation problem does not appear to be a major focus of attention. What is more, those arguing in favor of war are likely to be reluctant to include (and publicize) these longer-term costs. Nonetheless, good decisions cannot be made with insufficient data—especially if solid estimates of those data are possible. Having a sense of these longer-term costs of war may not prevent future conflict; perhaps key policymakers would still decide that the benefits are worth the costs. But solid estimates are necessary for transparent decision-making, especially in what has been a historically bellicose democracy.

#3. Invest in Medicine

As mentioned above, it might be easy (if facile) to conclude that because military medicine raises the costs of war, we should invest less in military medicine. If anything, the opposite is true. One of the positive externalities of medicine used in war is spillover into civilian life. The US military has joined forces with the National Football League to better understand the causes and consequences of traumatic brain injury. The Combat Application Tourniquet developed in Afghanistan and Iraq was used to help victims of the 2013 Boston Marathon bombing. And trauma centers around the country—indeed, around the world—have reverted to using whole blood for transfusion after a decades-long reliance on crystalloids.

Military medicine can also give countries an edge in war. In recent years, however, the United States has seriously considered major cuts to military medicine. For example, in 2019 the Defense Department announced that 13,000 military health jobs could be eliminated, creating concerns about the health of the force.[36] While these plans were disrupted by the COVID-19 pandemic, they have been recently resurrected.[37] On some level, these proposals reflect dissatisfaction with the Military Health System, which includes stateside care for military personnel and their families. But such cuts would inevitably undermine the quality of military medicine described in this book. While my own personal preference is for the United States to be involved in fewer wars, I harbor few illusions on that front.[38] Given this reality, doubling down on medicine—which generates spillover effects and is also, arguably, a force multiplier—is a compelling bet.

Conclusion

As long as war is about trying to kill other people, it will generate human costs. And as long as people are on the battlefield, they will need medical attention. As medicine improves in war, more lives will be saved. But these lives will also be altered indelibly.

Despite the claims of those who suggest that war is in decline, the evidence is to the contrary.[39] But those who decide to commit troops ought to do so better informed—and so should voters be. The information they should take into account includes not just intelligence estimates of the other side's capabilities but also the number and nature of casualties their own side will sustain. Considering these costs of war raises an unsettling counterfactual: if policymakers who chose war in the past had properly understood the long-term costs of war, would they have fought the same wars?

We can, of course, never know. Past presidents who are still living equivocate on this issue. George W. Bush, for example, has expressed regret over the US intelligence failures regarding Iraqi weapons of mass destruction that led to the Iraq War. This regret, however, does not necessarily extend to the war itself. According to Bush: "That's a do-over I can't do."[40] Nonetheless, this counterfactual raises a critical point: in debates over military action, we must always ask what we owe the future. We cannot answer that question unless we rectify existing systems of cost projection to include the wounded and subsequent veterans' care. Even if better cost assessments do not prevent future wars, we could at least better justify the costs of those wars to our children and grandchildren—who will inevitably pay the bill.

Henry Swan, a US military surgeon in the Second World War, wrote home in 1944: "It's a wonderful war—but for the wounded."[41] We cannot ignore the wounded in our understanding of wars past, present, and future. To do so not only dishonors their service, but hamstrings our choices. The decision to go to war is always fraught. Despite the chaos it unleashes, and the great suffering it brings, sometimes—albeit rarely—war is justified. And yet the decision to fight will always be morally suspect—not to mention economically disastrous—if it is made without a full acknowledgement of what will come after the fighting ends. The decision to go to war must be made in the knowledge that war creates multiple, and enduring, costs, both human and financial. Some will die, and some will survive. As the latter category increases with improved medical care in war, wounds of flesh and mind generate rising costs that overspill our individual bodies and last for generations. Ultimately, two rights—improvements in military medicine and the expansion of the veterans' benefits system—cannot undo the wrongs of war.

Notes

Introduction

1. Gragg 1991, ch. 10.
2. *MSHWR*, Vol. III, Part 2, 40.
3. Even though the minié bullet was cylindrical, it was commonly referred to as a "ball."
4. His mother did receive a pension of $8 per month until her death. Mother's Pension Certificate 162,060, Electa Bouton, mother of James Spaulding, Private, Company F, 112th New York Volunteers, National Archives Building, Washington, DC, Stack Area 18W3/Row 17/Compartment 29.
5. Linker 2011.
6. Kinder 2015, 61.
7. Bilmes 2021, 1.
8. National Material Capabilities dataset v. 6; Singer, Bremer, and Stuckey 1972.
9. Fazal 2021.
10. Mueller 1973, 61.
11. Eichenberg and Stoll 2004, 16; Lynaugh 2022.
12. Gartner 2008, 103; Gartner, Segura, and Wilkening 1997; Karol and Miguel 2007; Hayes and Myers 2009.
13. Horowitz and Levendusky 2011.
14. See, for example, Gelpi, Feaver, and Reifler 2009, 1n1. Kriner and Shen (2014, 1175) similarly define the human costs of war in terms of "combat deaths." Horowitz and Levendusky (2011, 530) equate high casualties with the number of US troops that might die in a conflict.
15. Mueller 1973, 36 (fig. 2.1), 168, and elsewhere.
16. The *Oxford English Dictionary* dates the first usage of the term "casualty" to the mid-sixteenth century, and defines it in terms of battlefield losses that include the wounded and those who deserted, as well as those killed.
17. Neufeldt and Guralnik 1988, 218–19. While there are exceptions to the rule that scholars of public opinion and the use of force have equated casualties with fatalities, they are relatively minor. Karol and Miguel (2007) include the wounded in their national-level analysis of casualty aversion, but not in the finer-grained analysis of the proximate casualty aversion hypothesis that most interests them. Gelpi, Feaver, and Reifler (2009) explicitly define casualties as fatalities on the first page of their book, but do conduct an experiment as a robustness check to assess casualty sensitivity to the wounded. Kriner and Shen (2016) likewise conduct experiments on nonfatal casualties as part of a larger analysis of the relationship between economic inequality and military participation. While others might mention the wounded as

part of the general concept of casualty, empirical analysis has focused on fatalities as the key measure of casualties.
18. Polling Report includes ten topics under the heading of national security: Afghanistan, China, Iran, Iraq, ISIS, Korea (North and South), Libya, Russia, and terrorism. There were no questions reported for 2015 for Afghanistan, China, or Korea (North and South). Only one question each on Iran and terrorism referred to military action, but without reference to ground troops or any other specifics. No questions on Libya or Russia referred to the possibility of US military deployment. See www.pollingreport.com, accessed August 21, 2015.
19. Pollingreport.com was the source for these questions.
20. WNYC 2009.
21. Clodfelter 2008, 4.
22. Kaysen 1990; Brooks 2005; Liberman 1996; Zacher 2001; Fazal 2007; Markowitz 2020.
23. Barnes 1870.
24. Keating 2022.
25. Wintermute 2011, 158, 162, 163.
26. Bump 2020.
27. Blum 2020.
28. On military medicine in the US Revolutionary War, see Gillett 2004; Applegate 1961; Gabriel 2013, 117–23.
29. For a comprehensive history of US military medicine, see Rostker 2013 and Rostker 2020.
30. Hacker 2011, 328–29; McPherson 1988, 619; McPherson 2011.

Chapter 1

1. Service Record for Moses Triplett, July 1862–June 1863, available via fold3.com, accessed June 26, 2023.
2. Volunteer Enlistment Form for Moses Triplett, August 1, 1864, National Archives Building, Washington, DC, Stack Area 7W3/Row 9/Compartment 15/Shelf 2.
3. Killian 2008.
4. Fox 2020.
5. "The Wound Dresser," in Whitman 1954, 261–64.
6. *MSHWR*, Vol. I, Part 1, iii.
7. As scholars like Sarah Handley-Cousins show, the politics around disability during and after the Civil War also deeply implicated prevailing views of American masculinity. Handley-Cousins 2019, 4.
8. "The war, Union surgeon-general William A. Hammond later observed, was fought at the 'end of the medical Middle ages.'" Faust 2008, 4.
9. Humphreys 2013, 24; Adler 2017, 4.
10. Donald 1995, 289.
11. Gunderson 1974, 930.

12. McPherson 1988, 312.
13. McPherson 1988, 318.
14. See, for example, Foner 1974; Gunderson 1974; Woods 2012. Notably, both Lincoln and Davis were more realistic about the duration of war than many in their administrations. Donald 1995, 296; McPherson 2014, 25.
15. Fearon 1995, 381.
16. Fearon 1995.
17. Kreidberg and Henry 1955, 102.
18. Humphreys 2013, 1.
19. Glasson 1918, 110.
20. Blum 2020; "Civil War Facts: 1861–1865," National Park Service, last updated October 27, 2021, https://www.nps.gov/civilwar/facts.htm.
21. Bell 2010, 116.
22. Freemon 1998, 37, 120.
23. Bollet 2002, 266; McPherson 1988, 472.
24. *MSHWR*, Vol. II, Part 1, 29.
25. Bollet 2002, 55.
26. Wintermute 2011, 5. On the US Sanitary Commission, see Maxwell 1956; Stillé 1868.
27. Brabin 2014.
28. Gibbons et al. 2012.
29. Bagozzi 2016.
30. *MSHWR*, Vol. I, Part 3, 77, 79–80. The 15,000 figure is a combination of Black and white Union troops.
31. *MSHWR*, Vol. I, Part 3, 111. Similarly, hypothesized causes of typhoid included "pythogenic misasm," overcrowding, poor ventilation, "a transmission of the disease from the localities whence the men were recruited," and rain. *MSHWR*, Vol. I, Part 3, 486.
32. "Malaria: Frequently Asked Questions," Centers for Disease Control and Prevention, last updated June 28, 2023, https://www.cdc.gov/malaria/about/faqs.html.
33. *MSHWR*, Vol. I, Part 3, 85.
34. Quoted in Bell 2010, 62.
35. Bell 2010, 62.
36. Bell 2010, 81.
37. Bell 2010, 82.
38. *MSHWR*, Vol. I, Part 3, 79–80; compare table XXII and table XXIII.
39. Bell 2010, 74.
40. Bell 2010, 101.
41. Smith 1982a, 192; Smith 1982b.
42. *MSHWR*, Vol. I, Part 3, 345, 348.
43. Smith 1982a, 220.
44. *MSHWR*, Vol. II, Part 1, 685, 715, 718.
45. Bell 2010, 33.
46. Shanks 2016; Bell 2010, 30.
47. Bell 2010, 6.

48. Bell 2010, 60, 83.
49. Bell 2010, 109.
50. See "Address to the Women of New York" in Moore 1862, 158–59.
51. For an in-depth discussion of the United States Sanitary Commission, see Maxwell 1956. The official history of the USSC is Stillé 1868. Most treatments of the USSC authored by men give most of the credit to the men who were appointed to high office within the commission, essentially writing out the critical role women played in the creation and continuance of the organization. As Bessie Z. Jones writes in the introduction to Louisa May Alcott's *Hospital Sketches*, women quickly realized that they needed prominent men to front the organization if their cause was to be taken seriously. Alcott 1960, xx.
52. "Blue mass" is different from "blue pill." "Blue mass" (*pilula hydragyri*), though, also contained mercury and was a cathartic. See "Union and Confederate Standard Supply Tables," Appendix A to Flannery 2004, http://www.siupress.com/sites/default/files/pdf/Flannery%20Appendixes.pdf.
53. Bollet 2002, 286.
54. Schmidt and Hasegawa 2009, 113.
55. Schmidt and Hasegawa 2009, 113; Reilly 2016.
56. *MSHWR*, Vol. I, Part 1, 636–41, cited in Sartin 1993. See also *MSHWR*, Vol. I, Part 3, 77.
57. *MSHWR*, Vol. I, Part 3, 155–56, 167.
58. *MSHWR*, Vol. I, Part 3, 489.
59. *MSHWR*, Vol. I, Part 3, 490, 493, 529.
60. Bell 2010, ch. 7.
61. Typhus was surprisingly uncommon in the Civil War. Humphreys 2006.
62. Bell 2010.
63. Blackford 1945, 27.
64. *MSHWR*, Vol. II, Part 3, 691.
65. *MSHWR*, Vol. I, Part 1, p. 34 of Appendix.
66. *MSHWR*, Vol. I, Part 1, p. 200 of Appendix.
67. Bollet 2002, 2.
68. Kinch and Clasper 2011; White 1944; Miller 2015.
69. *MSHWR*, Vol. II, Part 3, 563–72.
70. *MSHWR*, Vol. II, Part 3, 568.
71. Rostker 2013, 94.
72. Rowlands and Clasper 2003.
73. Blaisdell 2005.
74. *MSHWR*, Vol. II, Part 3, 572.
75. Pennington 2019, 167; Aldea and Shaw 1986, 565; Potter and Scoville 2006, 189; Rostker 2013, 199; Reister 1975, 90.
76. Cunningham 1958, 232.
77. One exception is Gillett 1995, ch. 3.
78. Rutkow 2005, 71–72.

79. Gillett 1987, 154.
80. McLaughlin and Beveridge 1977, 125. In other words, Olmsted had to wait hours until these meetings—which were, ultimately, very brief—would even begin.
81. Adams 1952, 5.
82. Young, Carpenter, and Murphy 2020.
83. Bollet 2002, 137.
84. Holmes 1862.
85. Bollet 2002, 103.
86. Shryock 1962, 161–62.
87. Adams 1952, 68, 75.
88. Bollet 2002, 103.
89. Bollet 2002, 105.
90. Gabriel 2013, 142–43.
91. Humphreys 2013, 46.
92. Stillé 1868, 134.
93. Bollet 2002, 105.
94. Bollet 2002, 124–27.
95. Rutkow 2005, 124–25, 201.
96. Maxwell 1956, 155.
97. Stillé 1868, 154, 485.
98. Gillett 1987, 153.
99. "The Innovative Design of Civilian Pavilion Hospitals," National Museum of Civil War Medicine, February 20, 2018, https://www.civilwarmed.org/pavilion-hospitals/.
100. Rutkow 2005, 157.
101. Humphreys 2013.
102. Alcott herself contracted typhoid fever and was retrieved from the hospital by her father.
103. Humphreys 2013, 33.
104. Alcott 1960, 66.
105. Schultz 2004, 2.
106. Schultz 2004, 15, 64; Rutkow 2005, 171; Erlandson 1920.
107. McPherson 1988, 483.
108. Bollet 2002, 410.
109. Bollet 2002, 421–23.
110. Schultz 2004, 15.
111. Maggie, "Civil War Women in Medicine," *History of American Women*, April 22, 2013, https://www.womenhistoryblog.com/2013/04/civil-war-women-doctors.html.
112. Bollet 2002, 188–89.
113. *MSHWR,* Vol. I, Part 1, xv.
114. *MSHWR*, Vol. I, Part 1, xxx.
115. *MSHWR*, Vol. I, Part 1, xxxi.
116. *MSHWR*, Vol. I, Part 1, xxxiv.

117. *MSHWR*, Vol. I, Part 1, xxxv.
118. *MSHWR*, Vol. I, Part 1, xxxvii.
119. Love, Hamilton, and Hellman 1958, ch. 2.
120. Wagner, Gallagher, and Finkelman 2002, 624; Faust 2008, 103, 251. Even twenty-first-century military medical record-keeping is challenging. Representatives of the Department of Defense Trauma Registry regularly exhort military medical personnel to fill out their Tactical Combat Casualty Care cards precisely because compliance is lower than they would like, a topic I will return to in Chapter 4.
121. Lamb 1916.
122. Bollet 2009, 59.
123. *MSHWR*, Vol. I, Part 1, xiii.
124. Humphreys 2008, xiii.
125. Downs 2012. For an analysis of the health effects of modern civil wars, see Stundal 2022.
126. Eli, Logan, and Miloucheva 2019.
127. Hacker 2011.
128. Cunningham 1958, 3.
129. "Statistics on the Civil War and Medicine," eHistory, Ohio State University, n.d., https://ehistory.osu.edu/exhibitions/cwsurgeon/cwsurgeon/statistics, accessed October 1, 2021. Also see "Civil War Facts: 1861–1865."
130. Blum 2020.
131. Levitan and Cleary 1973, 8.
132. "History of the National Home for Disabled Volunteer Soldiers," last updated November 14, 2017, https://www.nps.gov/articles/history-of-disabled-volunteer-soldiers.htm.
133. "History of the National Home for Disabled Volunteer Soldiers"; Plante 2004.
134. "History of the National Home for Disabled Volunteer Soldiers"; Kinder 2015, 27.
135. Resnick 2011; "$163 Bounty! Spinola's Empire Brigade! Hillhouse Light Infantry! Recruits Wanted for Comp'y I., Captain John B. Honstain," New-York Historical Society, ac03170s, PR-055-3-170, https://digitalcollections.nyhistory.org/islandora/object/islandora%3A160284.
136. "Pension! Bounty! Extra Pay! Col. J. Richter-Jones' Regiment of Pennsylvania," New-York Historical Society, ac03264s, PR-055-3-264, https://digitalcollections.nyhistory.org/islandora/object/islandora%3A159573.
137. Linker 2011, 12. This portion would have included the many veterans who had become addicted to opium as a result of medical treatment received during the war. Kinder 2015, 24.
138. Tretheway 2021.
139. Calculated using statistics from Glasson 1918, 144, combined with historical data from the Federal Reserve, https://fred.stlouisfed.org/series/M1505AUSM144NNBR, accessed April 27, 2023.
140. Severo and Milford 1989, 182.
141. Skocpol 1992, 1.
142. Kinder 2015, 26; Skocpol 1992, 114.
143. Holcombe 1999.

144. McConnell 1992; Linker 2011, 5.
145. Calculated using statistics from Glasson 1918, 144.
146. Ethelbert 1910, 586.
147. Glasson 1918, 144.
148. *MSHWR*, Vol. II, Part 3, 39.
149. Mother's Pension Certificate 176,663, Sophia Boner, mother of James Boner, Private, 48th Pennsylvania, National Archives Building, Washington, DC, Stack Area 18W3/Row 18/Compartment 8/Shelf 2.
150. Miller 2015.
151. Gunderson 1974, 926.
152. Faust 2008, 268.
153. Blum 2020.
154. Phillips 2020; Fox 2020.

Chapter 2

1. Gillett 1995, 87.
2. Linker 2011.
3. US Senate, *Congressional Record*, April 4, 1917, 201; US House of Representatives, *Congressional Record*, April 5, 1917, 305.
4. US House of Representatives, *Congressional Record*, April 5, 1917.
5. Pub. L. 65-2 (April 24, 1917), https://uslaw.link/citation/stat/40/35 p. 35, accessed September 19, 2022.
6. Sutch 2015. On US war financing, see Kreps 2018; Capella Zielinski 2016.
7. For example, that the United States would fight a defensive war against Germany. Kreidberg and Henry 1955, 235–40.
8. Schubert 1994.
9. Kinder 2015, 60–61.
10. Linker 2011, 2.
11. Cirillo 2000, 363.
12. Wintermute 2011, 159.
13. Lt. Col. Jacob Frank, "The Fate of Our Wounded in the Next War," 1916, Stanhope Bayne-Jones Papers, Archives and Modern Manuscripts Collection, History of Medicine Division, National Library of Medicine, Bethesda, MD; MS C 155, Box 7. Bayne-Jones served again in World War II and attained the rank of brigadier general. He is a major figure in the history of US medicine, including military medicine; see Cowdrey 1992.
14. Wintermute 2011, 77.
15. Adler 2017, 4–5.
16. Love 1936; Andrus, "Memorandum for Assistant Chief of Staff, G-1: Computation of Loss Replacements for War Plans," 1938, Records of the Office of the Surgeon General (Army), National Archives, College Park, MD, RG 165/Box 155/Stack 370/Row 077/Compartment 26/Shelf 2/Box 155/Folder 15460.

17. Lerwill 1954, 245.
18. "Memorandum for the Assistant Chief of Staff, G1: Loss Replacement for Air Combat Crews (Reference G-1/15460-3)," September 9, 1941, Records of the Office of the Surgeon General (Army), National Archives, College Park, MD, RG 165/Stack 370/Row 077/Compartment 26/Shelf 2/Box 155/Folder 15402.
19. War Department Operations Plan Rainbow No. 5 1941; Matloff and Snell 1990; Watson 1991, ch. XI.
20. Cosmas and Cowdrey 1992.
21. Smith 1956, 6, 33.
22. Herman 1997, 56.
23. The typhoid fever vaccine was field-tested among troops in 1909. It was deemed so effective that it became a mandatory immunization just prior to the 1911 Mexican border war. Wintermute 2011, 180.
24. Coffman 1968, 81–85.
25. Kinder 2015, 5.
26. Kirk 1945, 134.
27. Coates, Hoff, and Hoff 1958, 10.
28. Coffman 1968, 81.
29. Coffman 1968, 144–45.
30. 23rd Division, Sanitary Standing Orders for Summer, September 5, 1917, Stanhope Bayne-Jones Papers, MS C 155, Box 8, File: 23rd Division, 11th Sherwood Foresters, BEF Standing Orders.
31. Stanhope Bayne-Jones to E. Tante, July 15, 1918, Stanhope Bayne-Jones Papers, MS C 155, Box 7, File: Correspondence: March 19–November 11, 1918. Bayne-Jones would later serve in World War II and go on to have a distinguished career in medicine, including as dean of the medical schools at Yale and Cornell. Paul 1972.
32. Coates and Hoff 1955, 7–8. There was, of course, some local food purchased. Soldiers in the Seventh Army, for example, traded with the local population in France for eggs and milk. Kohlenberg 2000, 27.
33. Darling 1945, 380.
34. *Biennial Report of the Chief of Staff of the United States Army to the Secretary of War*, July 1, 1943 to June 30, 1945, p. 96, Michael DeBakey Papers, Archives and Modern Manuscripts Collection, History of Medicine Division, National Library of Medicine, Bethesda, MD, Box 27/File 21.
35. Rations were lettered according to the distance from a fully equipped kitchen. A-rations were the most desirable and closest to a traditional "hot meal." Going down the alphabet, D-rations were the easiest to transport, essentially consisting of what we might consider a very-high-calorie protein bar today. K-rations were similar to today's "meals ready-to-eat" (MREs)—high-calorie prepackaged food that could be eaten on the go.
36. Herman 1997, 92.
37. Simmons 1945, 144.
38. Atenstaedt 1999; Mayhew 2014, 46, 54.
39. Barry 2004, 2.

NOTES 181

40. Bylerly 2010, 86.
41. Coffman 1968, 81.
42. Coffman 1968, 83.
43. Stevenson 1976, 35.
44. Stevenson 1976, 35.
45. See, for example, the story of Sabra Regina Hardy, in Holmes 2017, 257.
46. Taubenberger and Morens, 15.
47. "WHO Coronavirus (COVID-19) Dashboard," World Health Organization, https://covid19.who.int, accessed February 13, 2023.
48. About 6.8 million out of an approximate world population of 7.9 billion.
49. Bylerly 2010.
50. Coates, Hoff, and Hoff 1955, 323.
51. Coates, Hoff, and Hoff 1955, 272–335. Also see Kohlenberg 2000, 44, 77; Fessler 1996, 200; Simmons 1945, 151.
52. Cowdrey 1994, 177.
53. Cowdrey and Condon-Rall 1998, 124 (emphasis added).
54. Wiltse 1965, 165.
55. Herman 1997, 83.
56. Coates and Hoff 1955, 218.
57. *Biennial Report of the Chief of Staff of the United States Army*, 109; Coates, Hoff, and Hoff 1963, 8–10.
58. Weina 1998, 635.
59. Cowdrey and Condon-Rall 1998, 123.
60. Monahan and Neidel-Greenlee 2003, 161.
61. Monahan and Neidel-Greenlee 2003, 295; Cowdrey and Condon-Rall 1998, 123.
62. Weina 1998, 636.
63. Monahan and Neidel-Greenlee 2003, 160.
64. Cowdrey 1994, 132.
65. Simmons 1945, 163.
66. Cowdrey 1994, 184.
67. Kohlenberg 2000, 28; Churchill 1972, 283; Cowdrey 1994, 148.
68. Monahan and Neidel-Greenlee 2003, 288.
69. *MDUSAWW*, vol. XI, part 1; Memo from Bayne-Jones (Surgeon, 2nd Battalion, 101st Infantry) to Surgeon, 101st Infantry, Subject: Report on Trench Foot in 2nd Battalion 101st Inf., May 1, 1918, Stanhope Bayne-Jones Papers, MS C 155, Box 9, File: 26th "Yankee" Division, AEF, Seicheprey, 1918.
70. Cosmas and Cowdrey 1992, 488; Monahan and Neidel-Greenlee 2003, 399.
71. Cosmas and Cowdrey 1992, 494.
72. Monahan and Neidel-Greenlee 2003, 288.
73. Monahan and Neidel-Greenlee 2003, 288; Cowdrey 1994, 267.
74. Cosmas and Cowdrey 1992, 491–92.
75. Cosmas and Cowdrey 1992, 492.
76. *Biennial Report of the Chief of Staff of the United States Army*; Kohlenberg 2000, 28.
77. Monahan and Neidel-Greenlee 2003, 425; Cowdrey 1994, 266.

78. Coffman 1968, 80.
79. Gillett 2009, 255.
80. Hibben 1943.
81. Hibben 1943.
82. Holmes; "Syphilis," Mayo Clinic, https://www.mayoclinic.org/diseases-conditions/syphilis/symptoms-causes/syc-20351756, accessed August 3, 2022.
83. Cosmas and Cowdrey 1992, 145; Monahan and Neidel-Greenlee 2003, 211.
84. Monahan and Neidel-Greenlee 2003, 211.
85. Monahan and Neidel-Greenlee 2003, 215.
86. Accorsi and Fazal 2022.
87. Simmons 1945, 158.
88. Parker 2014, 183–84.
89. Brooks 1966, 75; Parker 2014, 183, 242; Neiberg 2010, 46.
90. Howard E. Snyder and James W. Culbertson, *5th Army Hospital Study of Battle Casualty Deaths: An Analysis of Case Reports from Field and Evacuation Hospitals on 1450 Fatally Wounded American Soldiers: A Preliminary Report in Three Volumes* (ca. 1945), Edward D. Churchill Papers, Countway Library of Medicine, Center for the History of Medicine, World War II/Name Files H MS/C 62/Box 32/Folder 4.
91. Carter and DeBakey 1944.
92. Henry Swan, speech at Denver's Red Cross Blood Donor Center, ca. October 1945. For a description of artillery wounds in Flanders, see Mayhew 2014, 5.
93. Carter and DeBakey 1944; Monahan and Neidel-Greenlee 2003, 99.
94. Phibbs 1987, 224.
95. *MDUSAWW*, vol. XI, part 2, 399; Monahan and Neidel-Greenlee 2003, 337.
96. Fitzharris 2022.
97. Phibbs 1987, 132.
98. Monahan and Neidel-Greenlee 2003, 93.
99. Monahan and Neidel-Greenlee 2003, 287.
100. Moore 1945, 242.
101. *MDUSAWW*, vol. XIV, 54.
102. *MDUSAWW*, vol. XIV, 25.
103. *MDUSAWW*, vol. XIV, 273.
104. Stevenson 1976, 38; Stanhope Bayne-Jones to E. Tante, June 23, 1917, Stanhope Bayne-Jones Papers, MS C 155, Box 7, Correspondence, May 8–June 25, 1917.
105. Price 1997.
106. Churchill 1972, ch. 26.
107. *MDUSAWW*, vol. XII, sec. 2, 421.
108. *MDUSAWW*, vol. XII, sec. 2, 411–14.
109. Mihm 2022.
110. Monahan and Neidel-Greenlee 2003, 419.
111. Phibbs 1987, 79.
112. Monahan and Neidel-Greenlee 2003, 346.
113. Many of the doctors attending the conference lent aid following the attack. Fessler 1996, 18.

114. "Remembering Pearl Harbor: A Pearl Harbor Fact Sheet," National WWII Museum, 2001, https://www.census.gov/history/pdf/pearl-harbor-fact-sheet-1.pdf.
115. Herman 1997, 155.
116. Herman 1997, 156.
117. "US Navy Personnel in World War II: Service and Casualty Statistics," Naval History and Heritage Command, https://www.history.navy.mil/research/library/online-reading-room/title-list-alphabetically/u/us-navy-personnel-in-world-war-ii-service-and-casualty-statistics.html, accessed August 5, 2022.
118. Hawley 1945, 209.
119. Grant 1945, 286.
120. Hawley 1945, 210; Cowdrey 1994, 231–32.
121. Kirk 1945.
122. Hawley 1945, 210; Grant 1945, 284.
123. Mayhew 2014, 62.
124. Metcalf 2007.
125. *MDUSAWW*, vol. III, 140.
126. Churchill 1972, 169.
127. Herman 1997, 99; Churchill 1972, 192 (quoting from a memo: Restricted/Headquarters II Corps/Office of the Surgeon/APO 302/12 May 1943/Subject: Treatment of Casualties/To: All Unit Surgeons).
128. Churchill 1972, 280 (DeBakey to NRC, September 2, 1950).
129. Moore 1945, 242.
130. Rankin 1945, 189. Note, however, that DeBakey disagreed, arguing that fewer resources should be put toward blood vessel banks, for example. Churchill 1972, 280 (DeBakey to NRC, September 2, 1950).
131. Churchill 1972, 59–62.
132. Monahan and Neidel-Greenlee 2003, 215.
133. Monahan and Neidel-Greenlee 2003, 103; Rankin 1945, 189; Cowdrey 1994, 166.
134. "'Live-Blood' Banks" 1943; Monahan and Neidel-Greenlee 2003, 104.
135. Cowdrey 1994, 166.
136. Churchill 1972, 48; Monahan and Neidel-Greenlee 2003, 102.
137. Hawley 1945, 213.
138. Herman 1997, 212.
139. Churchill 1972, 53.
140. Calculations based on data from Biddle and Long 2004.
141. Monahan and Neidel-Greenlee 2003, 105.
142. Monahan and Neidel-Greenlee 2003, 383.
143. Henry Swan to Mary Fletcher, June 15, 1944, Henry Swan Papers (Digital Collection), Archives and Modern Manuscripts Collection, History of Medicine Division, National Library of Medicine, Bethesda, MD. Blood, like all medical supplies, raised ethical issues for doctors when treating prisoners of war. Swan describes operating on a German POW in 1945, and the only whole blood available was designated for American soldiers. As to the German: "We gave him every medical care, except the one which could save his life, and without which the rest were as nothing."

144. Cowdrey 1994, 170.
145. The Red Cross continued to segregate blood donations by race until 1950; Guglielmo 2010, 64. Note that in its very limited whole blood program, Nazi Germany only accepted "Aryan" blood; Giangrande 2000. Similarly, "Asian" blood was taken from Koreans and Vietnamese but not used to resuscitate US military personnel in Korea or Vietnam. Surgeon General Early Morning Conference Notes, entry from October 20, 1950, vol. 6, September–December 1950, National Archives and Records Administration, College Park, MD, RG 112/Records of the Office of the Surgeon General (Army)/Minutes of the Surgeon General's Early Morning Conferences/January 1950 to December 1951/Box 2/HM FY 1992.
146. *MDUSAWW*, vol. XIV, 388, 537.
147. Lyall 2020.
148. Stanhope Bayne-Jones to E. Tante, December 12, 1917, Stanhope Bayne-Jones Papers, MS C 155.
149. Henry Swan to Mary Fletcher, October 14, 1944, Henry Swan Papers.
150. *MDUSAWW*, vol. III.
151. *MDUSAWW*, vol. XI, part 1, p. 602.
152. Mayhew 2014, 30.
153. Stanhope Bayne-Jones Papers, MS C 155, Box 9, File: 26th "Yankee" Division, AEF, St. Mihiel.
154. *MDUSAWW*, vol. III.
155. Cowdrey and Condon-Rall 1998, 118.
156. Wiltse 1965, 120; Cowdrey and Condon-Rall 1998, 118.
157. Wiltse 1965, 240; Monahan and Neidel-Greenlee 2003, 223; Cowdrey and Condon-Rall 1998, 301.
158. Frank Berry to Elliot C. Cutler. July 2, 1943, Edward D. Churchill Papers, H MS C 62/Box 21.
159. Air evacuation did have some precedent in World War I, but it was so rudimentary that patients were stowed in cockpits. Page 1989, 7.
160. Cosmas and Cowdrey 1992, 483.
161. Cowdrey and Condon-Rall 1998, 75.
162. Smith 1956, 325.
163. Cosmas and Cowdrey 1992, 256.
164. Cosmas and Cowdrey 1992, 503.
165. Monahan and Neidel-Greenlee 2003, 332; Cowdrey 1994, 250.
166. Wiltse 1965, 279.
167. Page 1989, 7–8.
168. Herman 1997, 175.
169. Clark 2017.
170. Churchill 1944.
171. Henry Swan to Mary Fletcher, November 7, 1944, Henry Swan Papers.
172. Monahan and Neidel-Greenlee 2010, 11–15; Sarnecky 1999, 278.
173. Sarnecky 1999, 278.
174. Smith 1956, 109.

175. Sarnecky 1999, 273.
176. Cosmas and Cowdrey 1992, 119.
177. Monahan and Neidel-Greenlee 2003, 27.
178. Monahan and Neidel-Greenlee 2003, 134.
179. Monahan and Neidel-Greenlee 2003, 121.
180. Sarnecky 1999, 267; Monahan and Neidel-Greenlee 2003, 14.
181. Monahan and Neidel-Greenlee 2003, 151.
182. Wiltse 1965, 288. Also see Monahan and Neidel-Greenlee 2003, 285–86; Cowdrey 1994, 147.
183. Adler 2017, 64.
184. Cosmas and Cowdrey 1992, 122–23; Smith 1956, 110–17, 223; Monahan and Neidel-Greenlee 2003, 128, 434; Cowdrey 1994, 110–11.
185. Michael DeBakey to Edward Churchill, July 10, 1944, Edward D. Churchill Papers, H MS C 62/Box 21/Folder 21.
186. Linker 2011, 12.
187. Linker 2011, 2–3.
188. Adler 2017, 77.
189. Adler 2017, 87–89.
190. Douglas 1918, 469.
191. Bureau of War Risk Insurance 1920, 38.
192. Kinder 2015, 103.
193. Adler 2017, 91.
194. Kinder 2015, 103.
195. Kinder 2015; Adler 2017, 176–81; Severo and Milford 1989, 258–59.
196. Howenstine Jr. 1943.
197. Bureau of War Risk Insurance 1920, 53.
198. Adler 2017, 222.
199. Total expenditures were estimated at $3,505,754,727. Veterans Bureau expenditures were estimated at $455,232,702. The estimated Pensions Bureau budget was $252,350,000.
200. Ross 1969, 20.
201. Linker 2011, 138; Adler 2017, 108–10.
202. Adler 2017, 65–66, 110.
203. Adler 2017, 149.
204. Linker 2011, 116.
205. Linker 2011, 138.
206. Adler 2017, 18–19.
207. Kinder 2015, 181–83.
208. Kratz 2020.
209. See Figure 3.5 in Chapter 3.
210. Kinder 2015, 177.
211. Ross 1969, 25–26; Amenta and Skocpol 1988, 85–86; Altschuler and Blumin 2009, 31–32.
212. Altschuler and Blumin 2009, 40.

213. Altschuler and Blumin 2009, 59.
214. Ross 1969, 4.
215. Altschuler and Blumin 2009, chs. 2–3.
216. Ross 1969, 3.
217. Archuleta 2020.
218. Ross 1969, 112–16.
219. Schlesinger Jr. 1998, 61, cited in Mettler 2005, 7, 196.
220. 1944 Servicemen's Readjustment Act.
221. Mettler 2005, 23.
222. *Biennial Report of the Chief of Staff of the United States Army*, 109.
223. *Biennial Report of the Chief of Staff of the United States Army*, 109.
224. Mettler 2005, 36–37.
225. Marble 2008, ch. 3.
226. Marble 2008, 35.
227. Monahan and Neidel-Greenlee 2003, 456–57, 459–60; Mettler 2005, 21.
228. Severo and Milford 1989, 303.
229. Turner and Bound 2002; Cohen 2003, 167–71.
230. Humes 2006, ch. 8.
231. Griffith 1945, 322.
232. Office of Management and Budget 1947, A9, table 6.
233. Mettler 2005, 7.
234. Altschuler and Blumin 2009, 8.
235. Mettler 2005.
236. Simmons 1945.
237. *Time* magazine, December 13, 1943, Edward D. Churchill Papers, H MS/C 62/Box 21/Folder 20.
238. Henry Swan to Mary Fletcher, November 7, 1944, Henry Swan Papers.
239. Mettler 2005.

Chapter 3

1. Salazar Torreon and Plagakis 2022.
2. Stanton 1976.
3. King and Jatoi 2005.
4. See, for example, Krepinevich 1986.
5. Stiglitz and Bilmes 2008.
6. Memo, Donald Rumsfeld to Dov Zakheim, "Costs of Campaign," October 10, 2001, 8:41 a.m., National Security Archive, George Washington University, https://nsarchive.gwu.edu/document/16244-first-full-tranche-snowflakes.
7. Bush 2001.
8. Memo, Donald Rumsfeld to Richard Cheney, "Afghanistan," September 27, 2001, 6:13 p.m., National Security Archive, George Washington University, Accession No. DR00746.

9. Bronson 2002; Smock 2003, 8–10; Dobbs 2003.
10. Esterbrook 2002.
11. Russert 2003.
12. Fallows 2002.
13. O'Connell 2002.
14. Dreyfuss 2002.
15. Zunes 2002.
16. Cirincione 2002.
17. CRS 2003a.
18. CRS 2003b.
19. CRS 2003c.
20. Beehner 2006.
21. Cline 2013.
22. Ricks 2006, 213; interview of Dick Cheney by Tim Russert, *Meet the Press*, March 16, 2003.
23. Murphy 2003.
24. Shinkman 2013.
25. Woodward 2004, 327–28.
26. O'Hanlon 2003.
27. "Casualty Status as of 10 a.m. EDT September 17, 2019," Department of Defense, https://www.defense.gov/Newsroom/Casualty-Status/%EF%BB%BF/.
28. Eastridge et al. 2006, 1366–67.
29. Remick 2016, 107.
30. Zoom interview with Col. Stacy Shackelford. September 29, 2022.
31. Cubano 2018, ch. 35.
32. Bailey et al. 2012, 4.
33. Telephone interview with Dr. John Holcomb, June 2, 2023.
34. Remick 2016, 107–8.
35. See, for example, the papers collected in vols. III and IV of the *Battle Casualties of Korea* series (Howard 1955b).
36. Neel 1973, 131.
37. Perkins et al. 2012, 1042, 1043.
38. Holcomb et al. 2006, 397.
39. Holcomb, McMullin, et al. 2007, 986. As noted in an earlier chapter, the case fatality rate is the percentage of wounded who receive medical treatment and then die of their wounds.
40. Holcomb et al. 2006, 398, 399.
41. Bellamy 2000.
42. Robinson et al. 2016, 87.
43. Bailey et al. 2012, 6; Perkins et al. 2012, 1045.
44. Bailey et al. 2012, 4.
45. Remick 2016, 107.
46. Robinson et al. 2016, 87–88.
47. Kotwal et al. 2013, 2–3.

48. Cubano 2018, 6a.
49. Eastridge et al. 2012, S436. These were the main findings of a major study, "Death on the Battlefield."
50. Butler, Smith, and Carmona 2015, 321–22; Butler and Blackbourne 2012.
51. Eastridge et al. 2012, S435.
52. Kotwal et al. 2011.
53. Bellamy 1984.
54. Robinson et al. 2016, 91.
55. Perkins et al. 2012, 1048.
56. Perkins et al. 2012, 87.
57. Kragh and Dubick 2016, 30.
58. Robinson et al. 2016, 92.
59. Interview with Capt. John Maitha (US Army), Military Health System Research Symposium, Orlando, FL, September 14, 2022.
60. Cubano 2018, app. 3.
61. MSG HR Montgomery, TCCC update, Special Operations Medical Association Scientific Assembly, June 29, 2021.
62. Cubano 2018, ch. 3.
63. Holcomb, McMullin, et al. 2007, 989.
64. Holcomb, McMullin, et al. 2007, 987.
65. Eastridge et al. 2012, S432.
66. Eastridge et al. 2012, S431.
67. Cowdrey 1987, 93–96, 165, 341, 362; Howard 1955b, ch. 2.
68. Neel 1973, 70, 75; Dorland and Nancy 2008, 20.
69. Neel 1973, 72; Dorland and Nancy 2008, 30, 46, 54, 70–71.
70. Interview with Col. (Ret., USAF) Paul "Voodoo" Nelson and Col. Alex "Twitch" Keller, September 30, 2022.
71. Peoples et al. 2005; Rush et al. 2005.
72. Ingalls et al. 2014, 808.
73. For example, early helicopter evacuation flights in the Korean War were flown on relatively small helicopters that could not accommodate medical personnel. Pilots improvised a series of devices to keep patients warm, deliver fluids intravenously, and check blood pressure; helicopters at the time were so small that they did not permit more than a few people on board. Cowdrey 1987, 165.
74. Mabry et al. 2012; Ingalls et al. 2014, 812; Apodaca et al. 2013.
75. Rogers and Rittenhouse 2014; Clark 2017.
76. Shanker 2009.
77. Kotwal et al. 2016, 17.
78. Wojcik et al. 2016, 12, fig. 2.
79. Mathes et al. 2005; Cowdrey 1987, 145.
80. Beaumier et al. 2013.
81. Neel 1973, 34.
82. Garges, Taylor, and Pacha 2016, 161; Neel 1973, 34.
83. Garges, Taylor, and Pacha 2016, 164.

84. Garges, Taylor, and Pacha 2016, 163.
85. Neel 1973, 151.
86. Richards, Lundquist, and Richards 2016, 182–85.
87. Hauret et al. 2016, 17.
88. Several military medical personnel interviewed for this book questioned whether such nonbattle injuries should have been evacuated from theater.
89. These weapons were similar to those used against US forces in Vietnam, such as "mines, high-velocity missiles, and boobytraps." Small arms fire was also a major cause of injury to US forces in Vietnam. Neel 1973, 49, 53–54.
90. Cubano 2018, ch. 3, table 3-2.
91. Commandeur et al. 2012.
92. Stuhmiller 2008, 39.
93. Neel 1973, 55.
94. "Army Bans Privately" 2006. At the start of the Afghanistan and Iraq Wars, there was public outcry in the United States about how poorly supplied US troops were when it came to personal protective equipment. Families would fundraise to send PPE to their deployed loved ones. The logic behind these efforts was straightforward: that US troops should be as protected as possible from the weapons they encountered.
95. Mazurek and Ficke 2006, S20.
96. Bellamy 1984.
97. "Traumatic Brain Injury," Mayo Clinic, February 4, 2021, https://www.mayoclinic.org/diseases-conditions/traumatic-brain-injury/symptoms-causes/syc-20378557.
98. Cifu et al. 2010.
99. Cubano 2018, ch. 14.
100. Parker, Mossadegh, and McCrory 2014; Thomas et al. 2009.
101. Colyer and Jackson 2017.
102. Cubano 2018, ch. 1, fig. 1-1.
103. "COL Robert Mabry, MD, MC, USA," National Museum of Civil War Medicine, https://www.civilwarmed.org/people/mabry/, accessed September 23, 2022.
104. Mabry 2017, 120.
105. Jones 2008, 1.
106. Ibrahimi 2005.
107. Yun and Murray 2016, 114.
108. Robinson and O'Hanlon 2020.
109. Castro et al. 2015; Moyer 2021; Wood and Toppelberg 2017.
110. Department of Defense 2022a, 6.
111. Turchik and Wilson 2010.
112. Sadler et al. 2000, 475.
113. Gordon 2018, 125.
114. Sadler et al. 2000, 473; Suris and Lind 2008, 264.
115. Blais and Monteith 2019; Blais et al. 2017.
116. Schuyler et al. 2017.
117. Cross et al. 2011; McGarrah 2019.
118. Bilmes 2021, 10–11.

119. Bellamy 1984; Eastridge et al. 2012.
120. Eastridge et al. 2012; Kragh et al. 2012.
121. Welling et al. 2012.
122. Kragh et al. 2012, 248.
123. Howard 1955b, 102.
124. Butler and Blackbourne 2012, S396.
125. Kragh and Holcomb 2016.
126. Kragh and Holcomb 2016, 96.
127. Beekley et al. 2008; Kragh et al. 2008; Kragh et al. 2009; Kragh and Holcomb 2016, 97.
128. Georgoff, Rhee, and Alam 2016. For an account of the development of QuikClot, see Barber 2023.
129. Cowdrey 1987, 83, 244; Neel 1973, 125.
130. Cowdrey 1987, 244; Howard 1955a, 10; Scott and Howard 1955, 178, 185; Artz, Howard, and Frawley 1955.
131. Crystalloids are intravenous fluids used for transfusion.
132. Carrico, Canizaro, and Shires 1976; Hoyt 2009.
133. Soderdahl, Kniery, and Causey 2021, 5:40. Compartment syndrome occurs when pressure builds up in muscles. Blood is prevented from moving to that sector of the body. Swelling can lead to hypoxia and tissue death, killing the muscle.
134. Zoom interview with Dr. John Holcomb, November 10, 2022. See also Carmichael et al. 2021; Black et al. 2020.
135. Borgman et al. 2007; Holcomb et al. 2013; Holcomb et al. 2015.
136. Interview with LTC Manny Menendez. Army War College, Carlisle Barracks, PA, September 1, 2022.
137. Keynote address by Dr. John Holcomb, plenary session, Military Health Systems Research Symposium, Orlando, FL, September 12, 2022; Zoom interview with Dr. John Holcomb, November 10, 2022; Holcomb, Jenkins, et al. 2007; Borgman et al. 2007.
138. Spinella et al. 2009; Gurney et al. 2022.
139. See, for example, Neel 1973, 56.
140. For example, the June 2022 THOR meeting included several discussions of low-titer type O whole blood. Notably, low-titer type O whole blood was also a focus of transfusion efforts during the Vietnam War. Neel 1973, 56.
141. Cubano 2018, ch. 33; Graham et al. 2018.
142. For example, during a briefing on airway science as part of the 2022 Special Operations Medication Association Annual Meeting, Maj. Stephen Schauer pointed out that few advances beyond comparisons between devices available for intubation have been made. Maj. Stephen Schauer, "Improving Outcomes Associated with Prehospital Combat Airway Interventions—An Unrealized Opportunity," Special Operations Medical Association Scientific Assembly, May 3, 2022. See also Driver et al. 2021.
143. Kotwal et al. 2004; Johansson et al. 2013; Shackelford et al. 2015.
144. Diver 2008; White and Renz 2008; Chung et al. 2009; De Rond 2017, 101.
145. Kauvar et al. 2006.

NOTES 191

146. Kinder 2015, 272; Levitan and Cleary 1973, 11, 137.
147. Severo and Milford 1989, 330.
148. Desilver 2022.
149. "Budget," Department of Veterans Affairs, https://www.va.gov/budget/products.asp, accessed November 7, 2022; Shane 2022.
150. Skocpol 1993, 114.
151. Data from Office of Management and Budget, "Table 4.2—Percentage Distribution of Outlays by Agency: 1962–2021," https://obamawhitehouse.archives.gov/omb/budget/Historicals, accessed July 11, 2018. "Transition Quarter" refers to July–September 1976, after which the beginning of the fiscal year changed from July 1 to October 1. Data are in constant 2009 dollars.
152. Trynovsky 2014.
153. For example, Dana Priest, Anne Hull, and Michael du Cille of the *Washington Post* won a Pulitzer Prize in 2008 for their exposé of poor conditions at Walter Reed; see Priest and Hull 2007. Suzanne Gordon very much pushes back against the narrative of substandard care delivered by the VA, instead arguing that the level of care the VA provides should be a model for healthcare across the United States; Gordon 2018.
154. The military was edged out by small business as the most trusted institution for the first time in decades in 2021. Megan Brenan, "Americans' Confidence in Major U.S. Institutions Drops," Gallup, July 14, 2021, https://news.gallup.com/poll/352316/americans-confidence-major-institutions-dips.aspx.
155. Notably, this number represented an increase over results from a February 2013 survey, where education was first (at 60 percent) and veterans' benefits were second (at 53 percent). Pew Research Center 2017.
156. Data from Office of Management and Budget, "Table 4.2—Percentage Distribution of Outlays by Agency: 1962–2021," https://obamawhitehouse.archives.gov/omb/budget/Historicals, accessed July 11, 2018. "Transition Quarter" refers to July–September 1976, after which the beginning of the fiscal year changed from July 1 to October 1. Data are in constant 2009 dollars.
157. Based on Scott 2018.
158. In 2017, there were 7,271,000 Gulf War Veterans, 624,000 World War II veterans, 1,475,000 Korean War veterans, and 6,651,000 Vietnam War veterans. Department of Veterans Affairs 2017.
159. Bilmes 2021, 2.
160. As Bilmes points out, "Veterans from Iraq and Afghanistan are *applying* for VA benefits at much higher rates than in previous wars" (Bilmes 2021, 14; Bilmes 2014, 12). See also Archuleta 2020.
161. Dortch 2018.
162. US Army recruitment website, https://www.goarmy.com, accessed August 7, 2018.
163. "Take Charge of Your Present and Future," US Army recruitment website, https://www.goarmy.com/benefits.html, accessed August 7, 2018.
164. "Support for a Lifetime," US Army recruitment website, https://www.goarmy.com/benefits/after-the-army.html, accessed August 7, 2018.

192 NOTES

165. "Pay," US Navy recruitment website, https://www.navy.com/what-to-expect/navy-benefits-compensation-and-pay?activity=1224885&cid=ppc_gg_b_stan_core&mkwid=sofmRvm1Y%7Cpcrid%7C262988766611%7Cpkw%7Cunited%20states%20navy%7Cpmt%7Ce%7Cpdv%7Cc%7Ctargetids%7Ckwd-14887101%7Cgroupid%7C37367043353%7C, accessed August 7, 2018. Curiously, the Air Force website, while extremely slick on the first and second pages, is difficult to navigate on the question of benefits beyond the third page.
166. Archuleta 2020.
167. Bialik 2017; Department of Veterans Affairs, "Veterans Health Administration," https://www.va.gov/health/aboutvha.asp, accessed August 23, 2018; Gordon 2018.
168. Radford et al. 2016; Bilmes 2021.
169. Bilmes 2021, 8.
170. "About VA Disability Ratings," Department of Veterans Affairs, https://www.va.gov/disability/about-disability-ratings/#:~:text=What%27s%20a%20disability%20rating%3F,health%20and%20ability%20to%20function, accessed May 22, 2023.
171. Bilmes 2021, 2, 10.
172. Wong and Gerras 2021.
173. Mettler 2005, 20.
174. "Fast Facts," American Legion, https://www.legion.org/presscenter/facts; "About Us," VFW, https://www.vfw.org/about-us, accessed December 9, 2023.
175. IAVA 2021 Annual Report, https://iava.org/iavas-2021-annual-impact-report/.
176. Ingraham 2018.
177. "US Gun Control" 2022; IAVA 2021 Financial Statement, https://iava.org/about/iava-financials/iavas-2021-audited-financial-statement/; VFW 2021 Annual Report, https://vfworg-cdn.azureedge.net/-/media/VFWSite/Files/Media-and-Events/Press-Room/VFWAnnualReport; American Legion 2022 Annual Report, https://www.legion.org/documents/legion/pdf/2022_AnnualReport.pdf.
178. American Legion 2016.
179. Wilson and Dean 2022.
180. Lawrence 2017.
181. Board 2023.
182. This discrepancy was a constant issue that hovered over medical decision-making by US and NATO personnel. De Rond 2017, 46, 77.
183. Howard et al. 2019.
184. Kreps 2018.

Chapter 4

1. Homer 1883, book 20, sec. 503.
2. Shay 1991, 563, 570.
3. Shay 1991; Sherman 2015.
4. Babington 1997, 7–8.

5. Dean, for example, sees significant commonalities between the psychological trauma experienced during the US Civil War and the Vietnam War, while Young and also Jones and Wessely view wartime psychological trauma as specific to cultural time and context. Dean 1997; Young 1995; Jones and Wessely 2006; Engel 2004; Jones et al. 2002.
6. Summerfield 2001.
7. Kessler et al. 2007.
8. Recall that we have much better data for the Union Army than for the Confederate Army. We also have much better data for white soldiers than for Black soldiers. There is no systematic data on the mental health of women who served—officially or unofficially—as nurses in the Civil War.
9. More than 10 percent of the US population fought in the Civil War. On numbers of the Union and Confederate armies (totaling 3.9 million), see "Civil War Facts," National Park Service, https://www.nps.gov/civilwar/facts.htm, last updated October 27, 2021. On the US population in 1860 (over 31 million), see the Correlates of War National Material Capabilities Dataset v. 6; Singer, Bremer, and Stuckey 1972.
10. Kempster 1866, 350.
11. Babington 1997, 9; Jones and Wessely 2006, 9.
12. Jones and Wessely 2006, 10.
13. Quoted in Babington 1997, 15.
14. Quoted in Babington 1997, 15.
15. Babington 1997, 15.
16. Babington 1997, 17.
17. Hazlett, Olmstead, and Parks 1988, 28.
18. Babington 1997, 17.
19. Dean 1997, ch. 5.
20. Grob 1991, 423.
21. Dean 1997, ch. 6.
22. Dean 1997, 68.
23. Reid and White 1985, 64.
24. Quoted in Reid and White 1985, 70.
25. Kinder 2015, 24.
26. Humphreys 2013, 13–14.
27. Dean 1997, 138.
28. Skocpol 1992, ch. 2.
29. Glasson 1918, 138.
30. Dean 1997, 143.
31. Skocpol 1992, 110–11.
32. Dean 1997, 128; Lerner 1961, 124–25.
33. Lerner 1961, 124–25.
34. O'Callaghan 1954, 167–68. Taking advantage of land warrants was challenging for veterans even before 1862; see Oberly 1990.

35. "History of the National Home for Disabled Volunteer Soldiers," National Park Service, last updated November 14, 2017, https://www.nps.gov/articles/history-of-disabled-volunteer-soldiers.htm.
36. Myers 1915, 320. Note that Myers's subjects were French (not British) soldiers.
37. Babington 1997, 55–57; Shephard 2001, 67–71; Sweeney 1999.
38. *USAMDWW*, vol. X, 273–77. Pressure from the US Census Bureau for psychiatrists to systematize their diagnoses also helped professionalize the field; Grob 1991, 425.
39. Grob 1991, 427.
40. Salmon 1919.
41. Oral interview with Dr. Harry C. Solomon, Harry C. Solomon Papers, Countway Library of Medicine Center for the History of Medicine, H MS c368/Box 1/Tape 2 Side 1/Folder 2, p. 7.
42. Salmon 1919, 994.
43. *USAMDWW*, vol. X, 297.
44. "Circular No. 5—Duties of Medical Officers Detailed as Psychiatrists in Army Divisions in the Field," Headquarters, American Expeditionary Forces, Office of the Chief Surgeon, France, January 15, 1918, reprinted in *USAMDWW*, vol. X, 304–05.
45. *USAMDWW*, vol. X, 311.
46. *USAMDWW*, vol. X, 306.
47. Jones and Wessely 2006, 21.
48. Jones and Wessely 2006, 32.
49. *USAMDWW*, vol. X, sec. 2, ch. IV.
50. Fazal 2014, 110.
51. "Circular No. 35—The Management of Mental Diseases and War Neuroses in the American Expeditionary Forces," France, June 13, 1918, reprinted in *USAMDWW*, vol. X, 283. Thompson n.d.
52. *USAMDWW*, vol. X, 379.
53. Stagner 2014, 266.
54. Linker 2011; Skocpol 1992.
55. Oral interview with Dr. Harry C. Solomon, 40–41.
56. Stagner 2014, 267.
57. Kinder 2015, 112.
58. Babington 1997, 121–22; Kinder 2015, 207–8.
59. Stagner 2014, 267.
60. Adler 2017, 169–71.
61. Rates of shell shock among US military personnel were considerably lower than for the British. Whether this difference resulted from better US preparedness for shell shock or the fact that the United States was in the war for a much shorter time is difficult to say.
62. "Confidential Report to Federal Board of Hospitalization," August 19, 1940, Elizabeth Pritchard Papers, Archives and Modern Manuscripts Collection, History of Medicine Division, National Library of Medicine, Bethesda, MD, MS C 187. Box 1. File: Care of Sick and Wounded—Marine Hospitals.
63. Adler 2017, 36–39.

64. "Confidential Report to Federal Board of Hospitalization," 4–5.
65. "Confidential Report to Federal Board of Hospitalization," 1.
66. Menninger 1946, 109–10.
67. Ginzberg 1999, 523.
68. Dean 1997, 35.
69. Brill 1966, 229.
70. Brill 1966, 230–31.
71. Bartemeier et al. 1946, 370.
72. Bartemeier et al. 1946, 375–76.
73. For a discussion of the dangers of labeling patients with psychiatric illnesses in war, see Veatch 1977, 245–51.
74. Bartemeier et al. 1946, 387.
75. Brill 1966, 230.
76. Bartemeier et al. 1946, 359.
77. Brill 1966, 239–40.
78. Bartemeier et al. 1946.
79. Grob 1991, 428.
80. Bartemeier et al. 1946, 380.
81. BEMD 704.11, "Disposition of Neuropsychiatric Patients," July 31, 1944, Sanford Gifford Papers, Countway Library of Medicine, Center for Medical History, Box 23, Folder 14. As the war continued, physicians in the German and Austrian armies were more directly punished for failing to return psychologically traumatized patients to duty. This external constraint was meant to set an example, and likely succeeded in at least some quarters. Tatu and Bogousslavsky 2014.
82. Menninger 1946, 111.
83. Memorandum from 1st Lt. Sanford Gifford, Neuropsychiatric Section, 233rd Station Hospital, June 30, 1944, Sanford Gifford Papers, Box 23, Folder 14.
84. William H. Middleton to Charles S. Mayo, September 29, 1948, William H. Middleton Papers, Archives and Modern Manuscripts Collection, History of Medicine Division, National Library of Medicine, Bethesda, MD, Box 23/File 12. Middleton had served previously as a physician in the US Army Medical Corps in both world wars, and was then dean of the University of Wisconsin's School of Medicine and Public Health. Dr. Charles Mayo was also a physician, as well as the son of the founder of the Mayo Clinic.
85. Shephard 2001, 330.
86. "Summary and Review of History, Mission, Organization, Policies and Problems of the Veterans Administration Medical Program," prepared for Seminar on Federal Government Hospital Systems at Hotel Hershey, Hershey, Pennsylvania, November 28, 29, and 30, 1955, p. 12, William H. Middleton Papers, Box 23/File 12.
87. Pols 1999.
88. Montgomery 2017, 48.
89. Menninger 1946, 112.
90. De Rond 2017, 109.
91. Grob 1991, 427–28.

92. Andreasen 2010, 68; Grob 1991, 428.
93. APA 1952, 40.
94. Andreasen 2010, 68.
95. APA 1968.
96. Rostker 2013, 107.
97. Shephard 2001, 340.
98. Wilson 1993.
99. Scott 1990. As Wilson writes, "The homosexuality controversy seemed to show that psychiatric diagnoses were clearly wrapped up in social constructions of deviance." Wilson 1993, 404.
100. Shephard 2001, 340; Dean 1997, 14–15; Young 1995, 108–10.
101. Handwerk 2015.
102. Shay 2002; Levitan and Cleary 1973, 106.
103. "PTSD Basics," Department of Veterans Affairs, National Center for PTSD, https://www.ptsd.va.gov/understand/what/ptsd_basics.asp, accessed November 6, 2022.
104. APA 2013, s.v. "Posttraumatic Stress Disorder"; Friedman 2013. For descriptions of these changes, see Wilson 1994; Pai, Suris, and North 2017; Andreasen 1995.
105. Axelrod and Milner 1997; Pitman et al. 2006.
106. Interview with Dr. David Benedek, Dr. Joshua Morganstein, and Dr. Stephen Cozza, Uniformed Services University of the Health Sciences, April 27, 2018.
107. National Defense Authorization Act for Fiscal Year 2016, sec. 593, https://www.govinfo.gov/content/pkg/PLAW-114publ92/html/PLAW-114publ92.htm.
108. Department of Defense 2017.
109. Ferdinando 2018; Seck 2019; McClain 2008.
110. Wright et al. 2002; Warner et al. 2008.
111. Torreon and Plagakis 2019.
112. Shephard 2001, 370–71.
113. Smith et al. 2008; Kok et al. 2012, 444; Ferrier-Auerbach et al. 2010; Lapierre, Schwegler, and LaBauve 2007; Shen, Arkes, and Pilgrim 2009. Note, however, that Fear et al. report minimal, if any, correlation between combat deployment and PTSD onset in a study of UK military personnel (Fear et al. 2010).
114. Interian et al. 2014; Martin et al. 2008, 46.
115. Prince and Bruhns 2017.
116. Schneidermann, Braver, and Kang 2008; Hoge et al. 2008.
117. Stein and McAllister 2009.
118. Sbordone and Liter 1995; Warden et al. 1997.
119. Hickling et al. 1998, esp. 266; Bryant and Harvey 1999; Klein, Caspi, and Gil 2003; Menon et al. 2010. Note, however, that most studies on this relationship are based on civilian populations, typically those having been in motor vehicle accidents.
120. Nash et al. 2013.
121. Young 1995, 125.
122. Litz et al. 2009; Traci Pedersen, "Guerrilla Tactics Tied to Great PTSD Risk for Vets," PsychCentral. http://psychcentral.com/news/2015/12/30/guerilla-warfare-lin

ked-to-greater-risk-for-ptsd-in-veterans/96960.html, accessed November 1, 2017. No longer available.
123. Fontana and Rosenheck 1999.
124. Hoge et al. 2004.
125. Russell et al. 2014.
126. This particular finding, however, could be due to the fact that two different screening tests were used at different points in time. Milliken, Auchterlonie, and Hoge 2007.
127. Young 1995, 112–13.
128. Fazal 2018, 1.
129. "2023 Veterans Disability Compensation Rates," Department of Veterans Affairs, last updated November 29, 2022, https://www.va.gov/disability/compensation-rates/veteran-rates/.
130. Shephard 2001, 392; Gordon 2018, 142.
131. Crystalloids are fluids used for intravenous transfusion.
132. Bilmes 2021, 15.
133. Union of Concerned Scientists 2009.
134. Cummings 2016; Sonne 2018.
135. Ponton 2020.
136. Shephard 2001, 395.
137. Gallup, "Confidence in Institutions," 2018, https://news.gallup.com/poll/1597/confidence-institutions.aspx.
138. Montgomery 2017, 197.
139. Bachynski et al. 2012; Black et al. 2011; Bullman and Kang 1994; Hyman et al. 2012; Ilgen et al. 2012.
140. Department of Defense 2022b, 8 (fig. 1).
141. Fischer and Kaileh 2022.
142. Reger et al. 2015; Kang et al. 2015.
143. Schoenbaum et al. 2014.
144. Levi-Belz, Dichter, and Zerach 2022.
145. Finkel 2013, 253.
146. Lerner 2023; Checkroud et al. 2018.
147. Howell 2012.

Conclusion

1. Watson Institute 2021.
2. Peltier 2020.
3. Data on US casualties from "Casualty Status as of 10 a.m. EST November 21, 2023." US Department of Defense. https://www.defense.gov/casualty.pdf, accessed December 12, 2023. Data on Iraqi casualties from https://www.iraqbodycount.org/database/, accessed June 7, 2023.
4. Kreps 2018, 222.
5. I thank Linda Bilmes for this point.

6. Wohlforth 1991.
7. Katz and Insinna 2022; Strobel 2022.
8. See "The Role of Drones in Medical Practice Presented by Col Paul Parker," YouTube, posted by CPDme, September 16, 2021, https://www.youtube.com/watch?v=XgRaT2op8-c. See also Mesar, Lessig, and King 2018; Tucker 2019. Note that many of these capabilities depend on compliance with international humanitarian law around the protection of the wounded and medical personnel. These rules now also apply to remotely controlled vehicles, such as drones providing medical supplies. But it is too early to assess compliance with this new version of these laws.
9. Joshi 2022.
10. Telephone interview with Dr. P. K. Carlton Jr., October 13, 2022.
11. Dennis, *Prolonged Field Care Podcast*, https://anchor.fm/dennis3211/episodes/Prolonged-Field-Care-Podcast-100-The-Past--Present--and-Future-of-PFC-e1hp4eq/a-a7r0eit, accessed October 8, 2022.
12. Rubel 2011.
13. Eisenhauer et al. 2022. Notably, as Eisenhauer and coauthors mention, submarines have little to no medical capability on board.
14. Cubano 2018, ch. 28.
15. Luckenbaugh 2022.
16. Caverley 2014.
17. "Rangel Introduces Bill" 2003; Horowitz and Levendusky 2011.
18. Dao 2011.
19. The military could also change its fitness standards.
20. Asich 2019, 13–14.
21. Klay 2022, 118–21.
22. Trynovsky 2014, 45; Hicks 2014.
23. Trynovsky 2014.
24. Adler 2017, 187; Levitan and Cleary 1973, 171; Kinder 2015, 168; Linker 2011, 8; Severo and Milford 1989, 279. This concern becomes especially pointed when we consider that most veterans' benefits have benefited white men. Kinder 2015, 9–10.
25. Gordon 2018; Levitan and Cleary 1973, 171.
26. Priest and Hull 2007; Bowman 2011; Luo 2007.
27. Bronstein and Griffin 2014; Jaffe and O'Keefe 2014; Avila 2014.
28. Bellamy 1984; Eastridge et al. 2012.
29. Welling et al. 2012.
30. Bickell et al. 1994; Carrick et al. 2016; Holcomb et al. 2007; Carmichael et al. 2021.
31. Crombie et al. 2022.
32. Davis and Altenderfer 1945.
33. Stephen K. Trynovsky, "Physician-Soldier: The All-Volunteer Force and How it Changed Who Serves in Our Name," presentation given at the 134th American Public Health Association Annual Meeting, Boston, MA, November 6, 2006.
34. Accorsi and Fazal 2022.
35. D'Souza et al. 2019.
36. Kime and Kheel 2019.

37. Jowers 2021.
38. Fazal and Poast 2019.
39. Fazal 2014; Braumoeller 2019.
40. Bush 2008.
41. Henry Swan Papers, National Library of Medicine, https://profiles.nlm.nih.gov/ps/access/HPBBDC.pdf. Swan served in the US Army during World War II. After the war, Swan became known for developing the use of hypothermia in open-heart surgery.

Bibliography

Accorsi, Pedro, and Tanisha M. Fazal. 2022. "Military Medicine and Military Effectiveness." University of Minnesota.

Adams, George Worthington. 1952. *Doctors in Blue: The Medical History of the Union Army in the Civil War*. Baton Rouge: Louisiana State University Press.

Adler, Jessica. 2017. *Burdens of War: Creating the United States Veterans Health System*. Baltimore: Johns Hopkins University Press.

Alcott, Louisa May. 1960. *Hospital Sketches*. Edited by Bessie Z. Jones. Cambridge, MA: Harvard University Press.

Aldea, P., and W. Shaw. 1986. "The Evolution of the Surgical Management of Severe Lower Extremity Trauma." *Clinics in Plastic Surgery* 13, no. 4: 549–69.

Altschuler, Glenn C., and Stuart M. Blumin. 2009. *The GI Bill: A New Deal for Veterans*. New York: Oxford University Press.

Amenta, Edwin, and Theda Skocpol. 1988. "Redefining the New Deal: World War II and the Development of Social Provision in the United States." In *The Politics of Social Policy in the United States*, edited by Margaret Weir, Ann Shola Orloff, and Theda Skocpol, 81–122. Princeton, NJ: Princeton University Press.

American Legion. 2016. "Presumptive Service Connection for Gulf War Illness Is a Catch-22." March 22, 2016.

Andreasen, Nancy C. 1995. "Posttraumatic Stress Disorder: Psychology, Biology, and the Manichaean Warfare Between False Dichotomies." *American Journal of Psychiatry* 152, no. 7: 963–65.

Andreasen, Nancy C. 2010. "Posttraumatic Stress Disorder: A History and a Critique." *Annals of the New York Academy of Sciences* 1208, no. 1: 67–71.

APA. 1952. *Diagnostic and Statistical Manual: Mental Disorders*. Washington, DC: American Psychiatric Association.

APA. 1968. *Diagnostic and Statistical Manual of Mental Disorders*. 2nd ed. Washington, DC: American Psychiatric Association.

APA. 2013. *Diagnostic and Statistical Manual of Mental Disorders*. 5th ed. Washington, DC: American Psychiatric Association.

Apodaca, Amy, Chris M. Olson, Jeffrey A. Bailey, Frank K. Butler, Brian J. Eastridge, and Eric Kuncir. 2013. "Performance Improvement Evaluation of Forward Aeromedical Evacuation Platforms in Operation Enduring Freedom." *Journal of Trauma and Acute Care Surgery* 75, no. 2: S157–63.

Applegate, Howard Lewis. 1961. "The Need for Further Study in the Medical History of the American Revolutionary Army." *Military Medicine*, August 1961: 616–18.

Archuleta, Brandon J. 2020. *Twenty Years of Service: the Politics of Military Pension Policy and the Long Road to Reform*. Lawrence: University Press of Kansas.

"Army Bans Privately Bought Body Armor." 2006. *New York Times*, April 1, 2006.

Artz, Curtis P., John M. Howard, and John P. Frawley. 1955. "Clinical Observations on the Use of Dextran and Modified Fluid Gelatin in Combat Casualties." In *Battle Casualties in Korea: Studies of the Surgical Research Team*, edited by John M. Howard, 236–45. Washington, DC: Walter Reed Army Medical Center, Army Medical Service Graduate School.

Asich, Beth J. 2019. "Navigating Current and Emerging Army Recruiting Challenges." RAND Corporation, Santa Monica, CA.

Atenstaedt, R. L. 1999. "Trench Fever: The British Medical Response in the Great War." *Journal of the Royal Society of Medicine* 99, no. 11: 564–68.

Avila, Jim. 2014. "Phoenix Wait-Lists 'Contributed' to VA Deaths." ABC News, September 17.

Axelrod, Bradley N., and I. Boaz Milner. 1997. "Neuropsychological Findings in a Sample of Operation Desert Storm Veterans." *Journal of Neuropsychiatry and Clinical Neurosciences* 9, no. 1: 23–28.

Babington, Anthony. 1997. *Shell-Shock: A History of the Changing Attitudes to War Neurosis*. London: Leo Cooper.

Bachynski, K. E., M. Canham-Chervak, S. A. Black, E. O. Dada, A. M. Millikan, and B. H. Jones. 2012. "Mental Health Risk Factors for Suicides in the US Army, 2007–8." *Injury Prevention* 18: 405–12.

Bagozzi, Benjamin E. 2016. "On Malaria and the Duration of Civil War." *Journal of Conflict Resolution* 60, no. 5: 813–39.

Bailey, Jeffrey A., Mary Ann Spott, George P. Costanzo, James R. Dunner, Warren Dorlac, and Brian Eastridge. 2012. "Joint Trauma System: Development, Conceptual Framework, and Optimal Elements." US Department of Defense, US Army Institute for Surgical Research, Fort Sam Houston, TX.

Barber, Charles. 2023. *In the Blood: How Two Outsiders Solved a Centuries-Old Medical Mystery and Took on the US Army*. New York: Grand Central Publishing.

Barnes, Joseph K. 1870. *The Medical and Surgical History of the War of the Rebellion (1861–65)*. 3 vols. Washington, DC: Government Printing Office.

Barry, John M. 2004. "The Site of Origin of the 1918 Influenza Pandemic and Its Public Health Implications." *Journal of Translational Medicine* 2, no. 3.

Bartemeier, Leo H., Lawrence S. Kubie, Karl A. Menninger, John Romano, and John C. Whitehorn. 1946. "Combat Exhaustion." *Journal of Nervous and Mental Disease* 104, no. 4: 358–89.

Beaumier, Coreen M., Ana Maria Gomez-Rubio, Peter J. Hotez, and Peter J. Weina. 2013. "United States Military Tropical Medicine: Extraordinary Legacy, Uncertain Future." *PLOS Neglected Tropical Diseases* 7, no. 12: E2248.

Beehner, Lionel. 2006. "The Cost of the Iraq War." CFR Backgrounder. Council on Foreign Relations, New York.

Beekley, Alec C., James A. Sebesta, Lorne H. Blackbourne, Garth S. Herbert, David S. Kauvar, David G. Baer, Thomas J. Walters, Philip S. Mullenix, and John B. Holcomb. 2008. "Prehospital Tourniquet Use in Operation Iraqi Freedom: Effect on Hemorrhage Control and Outcomes." *Journal of Trauma, Injury, Infection, and Critical Care* 64, 2(Suppl): S28–37.

Bell, Andrew McIlwaine. 2010. *Mosquito Soldiers: Malaria, Yellow Fever, and the Course of the American Civil War*. Baton Rouge: Louisiana State University Press.

Bellamy, Ronald F. 1984. "The Causes of Death in Conventional Land Warfare: Implications for Combat Casualty Care Research." *Military Medicine* 149, no. 2: 55–62.

Bellamy, Ronald F. 2000. "Why Is Marine Combat Mortality Less Than That of the Army?" *Military Medicine* 165, no. 5: 362–67.

Bialik, Kristen. 2017. "The Changing Face of America's Veteran Population." Pew Research Center.
Bickell, William H., Matthew J. Wall, Paul E. Pepe, R. Russell Martin, Victoria F. Ginger, Mary K. Allen, and Kenneth L. Mattox. 1994. "Immediate Versus Delayed Fluid Resuscitation for Hypotensive Patients with Penetrating Torso Injuries." *New England Journal of Medicine* 331, no. 17: 1105–109.
Biddle, Stephen, and Stephen Long. 2004. "Democracy and Military Effectiveness: A Deeper Look." *Journal of Conflict Resolution* 48, no. 4: 525–46.
Bilmes, Linda J. 2014. "The Financial Legacy of Afghanistan and Iraq: How Wartime Spending Decisions Will Constrain Future U.S. National Security Budgets." *Economics of Peace and Security Journal* 9, no. 1: 5–18.
Bilmes, Linda J. 2021. "Veterans of the Iraq and Afghanistan Wars: The Long-Term Costs of Providing Disability Benefits and Medical Care, 2001–2050." Working Paper No. RWP21-024, Harvard Kennedy School.
Black, Jonathan, Virginia S. Pierce, Jeffrey D. Kerby, and John B. Holcomb. 2020. "The Evolution of Blood Transfusion in the Trauma Patient: Whole Blood Has Come Full Circle." *Seminars in Thrombosis and Hemostasis* 46, no. 2: 215–20.
Black, S. A., M. S. Gallaway, M. R. Bell, and E. C. Ritchi. 2011. "Prevalence and Risk Factors Associated with Suicides of Army Soldiers 2001–2009." *Military Psychology* 23: 433–51.
Blackford, W. W. 1945. *War Years with Jeb Stuart*. New York: Charles Scribner's Sons.
Blais, Rebecca, Emily Brignone, Shira Maguen, Marjorie E. Carter, Jamison D. Fargo, and Adi V. Gundlapalli. 2017. "Military Sexual Trauma Is Associated with Post-Deployment Eating Disorders Among Afghanistan and Iraq Veterans." *International Journal of Eating Disorders* 50, no. 7: 808–16.
Blaisdell, F. William. 2005. "Civil War Vascular Injuries." *World Journal of Surgery* 29: S21–S24.
Blais, Rebecca K., and Lindsey L. Monteith. 2019. "Suicide Ideation in Female Survivors of Military Sexual Trauma: The Trauma Source Matters." *Suicide and Life-Threatening Behavior* 49, no. 3: 643–52.
Blum, David A. 2020. "American War and Military Operations Casualties: Lists and Statistics." Congressional Research Service, Washington, DC.
Bollet, Alfred J. 2002. *Civil War Medicine: Challenges and Triumphs*. Tuscon, AZ: Galen Press.
Bollet, Alfred J. 2009. "Amputations in the Civil War." In *Years of Change and Suffering: Modern Perspectives on Civil War Medicine*, edited by James M. Schmidt and Guy R. Hasegawa, 57–67. Roseville, MN: Edinborough Press.
Borgman, Matthew A., Philip C. Spinella, Jeremy G. Perkins, Kurt W. Grathwohl, Thomas Repine, Alec C. Beekley, James A. Sebesta, Donald H. Jenkins, Charles Wade, and John B. Holcomb. 2007. "The Ratio of Blood Products Transfused Affects Mortality in Patients Receiving Massive Transfusions at a Combat Support Hospital." *Journal of Trauma, Injury, Infection, and Critical Care* 63, no. 4: 805–13.
Bowman, Tom. 2011. "Walter Reed Was the Army's Wake-Up Call in 2007." National Public Radio, August 31.
Brabin, Bernard J. 2014. "Malaria's Contribution to World War One—The Unexpected Adversary." *Malaria Journal* 13, no. 497.
Braumoeller, Bear. 2019. *Only the Dead: The Persistence of War in the Modern Age*. New York: Oxford University Press.

Brevard, Sidney B., Howard R. Champion, and Dan Katz. 2012. "Weapon Effects." In *Combat Casualty Care: Lessons Learned from OEF and OIF*, edited by Martha K. Lenhart, Eric Savitsky, and Brian Eastridge, 39–83. Fort Detrick, MD: Borden Institute.

Brill, Norman Q. 1966. "Hospitalization and Disposition." In *Neuropsychiatry in World War II: Zone of Interior*, edited by Albert J. Glass and Robert J. Bernucci, 195–253. Washington, DC: Office of the Surgeon General, Department of the Army.

Bronstein, Scott, and Drew Griffin. 2014. "A Fatal Wait: Veterans Languish and Die on a VA Hospital's Secret List." CNN, April 23.

Brooks, S. 1966. *Civil War Medicine*. Springfield, IL: Thomas Books.

Brooks, Stephen G. 2005. *Producing Security: Multinational Corporations, Globalization, and the Changing Calculus of Conflict*. Princeton, NJ: Princeton University Press.

Bryant, Richard A. and Harvey, Allison G. 1999. "The Influence of Traumatic Brain Injury on Acute Stress Disorder and Post-Traumatic Stress Disorder Following Motor Vehicle Accidents." *Brain Injury* 13(1): 15–22.

Bullman, T. A., and H. K. Kang. 1994. "Posttraumatic Stress Disorder and the Risk of Traumatic Deaths Among Vietnam Veterans." *Journal of Nervous and Mental Disease* 182: 604–10.

Bump, Philip. 2020. "Nearly a Quarter of Americans Have Never Experienced the U.S. in a Time of Peace." *Washington Post*, January 8, 2020.

Bureau of War Risk Insurance. 1920. *Annual Report of the Director of the Bureau of War Risk Insurance for the Fiscal Year Ended June 30 1920*. Washington, DC: Government Printing Office.

Bush, George W. 2001. "Presidential Address to the Nation." The White House, October 7.

Bush, George W. 2008. "Transcript: Charlie Gibson Interviews President Bush." ABC News, November 28.

Butler, Frank K., and Lorne H. Blackbourne. 2012. "Battlefield Trauma Care Then and Now: A Decade of Tactical Combat Casualty Care." *Journal of Trauma and Acute Care Surgery* 73, no. 6: S395–402.

Butler, Frank K., David J. Smith, and Richard H. Carmona. 2015. "Implementing and Preserving the Advances in Combat Casualty Care from Iraq and Afghanistan Throughout the US Military." *Journal of Trauma and Acute Care Surgery* 79, no. 2: 321–26.

Byerly, Carol R. 2010. "The U.S. Military and the Influenza Pandemic of 1918–1919." *Public Health Reports* 125: 82–91.

Capella Zielinski, Rosella. 2016. *How States Pay for Wars*. Ithaca, NY: Cornell University Press.

Carmichael, Samuel P., Nicholas Lin, Meagan E. Evangelista, and John B. Holcomb. 2021. "The Story of Blood for Shock Resuscitation: How the Pendulum Swings." *Journal of the American College of Surgeons* 233, no. 5: 644–53.

Carrick, Matthew M., Jan Leonard, Denetta S. Slone, Charles W. Mains, and David Bar-Or. 2016. "Hypotensive Resuscitation Among Trauma Patients." *BioMed Research International*.

Carrico, Charles J., Peter C. Canizaro, and Tom Shires. 1976. "Fluid Resuscitation Following Injury: Rationale for the Use of Balanced Salt Solution." *Critical Care Medicine* 4, no. 2: 46–54.

Carter, Noland, and Michael E. DeBakey. 1944. "War Wounds of the Extremities." *Bulletin of the American College of Surgeons* 29: 117–21.

Castro, Carl Andrew, Sara Kintzle, Ashley C. Schuyler, Carrie L. Lucas, and Christopher H. Warner. 2015. "Sexual Assault in the Military." *Current Psychiatry Reports* 17, no. 7 (July): 54.

Caverley, Jonathan D. 2014. *Democratic Militarism: Voting, Wealth, and War*. New York: Cambridge University Press.

Checkroud, Adam M., Hieronimus Loho, Martin Paulus, and John H. Krystal. 2018. "PTSD and the War of Words." *Chronic Stress* 2.

Chung, Kevin K., Steven E. Wolf, Leopoldo C. Cancio, Ricardo Alvarado, John A. Jones, Jeffery McCorcle, Booker T. King, David J. Barillo, Evan M. Renz, and Lorne H. Blackbourne. 2009. "Resuscitation of Severely Burned Military Casualties: Fluid Begets More Fluid." *Journal of Trauma* 67, no. 2: 231–37.

Churchill, Edward D. 1944. "The Surgical Management of the Wounded in the Mediterranean Theater at the Time of the Fall of Rome." *Annals of Surgery*, September 1944, 269–83.

Churchill, Edward D. 1972. *Surgeon to Soldiers: Diary and Records of Surgical Consultant, Allied Force Headquarters, World War II*. Philadelphia: J. B. Lippincott.

Cifu, David X., Sara I. Cohen, Henry L. Lew, Michael Jaffee, and Barbara Sigford. 2010. "The History and Evolution of Traumatic Brain Injury Rehabilitation in Military Service Members and Veterans." *American Journal of Physical Medicine and Rehabilitation* 89, no. 8: 688–94.

Cirillo, Vincent J. 2000. "Fever and Reform: the Typhoid Epidemic in the Spanish-American War." *Journal of the History of Medicine and Allied Sciences* 55, no. 4: 363–97.

Cirincione, Joseph. 2002. "Iraq's WMD Arsenal: Deadly but Limited." Carnegie Endowment for International Peace.

Clark, David E. 2017. "RA Cowley, the 'Golden Hour,' the 'Momentary Pause,' and the 'Third Space.'" *The American Surgeon* 83, no. 12: 1401–6.

Cline, Seth. 2013. "The Underestimated Costs, and Price Tag, of the Iraq War." *US News and World Report*, March 20, 2013.

Clodfelter, Micheal. 2008. *Warfare and Armed Conflicts: A Statistical Encyclopedia of Casualty and Other Figures, 1494–2007*. 3rd ed. Jefferson, NC: McFarland.

Coates, John Boyd, and Ebbe Curtis Hoff, eds. 1955. *Environmental Hygiene*, vol. II, *Preventive Medicine in World War II*. Washington, DC: Office of the Surgeon General Department of the Army.

Coates, John Boyd, Ebbe Curtis Hoff, and Phebe Hoff, eds. 1955. *Personal Health Measures and Immunization, Preventive Medicine in World War II*. Washington, DC: Office of the Surgeon General, Department of the Army.

Coates, John Boyd, Ebbe Curtis Hoff, and Phebe Hoff, eds. 1958. *Communicable Diseases Transmitted Chiefly Through Respiratory and Alimentary Tracts*. Edited by S. B. Hays. Vol. IV, Preventive Medicine in World War II. Washington, DC: Office of the Surgeon General.

Coates, John Boyd, Ebbe Curtis Hoff, and Phebe Hoff, eds. 1963. *Communicable Diseases: Malaria*. Edited by Leonard D. Heaton. Vol. VI, Preventive Medicine in World War II. Washington, DC: Office of the Surgeon General, Department of the Army.

Coffman, Edward M. 1968. *The War to End All Wars: The American Military Experience in World War I*. New York: Oxford University Press.

Cohen, Lizabeth. 2003. *A Consumers' Republic: The Politics of Mass Consumption in Postwar America*. New York: Alfred A. Knopf.

Colyer, Marcus H., and Kevin M. Jackson. 2017. "Combat Ocular Trauma." In *Out of the Crucible: How the US Military Transformed Combat Casualty Care in Iraq and Afghanistan*, edited by Arthur L. Kellermann and Eric Elster, 197–202. Fort Sam Houston, TX: Borden Institute.

Commandeur, Joris, Robert Jan Derksen, Damian MacDonald, and Roelf Breederveld. 2012. "Identical Fracture Patterns in Combat Vehicle Blast Injuires Due to Improvised Explosive Devices; A Case Series." *BMC Emergency Medicine* 12, no. 12: 1–5.

Cosmas, Graham A., and Albert E. Cowdrey. 1992. *Medical Service in the European Theater of Operations, United States Army in World War II. The Technical Services*. Washington, DC: Center of Military History, United States Army.

Cowdrey, Albert E. 1987. *The Medics' War: United States Army in the Korean War*. Washington, DC: Center of Military History, United States Army.

Cowdrey, Albert E. 1992. *War and Healing: Stanhope Bayne-Jones and the Maturing of American Medicine*. Baton Rouge: Louisiana State University Press.

Cowdrey, Albert E. 1994. *Fighting for Life: American Military Medicine in World War II*. New York: Free Press.

Cowdrey, Albert E., and Mary E. Condon-Rall. 1998. *Medical Service in the War Against Japan, United States Army in World War II. The Technical Services*. Washington, DC: Center of Military History, United States Army.

Crombie, Nicholas, Heidi A. Doughty, Jonathan R. B. Bishop, Amisha Desai, Emily F. Dixon, James M. Hancox, Mike J. Herbert, Caroline Leech, Simon J. Lewis, Mark R. Nash, David N. Naumann, Gemma Slinn, Hazel Smith, Ian M. Smith, Rebekah K. Wale, Alastair Wilson, Natalie Ives, and Gavin D. Perkins. 2022. "Resuscitation with Blood Products in Patients with Trauma-Related Haemorrhagic Shock Receiving Prehospital Care (RePHILL): A Multicentre, Open-Label, Randomised, Controlled, Phase 3 Trial." *Lancet Haematology* 9, no. 4: E250–61.

Cross, Jessica D., Anthony E. Johnson, Joseph C. Wenke, Michael J. Bosse, and James R. Ficke. 2011. "Mortality in Female War Veterans of Operations Enduring Freedom and Iraqi Freedom." *Clinical Orthopedics and Related Research* 469: 1956–61.

Crown, Ellen. 2016a. "Soldiers Getting Junctional Tourniquet Designed to Save Lives." US Army, March 2. https://www.army.mil/article/163229/soldiers_getting_junctional_tourniquet_designed_to_save_lives.

Crown, Ellen. 2016b. "Here Are the Details on the New Combat Tourniquet." US Army, October 12. https://www.army.mil/article/176507/here_are_the_details_on_the_new_combat_tourniquet.

CRS. 2003a. "Iraq: Potential Post-War Foreign Aid Issues." Congressional Research Service, Washington, DC.

CRS. 2003b. "U.S. Occupation of Iraq? Issues Raised by Experiences in Japan and Germany." Congressional Research Service, Washington, DC.

CRS. 2003c. "Potential Humanitarian Issues in Post-War Iraq: An Overview for Congress." Congressional Research Service, Washington, DC.

Cuban, Michael A. 2018. *Emergency War Surgery Handbook*.

Cubano, Miguel A., ed. 2018. *Emergency War Surgery*. 5th ed. Fort Sam Houston, TX: Borden Institute and Office of the Surgeon General.

Cummings, William. 2016. "Trump PTSD Comments Spark Emotional Debate." *USA Today*, October 3, 2016.

Cunningham, H. H. 1958. *Doctors in Gray: The Confederate Medical Service*. Baton Rouge: Louisiana State University Press.

D'Souza, Edwin, James Zouris, Trevor Elkins, Vern Wing, and Andrew Olson. 2019. "Forecasting Wounded-in-Action Casualty Rates for Ground Combat Operations." Naval Health Research Center, San Diego, CA. https://apps.dtic.mil/sti/citations/AD1105971.
Dao, James. 2011. "They Signed Up to Fight." *New York Times*, September 6, 2011.
Darling, George B. 1945. "How the National Research Council Streamlined Medical Research for War." In *Doctors at War*, edited by Morris Fishbein, 363–98. New York: E. P. Dutton.
Davis, Burnet M., and Marion E. Altenderfer. 1945. "Effect of the War on the Distribution of Full-Time Local Health Officers." *American Journal of Public Health* 35, no. 10: 1047–52.
Dean, Eric T. 1997. *Shook over Hell: Post-Traumatic Stress, Vietnam, and the Civil War*. Cambridge, MA: Harvard University Press.
Department of Defense. 2017. "Report on Section 593 of the National Defense Authorization Act for Fiscal Year 2016, (Public Law 114-92): Report on Preliminary Mental Health Screenings for Individuals Becomeing Members of the Armed Forces." Department of Defense, Washington, DC.
Department of Defense. 2022a. "Annual Report on Sexual Assault in the Military, Fiscal Year 2021." Department of Defense, Washington, DC.
Department of Defense. 2022b. "Annual Report on Suicide in the Military: Calendar Year 2021." Undersecretary of Defense for Personnel and Readiness, Department of Defense, Washington, DC.
Department of Veterans Affairs. 2017. "Veteran Population Projections 2017–2037." https://www.va.gov/vetdata/docs/Demographics/New_Vetpop_Model/Vetpop_Infographic_Final31.pdf.
De Rond, Mark. 2017. *Doctors at War: Life and Death in a Field Hospital*. Ithaca, NY: Cornell University Press.
Desilver, Drew. 2022. "The Polarization in Today's Congress Has Roots That Go Back Decades." Pew Research Center.
Diver, Andrew J. 2008. "The Evolution of Burn Fluid Resuscitation." *International Journal of Surgery* 6: 345–50.
Dobbs, Michael. 2003. "Wolfowitz Shifts Rationales on Iraq War." *Washington Post*, September 12, 2003.
Donald, David Herbert. 1995. *Lincoln*. New York: Simon & Schuster.
Dorland, Peter, and James Nancy. 2008. *Dust Off: Army Aeromedical Evacuation in Vietnam*. Washington, DC: Center of Military History, United States Army.
Dortch, Cassandria. 2018. "The Post-9/11 GI Bill: A Primer." Congressional Research Service, Washington, DC.
Douglas, Paul H. 1918. "The War Risk Insurance Act." *Journal of Political Economy* 26: 461–83.
Downs, Jim. 2012. *Sick from Freedom: African-American Illness and Suffering During the Civil War and Reconstruction*. New York: Oxford University Press.
Dreyfuss, Robert. 2002. "Tinker, Banker, NeoCon, Spy." *American Prospect*, October 23, 2002.
Driver, Brian E., Matthew W. Semler, Wesley H. Self, Adit A. Ginde, Stacy A. Trent, Gandotra-Sheetal, Lane M. Smith, David B. Page, Derek J. Vonderhaar, Jason R. Wast, Aaron M. Joffe, Steven H. Mitchell, Kevin C. Koerschug, Christopher G. Hughes, Kevin High, Janna S. Landsperger, Karen E. Jackson, Michelle P. Howell, Sarah W. Rosison,

John P. Gaillard, Micah R. Whitson, Christopher M. Barnes, Andrew J. Latimer, Vikas S. Koppurapu, Bret D. Alvis, Derek W. Russell, Kevin W. Gibbs, Li Wang, Christopher J. Lindsell, David R. Janz, Todd W. Rice, Matthew E. Prekker, and Jonathan D. Casey. 2021. "Effect of Use of a Bougie vs. Endotracheal Tube with Stylet on Successful Intubation on the First Attempt Among Critically Ill Patients Undergoing Tracheal Intubation: A Randomized Clinical Trial." *JAMA* 326, no. 24: 2488–97.

Eastridge, Brian J., Donald Jenkins, Stephen Flaherty, Henry Schiller, and John B. Holcomb. 2006. "Trauma System Development in a Theater of War: Experiences from Operation Iraqi Freedom and Operation Enduring Freedom." *Journal of Trauma, Injury, Infection, and Critical Care* 61: 1366–73.

Eastridge, Brian, Robert L. Mabry, Peter Seguin, Joyce Cantrell, Terrill Tops, Paul Uribe, Olga Mallett, Tamara Zubko, Lynne Oetjen-Gerdes, Todd Rasmussen, Frank K. Butler, Russell S. Kotwal, John B. Holcomb, Charles Wade, Howard Champion, Mimi Lawnick, Leon Moores, and Lorne H. Blackbourne. 2012. "Death on the Battlefield (2001–2011): Implications for the Future of Combat Casualty Care." *Journal of Trauma and Acute Care Surgery* 73, no. 6: S431–37.

Eichenberg, Richard C., and Richard J. Stoll. 2004. "The Political Fortunes of War: Iraq and the Domestic Standing of President George W. Bush." Foreign Policy Centre, London.

Eisenhauer, Ian F., Benjamin D. Walrath, Vikhyat S. Bebarta, Matthew D. Tadlock, Jay B. Baker, and Steven G. Schauer. 2022. "Navy En-Route Care in Future Distributed Maritime Operations: A Review of Clinician Capabilities and Roles of Care." *Prehospital Emergency Care* 27, no. 4: 465–72.

Eli, Shari, Trevon D. Logan, and Boriana Miloucheva. 2019. "Physician Bias and Racial Disparities in Health: Evidence from Veterans' Pensions." NBER Working Paper 25846, National Bureau of Economic Research, Cambridge, MA.

Engel, Charles C. 2004. "Post-War Syndromes: Illustrating the Impact of the Social Psyche on Notions of Risk, Responsibility, Reason, and Remedy." *Journal of the American Academy of Pschoanalysis and Dynamic Psychiatry* 32, no. 3: 321–34.

Erlandson, E. V. 1920. "The Story of Mother Bickerdyke." *American Journal of Nursing* 20, no. 8: 628–31.

Esterbrook, John. 2002. "Rumsfeld: It Would Be a Short War." CBS News, November 15.

Ethelbert, Stewart. 1910. "Wages and Hours of Labor of Union Carpenters in the United States in in English-Speaking Foreign Countries." *Bulletin of the United States Bureau of Labor*, no. 87: 583–98.

Lawrence, Quil. 2017. "Fact Checking Trump on Veterans Affairs." *All Things Considered*, National Public Radio, August 23, 2017.

Fallows, James. 2002. "The Fifty-First State?" *Atlantic Monthly* (November): 53–64.

Faust, Drew Gilpin. 2008. *The Republic of Suffering: Death and the American Civil War*. New York: Alfred A. Knopft.

Fazal, Tanisha M. 2007. *State Death: The Politics and Geography of Conquest, Occupation, and Annexation*. Princeton, NJ: Princeton University Press.

Fazal, Tanisha M. 2014. "Dead Wrong? Battle Deaths, Military Medicine, and the Exaggerated Reports of War's Demise." *International Security* 39, no. 1: 95–125.

Fazal, Tanisha M. 2018. "PTSD and Veterans' Benefits in the United States: A Historical Backgrounder." Modern War Institute, West Point, NY.

Fazal, Tanisha M. 2021. "Life and Limb: New Estimates of Casualty Aversion in the United States." *International Studies Quarterly* 65, no. 1: 160–72.

Fazal, Tanisha M., and Paul Poast. 2019. "War Is Not Over: What the Optimists Get Wrong About Conflict." *Foreign Affairs* 98, no. 6: 74–83.

Fear, Nicola T., Margaret Jones, Dominic Murphy, Lisa Hull, Amy C. Iversen, Bolaji Coker, Louise Machell, Josefin Sundin, Charlotte Woodhead, Norman Jones, Neil Greenberg, Sabine Landau, Christopher Dandeker, Roberto J. Rana, Matthew Hotopf, and Simon Wessely. 2010. "What Are the Consequences of Deployment to Iraq and Afghanistan on the Mental Health of the UK Armed Forces? A Cohort Study." *Lancet* 375: 1783–97.

Fearon, James D. 1995. "Rationalist Explanations for War." *International Organization* 49, no. 3: 379–414.

Ferdinando, Lisa. 2018. "Military Recruiters Highlight Efforts, Challenges in Recruiting, Retention." *DOD News*, April 13.

Ferrier-Auerbach, Amanda G., Christopher R. Erbes, Melissa A. Polusny, Michael Rath, and Scott R. Sponheim. 2010. "Predictors of Emotional Distress Reported by Soldiers in the Combat Zone." *Journal of Psychiatric Research* 44: 470–76.

Fessler, Diane Burke. 1996. *No Time for Fear: Voices of American Military Nurses in World War II*. East Lansing: Michigan State University Press.

Finkel, David. 2013. *Thank You for Your Service*. New York: Farrar, Straus and Giroux.

Fischer, Hannah, and Hibbah Kaileh. 2022. "Trends in Active-Duty Military Deaths from 2006 Through 2021." Congressional Research Service, Washington, DC.

Fitzharris, Lindsey. 2022. *The Facemaker: A Visionary Surgeon's Battle to Mend the Disfigured Soldiers of World War I*. New York: Macmillan.

Flannery, Michael A. 2004. *Civil War Pharmacy: A History of Drugs, Drug Supply and Provision, and Therapeutics for the Union and Confederacy*. Binghamton, NY: Pharmaceutical Products Press.

Foner, Eric. 1974. "The Causes of the American Civil War: Recent Interpretations and New Directions." *Civil War History* 20, no. 3: 197–214.

Fontana, Alan, and Robert Rosenheck. 1999. "A Model of War Zone Stressors and Posttraumatic Stress Disorder." *Journal of Traumatic Stress* 12, no. 1: 111–26.

Fox, Alex. 2020. "The Last Person to Receive a Civil War Pension Dies at Age 90." *Smithsonian Magazine*, June 8, 2020.

Freemon, Frank R. 1998. *Gangrene and Glory: Medical Care During the American Civil War*. Madison, NJ: Farleigh Dickinson University Press.

Friedman, Matthew. 2013. "Finalizing PTSD in *DSM-5:* Getting Here from There and Where to Go Next." *Journal of Traumatic Stress* 26, no. 5: 548–56.

Gabriel, Richard A. 2013. *Between Flesh and Steel: A History of Military Medicine from the Middle Ages to the War in Afghanistan*. Washington, DC: Potomac Books.

Garges, Eric C., Kevin M. Taylor, and Laura A. Pacha. 2016. "Select Public Health and Communicable Disease Lessons Learned During Operations Iraqi Freedom and Enduring Freedom." *United States Army Medical Department Journal*, April–September 2016: 161–66.

Gartner, Scott Sigmund. 2008. "The Multiple Effects of Casualties on Public Support for War: An Experimental Approach." *American Political Science Review* 102, no. 1: 95–106.

Gartner, Scott Sigmund, Gary M. Segura, and Michael Wilkening. 1997. "All Politics Are Local: Local Losses and Individual Attitudes Toward the Vietnam War." *Journal of Conflict Resolution* 41, no. 5: 669–94.

Gelpi, Christopher, Peter D. Feaver, and Jason Reifler. 2009. *Paying the Human Costs of War: American Public Opinion & Casualties in Military Conflicts*. Princeton, NJ: Princeton University Press.

Georgoff, Patrick, Peter Rhee, and Hassan Alam. 2016. "Topical Hemostatic Agents." In *Out of the Crucible: How the US Military Transformed Combat Casualty Care in Iraq and Afghanistan*, edited by Arthur L. Kellermann and Eric Elster, 111–18. Fort Sam Houston, TX: Borden Institute.

Giangrande, Paul L. F. 2000. "The History of Blood Transfusion." *British Journal of Haematology* 110, no. 4: 758–67.

Gibbons, Robert V., Matthew Streitz, Tatyana Babina, and Jessica R. Fried. 2012. "Dengue and US Military Operations from the Spanish-American War Through Today." *Emerging Infectious Diseases* 18, no. 4: 623–30.

Gillett, Mary C. 1987. *The Army Medical Department, 1818–1865*. Washington, DC: Center of Military History, United States Army.

Gillett, Mary C. 1995. *The Army Medical Department, 1865–1917*. Washington, DC: Center of Military History, US Army.

Gillett, Mary C. 2004. *The Army Medical Department, 1775–1818*. Washington, DC: Center of Military History, US Army.

Gillett, Mary C. 2009. *The Army Medical Department, 1917–1941*. Washington, DC: Center of Military History, United States Army.

Ginzberg, Eli. 1999. "The Shift to Specialism in Medicine: The US Army in World War II." *Academic Medicine* 74, no. 5: 522–25.

Glasson, William H. 1918. *Federal Military Pensions in the United States*. New York: Oxford University Press.

Global Views. 2016. "US Public Topline Report." Chicago Council on Global Affairs.

Gordon, Suzanne. 2018. *Wounds of War: How the VA Delivers Health, Healing, and Hope to the Nation's Veterans*. Ithaca, NY: ILR Press.

Gragg, Rod. 1991. *Confederate Goliath: The Battle of Fort Fisher*. New York: HarperCollins.

Graham, Brendan C., Lindsey J. Graham, Carl H. Rose, and Jeffrey L. Winters. 2018. "How Shall We Transfuse Hippolyta?" *American Journal of Obstetrics and Gynecology*, February 2018: 219–20.

Grant, David N. W. 1945. "The Medical Mission in the Army Air Forces." In *Doctors at War*, edited by Morris Fishbein, 275–301. New York: E. P. Dutton.

Griffith, Charles M. 1945. "The Veterans Administration." In *Doctors at War*, edited by Morris Fishbein, 321–35. New York: E. P. Dutton.

Grob, Gerald N. 1991. "Origins of *DSM-I*: A Study in Appearance and Reality." *American Journal of Psychiatry* 148, no. 4: 421–31.

Guglielmo, Thomas A. 2010. "'Red Cross, Double Cross': Race and America's World War II–Era Blood Donor Service." *Journal of American History* 97, no. 1: 63–90.

Gunderson, Gerald. 1974. "The Origins of the American Civil War." *Journal of Economic History* 34, no. 4: 915–50.

Gurney, Jennifer M., Amanda M. Staudt, Deborah J. del Junco, Stacy A. Shackelford, Elizabeth Mann-Salinas, Andrew P. Cap, Philip C. Spinella, and Matthew J. Martin. 2022. "Whole Blood at the Tip of the Spear: A Retrospective Cohort Analysis of Warm Fresh Whole Blood Resuscitation Versus Component Therapy in Severely Injured Combat Casualties." *Surgery* 171: 518–25.

Gwertzman, Bernard. 2002. "U.S. Has 'Strategically Sound and Morally Just' Reasons to Invade Iraq, Says Council's Middle East Director Rachel Bronson." Council on Foreign Relations, December 12, 2002.

Hacker, J. David. 2011. "A Census-Based Count of the Civil War Dead." *Civil War History* 57, no. 4: 307–48.

Handley-Cousins, Sarah. 2019. *Bodies in Blue: Disability in the Civil War North*. Athens: University of Georgia Press.

Handwerk, Brian. 2015. "Over a Quarter-Million Vietnam War Veterans Still Have PTSD." *Smithsonian Magazine*, July 22, 2015.

Hauret, Keith G., Laura A. Pacha, Bonnie J. Taylor, and Bruce H. Jones. 2016. "Surveillance of Disease and Nonbattle Injuries During US Army Operations in Afghanistan and Iraq." *United States Army Medical Department Journal* (April–September): 15–23.

Hawley, Paul R. 1945. "How Medicine in the European Theater of Operations Prepared for D-Day." In *Doctors at War*, edited by Morris Fishbein, 195–217. New York: E. P. Dutton.

Hayes, Andrew F., and Teresa A. Myers. 2009. "Testing the 'Proximate Casualties Hypothesis': Local Troop Loss, Attention to News, and Support for Military Intervention." *Mass Communication and Society* 12, no. 4: 379–402.

Hazlett, James C., Edwin Olmstead, and M. Hume Parks. 1988. *Field Artillery Weapons of the Civil War*. Urbana: University of Illinois Press.

Herman, Jan K. 1997. *Battle Station Sick Bay: Navy Medicine in World War II*. Annapolis: Naval Institute Press.

Hibben, M. C. 1943. "Venereal Disease in the Armed Forces." *Editorial Research Reports* 1: 21–36.

Hickling, E. J., R. Gillen, E. B. Blanchard, T. Buckley, and A. Taylor. 1998. "Traumatic Brain Injury and Posttraumatic Stress Disorder: A Preliminary Investigation of Neuropsychological Test Results in PTSD Secondary to Motor Vehicle Accidents." *Brain Injury* 12(4): 265–74.

Hicks, Josh. 2014. "The VA's 2-Page Justification for a $17 Billion Funding Request." *Washington Post*, July 24, 2014.

Hill and Ponton, P.A. 2020. "PTSD Veterans: Need to Watch This Ultimate Guide for VA Benefits." YouTube, posted by Hill and Ponton, P.A., September 4, 2020, https://www.youtube.com/watch?v=uU1SxSCm4sU.

Hoge, Charles W., Carl A. Castro, Stephen C. Messer, Dennis McGurk, Dave I. Cotting, and Robert L. Koffman. 2004. "Combat Duty in Iraq and Afghanistan, Mental Health Problems, and Barriers to Care." *New England Journal of Medicine* 351, no. 1: 13–22.

Hoge, Charles W., Dennis McGurk, Jeffrey L. Thomas, Anthony L. Cox, Charles C. Engel, and Carl A. Castro. 2008. "Mild Traumatic Brain Injury in US Soldiers Returning from Iraq." *New England Journal of Medicine* 358, no. 5: 453–63.

Holcomb, John B., Deborah J. del Junco, Erin E. Fox, Charles E. Wade, Mitchell J. Cohen, Martin A. Schreiber, Louis H. Alarcon, Yu Bai, Karen J. Brasel, Eileen M. Bulger, Bryan A. Cotton, Nena Matijevic, Peter Muskat, John G. Myers, Herb A. Phelan, Christopher E. White, Jiajie Zhang, and Mohammad H. Rahbar. 2013. "The Prospective, Observation, Multicenter, Major Trauma Transfusion (PROMMTT) Study." *JAMA Surgery* 148, no. 2: 127–36.

Holcomb, John B., David B. Jenkins, Peter Rhee, Jay Johannigman, Peter Mahoney, Sumeru Mehta, E. Darrin Cox, Michael J. Gehrke, Greg J. Beilman, Martin Schreiber, Stephen F. Flaherty, Kurt W. Grathwohl, Philip C. Spinella, Jeremy G. Perkins, Alec C. Beekley, Neil R. McMullin, Muyng S. Park, Ernest A. Gonzalez, Charles E. Wade,

Michael A. Dubick, William Schwab, Fred A. Moore, Howard R. Champion, David B Hoyt, and John R. Hess. 2007. "Damage Control Resuscitation: Directly Addressing the Early Coagulopathy of Trauma." *Journal of Trauma, Injury, Infection, and Critical Care* 62, no. 2: 307–10.

Holcomb, John B., Neil R. McMullin, Lisa Pearse, Jim Caruso, Charles E. Wade, Lynne Oetjen-Gerdes, Howard R. Champion, Mimi Lawnick, Warner Farr, Sam Rodriguez, and Frank K. Butler. 2007. "Causes of Death in U.S. Special Operations Forces in the Global War on Terrorism, 2001–2004." *Annals of Surgery* 245, no. 6: 986–91.

Holcomb, John B., Lynn G. Stansbury, Howard R. Champion, Charles Wade, and Ronald F. Bellamy. 2006. "Understanding Combat Casualty Care Statistics." *Journal of Trauma, Injury, Infection, and Critical Care* 60, no. 2: 397–401.

Holcomb, John B., Barbara C. Tilley, Sarah Baraniuk, Erin E. Fox, Charles E. Wade, Jeanette M. Podbielski, Deborah J. del Junco, Karen J. Brasel, Eileen M. Bulger, Rachael A. Callcut, Michell Jay Cohen, Bryan A. Cotton, Timothy C. Fabian, Kenji Inaba, Jeffrey D. Kerby, Peter Muskat, Terence O'Keefe, Sandro Rizoli, Bryce R. H. Robinson, Thomas M. Scalea, Martin A. Schreiber, Deborah M. Stein, Jordan A. Weinberg, Jeannie L. Callum, John R. Hess, Nena Matijevic, Christopher N. Miller, Jean-Francois Pittet, David B Hoyt, Gail D. Pearson, Brian Leroux, and Gerald van Belle. 2015. "Transfusion of Plasma, Platelets, and Red Blood Cells in a 1:1:1 vs a 1:1:2 Ratio and Mortality in Patients with Severe Trauma: The PROPPR Randomized Clinical Trial." *JAMA* 313, no. 5: 471–82.

Holcombe, Randall G. 1999. "Veterans Interests and the Transition to Government Growth: 1870–1915." *Public Choice* 99: 311–26.

Holmes, Frederick. n.d. "Venereal Disease." Medicine in the First World War, KU Medical Center. https://www.kumc.edu/school-of-medicine/academics/departments/history-and-philosophy-of-medicine/archives/wwi/essays/medicine/venereal-disease.html.

Holmes, Grace E. F. 2017. *North Dakota Nurses over There, 1917–1919*. Fargo, ND: American Legion Auxiliary, Department of North Dakota.

Holmes, Oliver Wendell. 1862. "My Hunt After the Captain." *The Atlantic* (December): 738–64.

Homer. 1883. *Iliad of Homer*. Translated by Theodore Alois Buckley. New York: Harper & Brothers.

Horowitz, Michael C., and Matthew S. Levendusky. 2011. "Drafting Support for War: Conscription and Mass Support for Warfare." *American Journal of Political Science* 73, no. 2: 524–34.

Howard, Jeffrey T., Russ S. Kotwal, Caryn Stern, Jud C. Janak, Edward L. Mazuchowski, Frank K. Butler, Zsolt T. Stockinger, Barbara R. Holcomb, Raquel C. Bono, and David J. Smith. 2019. "Use of Combat Casualty Care Data to Assess the US Military Trauma System During the Afghanistan and Iraq Conflicts, 2001–2017." *JAMA Surgery* 154, no. 7: 600–608.

Howard, John M. 1955a. "Introduction—Historical Background and Development." In *Battle Casualties in Korea: Studies of the Surgical Research Team*, edited by John M. Howard, Washington, DC: Army Medical Service Graduate School, Walter Reed Army Medical Center.

Howard, John M., ed. 1955b. *Battle Casualties in Korea: Studies of the Surgical Research Team*, vol. III, *The Battle Wound: Clinical Experiences*. Washington, DC: Army Medical Service Graduate School Walter Reed Army Medical Center.

Howell, Alison. 2012. "The Demise of PTSD: From Governing Through Trauma to Governing Resilience." *Alternatives: Global, Local, Political* 37, no. 3: 214–26.

Howenstine, E. Jay, Jr. 1943. "Demobilization After the First World War." *Quarterly Journal of Economics* 58, no. 1: 91–105.

Hoyt, David B. 2009. "Blood and War—Lest We Forget." *Journal of the American College of Surgeons* 209, no. 6: 681–86.

Humes, Edward. 2006. *Over Here: How the G.I. Bill Transformed the American Dream.* New York: Harcourt.

Humphreys, Margaret. 2006. "A Stranger to Our Camps: Typhus in American History." *Bulletin of the History of Medicine* 80, no. 2: 269–90.

Humphreys, Margaret. 2008. *Intensely Human: The Health of the Black Soldier in the American Civil War.* Baltimore: Johns Hopkins University Press.

Humphreys, Margaret. 2013. *Marrow of Tragedy: The Health Crisis of the American Civil War.* Baltimore: Johns Hopkins University Press.

Hyman, J., R. Ireland, L. Frost, and L. Cottrell. 2012. "Suicide Incidence and Risk Factors in an Active Duty US Military Population." *American Journal of Public Health* 102: S138–46.

Ibrahimi, Sayed Yaqub. 2005. "Afghan Gun Culture Costs Lives." Institute for War and Peace Reporting.

Ilgen, M. A., J. F. McCarthy, R. V. Ignacio, A. S. Bohnert, M. Valenstein, F. C. Blow, and I. R. Katz. 2012. "Psychopathology, Iraq and Afghanistan Service, and Suicide Among Veterans Health Administration Patients." *Journal of Consulting and Clinical Psychology* 80: 323–30.

Ingalls, Nichole, David Zonies, Jeffrey A. Bailey, Kathleen D. Martin, Bart O. Iddins, Paul K. Carlton, Dennis Hanseman, Richard Branson, Warren Dorlac, and Jay Johannigman. 2014. "A Review of the First 10 Years of Critical Care Aeromedical Transport During Operation Iraqi Freedom and Operation Enduring Freedom: The Importance of Evacuation Timing." *JAMA Surgery* 149, no. 8: 807–13.

Ingraham, Christopher. 2018. "Nobody Knows How Many Members the NRA Has, but Its Tax Returns Offer Some Clues." *Washington Post*, February 26, 2018.

Institute of Medicine and National Research Council. 2007. *PTSD Compensation and Military Service.* Washington, DC: National Academies Press.

Interian, Alejandro, Anna Kline, Malvin Janal, Shirley Glynn, and Miklos Losonczy. 2014. "Multiple Deployments and Combat Trauma: Do Homefront Stressors Increase the Risk for Posttraumatic Stress Symptoms?" *Journal of Traumatic Stress* 27: 90–97.

Jaffe, Greg, and Ed O'Keefe. 2014. "Obama Accepts Resignation of VA Secretary Shinseki." *Washington Post*, May 30, 2014.

Johansson, Joakim, Jonas Sjöberg, Marie Nordgren, Erik Sandström, Folke Sjöberg, and Henrik Zetterström. 2013. "Prehospital Analgesia Using Nasal Administration of S-ketamine—A Case Series." *Scandinavian Journal of Trauma, Resuscitation and Emergency Medicine* 21: 21–38.

Jones, Edgar, Robert Hodgins-Vermaas, Helen McCartney, Brian Everitt, Charlotte Beech, Denise Poynter, Ian Palmer, Kenneth Kyams, and Simon Wessely. 2002. "Post-Combat Syndromes from the Boer War to the Gulf War: A Cluster Analysis of Their Nature and Attribution." *British Medical Journal* 324, no. 7333: 321–24.

Jones, Edgar, and Simon Wessely. 2006. *Shell Shock to PTSD: Military Psychiatry from 1900 to the Gulf War.* New York: Psychology Press.

Jones, Seth G. 2008. "Counterinsurgency in Afghanistan." RAND Corporation, Santa Monica, CA.

Joshi, Shashank. 2022. "How Heavy Are Russian Casualties in Ukraine?" *The Economist*, July 24, 2022.

Jowers, Karen. 2021. "New Plan Scales Back Massive Cuts in Military Medical Billets." *Military Times*, September 10, 2021.

Kang, Han K., Tim A. Bullman, Derek J. Smolenski, Nancy A. Skopp, Gregory A. Gahm, and Mark A. Reger. 2015. "Suicide Risk Among 1.3 Million Veterans Who Were on Active Duty During the Iraq and Afghanistan Wars." *Annals of Epidemiology* 25, no. 2: 96–100.

Karol, David, and Edward Miguel. 2007. "The Electoral Cost of War: Iraq Casualties and the 2004 US Presidential Election." *Journal of Politics* 69, no. 3: 633–48.

Katz, Justin, and Valerie Insinna. 2022. "'A Bloody Mess' with 'Terrible Loss of Life': How a China-US Conflict over Taiwan Could Play Out." *Breaking Defense*, August 11, 2022.

Kauvar, David S., Steven E. Wolf, Charles E. Wade, Leopoldo C. Cancio, Evan M. Renz, and John B. Holcomb. 2006. "Burns Sustained in Combat Explosions in Operations Iraqi and Enduring Freedom (OEF/OIF Explosion Burns)." *Burns* 32: 853–57.

Kaysen, Carl. 1990. "Is War Obsolete? A Review Essay." *International Security* 14, no. 4: 42–64.

Keating, Joshua 2022. "How Many Russian Soldiers Have Been Killed in Ukraine? What We Know, How We Know It and What It Really Means." *Grid News*, August 16, 2022.

Kempster, W. 1866. "Entero-colitis, or Chronic Diarrhoea. With Some Practical Observations upon Its Nature and Treatment." *American Journal of the Medical Sciences*, July 1866, 337–51.

Kessler, Ronald C., G. Paul Amminger, Sergio Aguilar-Gaxiola, Jordi Alonso, Sing Lee, and T. Bedirhan Ustun. 2007. "Age of Onset of Mental Disorders: A Review of Recent Literature." *Current Opinion in Psychiatry* 20, no. 4: 359–64.

Killian, Ron V. 2008. *A History of the North Carolina Third Mounted Infantry Volunteers U.S.A.: March 1864 to August 1865*. Westminster, MD: Heritage Books.

Kime, Patricia, and Rebecca Kheel. 2019. "Medical Forces Could Be Shorthanded During War Due to Planned Cuts, Milley Says." Military.com, May 11, 2019.

Kinch, Kevin, and J. C. Clasper. 2011. "A Brief History of War Amputation." *BMJ Military Health* 157: 374–80.

Kinder, John. 2015. *Paying with Their Bodies: American War and the Problem of the Disabled Veteran*. Chicago: University of Chicago Press.

King, Booker, and Ismail Jatoi. 2005. "The Mobile Army Surgical Hospital (MASH): A Military and Surgical Legacy." *JAMA* 97, no. 5: 648–56.

Kirk, Norman T. 1945. "The Army Doctor in Action." In *Doctors at War*, edited by Morris Fishbein, 109–35. New York: E.P. Dutton & Company, Inc.

Klay, Phil. 2022. *Uncertain Ground: Citizenship in an Age of Endless, Invisible War*. New York: Penguin Press.

Klein, Ehud, Yael Caspi, and Sharon Gil. 2003. "The Relation Between Memory of the Traumatic Event and PTSD: Evidence from Studies of Traumatic Brain Injury." *Canadian Journal of Psychiatry* 48, no. 1: 28–33.

Kohlenberg, Mary Jane. 2000. *Hospital on the Move: Life with the 79th Field Hospital in World War II*. Kirksville, MO: Truman State University Press.

Kok, Brian C., Richard K. Herrell, Jeffrey L. Thomas, and Charles W. Hoge. 2012. "Posttraumatic Stress Disorder Associated with Combat Service in Iraq or Afghanistan." *Journal of Nervous and Mental Disease* 200, no. 5: 444–50.

Kotwal, Russ S., Frank K. Butler, Harold R. Montgomery, Tyson Brunstetter, George Y. Diaz, James W. Kirkpatrick, Nancy L. Summers, Stacy A. Shackelford, John B. Holcomb, and Jeffrey A. Bailey. 2013. "The Tactical Combat Casualty Card TCCC Guidelines: Proposed Changed 1301." *Journal of Special Operations Medicine* 13, no. 2: 82–87.

Kotwal, Russ S., Jeffrey T. Howard, Jean A. Orman, Bruce W. Tarpey, Jeffrey A. Bailey, Howard R. Champion, Robert L. Mabry, John B. Holcomb, and Kirby R. Gross. 2016. "The Effect of a Golden Hour Policy on the Morbidity and Mortality of Combat Casualties." *JAMA Surgery* 151, no. 1: 15–24.

Kotwal, Russ S., Harold R. Montgomery, Bari M. Kotwal, Howard R. Champion, Frank K. Butler, Robert L. Mabry, Jeffrey S. Cain, Lorne H. Blackbourne, Kathy K. Mechler, and John B. Holcomb. 2011. "Eliminating Preventable Death on the Battlefield." *Archives of Surgery* 146, no. 12: 1350–58.

Kotwal, Russ S., Kevin C. O'Connor, Troy R. Johnson, Dan S. Mosely, David E. Meyer, and John B. Holcomb. 2004. "A Novel Pain Management Strategy for Combat Casualty Care." *Annals of Emergency Medicine* 44, no. 2: 121–27.

Kragh, John F., Kenneth G. Swam, Dale C. Smith, Robert L. Mabry, and Lorne H. Blackbourne. 2012. "Historical Review of Emergency Tourniquet Use to Stop Bleeding." *American Journal of Surgery* 203: 242–52.

Kragh, John F., and Michael A. Dubick. 2016. "Battlefield Tourniquets: Lessons Learned in Moving Current Care Toward Best Care in an Army Medical Department at War." *United States Army Medical Department Journal*, April–September 2016, 29–36.

Kragh, John F., and John B. Holcomb. 2016. "Battlefield Tourniquets." In *Out of the Crucible: How the US Military Transformed Combat Casualty Care in Iraq and Afghanistan*, edited by Arthur L. Kellermann and Eric Elster, 93–102. Fort Sam Houston, TX: Borden Institute.

Kragh, John F., Thomas J. Walters, David G. Baer, Charles J. Fox, Charles E. Wade, Jose Salinas, and John B. Holcomb. 2009. "Survival with Emergency Tourniquet Use to Stop Bleeding in Major Limb Trauma." *Annals of Surgery* 249, no. 1: 1–7.

Kragh, John F., Thomas J. Walters, David G. Baer, Charles J. Fox, Charles Wade, Jose Salinas, and John B. Holcomb. 2008. "Practical Use of Emergency Tourniquets to Stop Bleeding in Major Limb Trauma." *Journal of Trauma, Injury, Infection, and Critical Care* 64: S38–50.

Kratz, Jessie. 2020. "The 1932 Bonus Army: Black and White Americans Unite in March on Washington." National Archives, Washington, DC.

Kreidberg, Marvin A., and Merton G. Henry. 1955. "History of Military Mobilization in the United States Army, 1775–1945." Washington, DC: Office of the Chief of Military History, Department of the Army.

Krepinevich, Andrew F. 1986. *The Army and Vietnam*. Baltimore: Johns Hopkins University Press.

Kreps, Sarah. 2018. *Taxing Wars: The American Way of War Finance*. New York: Oxford University Press.

Kriner, Douglas L., and Francis X. Shen. 2014. "Reassessing American Casualty Sensitivity: The Mediating Influence of Inequality." *Journal of Conflict Resolution* 58, no. 7: 1174–201.

Kriner, Douglas, and Francis X. Shen. 2016. "Invisible Inequality: The Two Americas of Military Sacrifice." *Memphis Law Review* 46: 545–635.

Lamb, David S. 1916. "The Army Medical Museum—A History." *Washington Medical Annals* 15, no. 1: 15–24.

Lapierre, Coady B., Andria F. Schwegler, and Bill J. LaBauve. 2007. "Posttraumatic Stress and Depression Symptoms in Soldiers Returning from Combat Operations in Iraq and Afghanistan." *Journal of Traumatic Stress* 20, no. 6: 933–43.

Lerner, Adam B. 2023. "Blurring the Boundaries of War: PTSD in American Foreign Policy Discourse." *Perspectives on Politics* 21, no. 2: 569–86.

Lerner, Harry V. 1961. "Effect of Character of Discharge and Length of Service on Eligibility to Veterans' Benefits." *Military Law Review* 13: 121–42.

Lerwill, Leonard. 1954. *The Personnel Replacement System in the United States Army*. Washington, DC: Center of Military History, Department of the Army.

Levi-Belz, Yossi, Neta Dichter, and Gadi Zerach. 2022. "Moral Injury and Suicide Ideation Among Israeli Combat Veterans: The Contribution of Self-Forgiveness." *Journal of Interpersonal Violence* 37, nos. 1–2: NP1031–57.

Levitan, Sar A., and Karen Cleary. 1973. *Old Wars Remain Unfinished: The Veteran Benefits System*. Baltimore: Johns Hopkins University Press.

Liberman, Peter. 1996. *Does Conquest Pay? The Exploitation of Occupied Industrial Societies*. Princeton, NJ: Princeton University Press.

Linker, Beth. 2011. *War's Waste: Rehabilitation in World War I America*. Chicago: University of Chicago Press.

Litz, Brett T., Nathan Stein, Eileen Delaney, Leslie Lebowitz, William P. Nash, Caroline Silva, and Shira Maguen. 2009. "Moral Injury and Moral Repair in War Veterans: A Preliminary Model and Intervention Strategy." *Clinical Psychology Review* 29: 695–706.

"'Live-Blood' Banks Save Soldiers' Lives in Sicily When Plasma Proves Inadequate." 1943. *New York Times*, August 27, 1943.

Love, Albert G. 1931. "War Casualties: Their Relation to Medical Service and Replacements." *Army Medical Bulletin* 24: 5–177.

Love, Albert G., Eugene L. Hamilton, and Ida Levin Hellman. 1958. *Tabulating Equipment and Army Medical Statistics*. Washington, DC: Department of the Army.

Luckenbaugh, Josh. 2022. "Drones Modified for Medical Supply Drops in Ukraine." *National Defense*, August 22.

Luo, Michael. 2007. "Soldiers Testify to Lawmakers over Poor Care at Walter Reed." *New York Times*, March 6, 2007.

Lyall, Jason. 2020. *Divided Armies: Inequality and Battlefield Performance in Modern War*. Princeton, NJ: Princeton University Press.

Lynaugh, Kyle. 2022. "Public Opinion on Civilian Casualties in the War on Terror." Running Numbers blog. Chicago Council on Global Affairs, March 9. https://globalaffairs.org/commentary-and-analysis/blogs/public-opinion-civilian-casualties-war-terror. Accessed January 5, 2024.

Lynch, Charles, ed. 1921–29. *The Medical Department of the United States Army in the World War*. Washington, DC: Government Printing Office.

Mabry, Robert L. 2017. "MEDEVAC Lessons from the Iraq and Afghan Wars." In *Out of the Crucible: How the US Military Transformed Combat Casualty Care in Iraq and Afghanistan*, edited by Arthur L. Kellermann and Eric Elster, 119–30. Fort Sam Houston, TX: Borden Institute.

Mabry, Robert L., Amy Apodaca, Jason Penrod, Jean A. Orman, Robert T. Gerhardt, and Warren Dorlac. 2012. "Impact of Critical Care-Trained Flight Paramedics on Casualty Survival During Helicopter Evacuation in the Current War in Afghanistan." *Journal of Trauma and Acute Care Surgery* 73, no. 2: S32–37.

Marble, Sanders. 2008. *Rehabilitating the Wounded: Historical Perspective on Army Policy.* Washington, DC: Office of Medical History.

Markowitz, Jonathan N. 2020. *Perils of Plenty: Arctic Resource Competition and the Return of the Great Game?* New York: Oxford University Press.

Martin, Elisabeth Moy, Wei C. Lu, Katherine Helmick, Louis French, and Deborah L. Warden. 2008. "Brain Injuries Sustained in the Afghanistan Wars." *American Journal of Nursing* 108, no. 4: 40–48.

Mathes, Robert W., William H. Page, Harriet M. Crawford, A. Marshal McBean, and Richard N. Miller. 2005. "Long-Term Sequelae of Hemorrhagic Fever with Renal Syndrome Attributable to Hantaan Virus in Korean War Veterans." *Military Medicine* 170, no. 4: 315–19.

Matloff, Maurice, and Edwin M. Snell. 1990. *Strategic Planning for Coalition Warfare, 1941–1942.* Washington, DC: Center of Military History.

Maxwell, William Quentin. 1956. *Lincoln's Fifth Wheel: The Political History of the United States Sanitary Commission.* New York: Longmans, Green.

Mayhew, Emily. 2014. *Wounded: The Long Journey Home from the Great War.* London: Vintage Books.

Mazurek, Michael T., and James R. Ficke. 2006. "The Scope of Wounds Encountered in Casualties from the Global War on Terrorism: From the Battlefield to the Tertiary Treatment Facility." *Journal of the American Academy of Orthopaedic Surgeons* 14: S18–23.

McClain, Jeffrey D. 2008. "Army Recruiting Challenges in the 21st Century." US Army War College, Carlisle Barracks, PA.

McConnell, Stuart. 1992. *Glorious Contentment: The Grand Army of the Republic, 1865–1900.* Chapel Hill: University of North Carolina Press.

McGarrah, Daniel P. 2019. "The Gender Gap in Trauma Training." *Joint Forces Quarterly*, 55–59.

McLaughlin, Charles Capen, and Charles E. Beveridge, eds. 1977. *The Papers of Frederick Law Olmsted.* Vol. 4. Baltimore: Johns Hopkins University Press.

McPherson, James M. 1988. *Battle Cry of Freedom: The Civil War Era.* New York: Oxford University Press.

McPherson, James M. 2011. "Commentary on 'A Census-Based Count of the Civil War Dead.'" *Civil War History* 57, no. 4: 309–10.

McPherson, James M. 2014. *Embattled Rebel: Jefferson Davis as Commander in Chief.* New York: Penguin.

Menninger, William C. 1946. "The Future Role of Psychiatry in the Army." *The Military Surgeon*, February 1946, 108–113.

Menon, David K., Karen Schwab, David W. Wright, and Andrew I. Maas. 2010. "Position Statement: Definition of Traumatic Brain Injury." *Archives of Physical Medicine and Rehabilitation* 91, no. 11: 1637–40.

Mesar, Tomaz, Aaron Lessig, and David R. King. 2018. "Use of Drone Technology for Delivery of Medical Supplies During Prolonged Field Care." *Journal of Special Operations Medicine* 18, no. 4: 34–35.

Metcalf, N. H. 2007. "The Effect of the First World War (1914–1918) on the Development of British Anaesthesia." *European Journal of Anaesthesiology* 24: 649–57.

Mettler, Suzanne. 2005. *Soldiers to Citizens: The G.I. Bill and the Making of the Greatest Generation*. New York: Oxford University Press.

Mihm, Stephen. 2022. "Battle Tanks Are Always Outmoded but Never Obsolete." *Washington Post*, March 28, 2022.

Miller, Brian Craig. 2015. *Empty Sleeves: Amputation in the Civil War South*. Athens: University of Georgia Press.

Milliken, Charles S., Jennifer L. Auchterlonie, and Charles W. Hoge. 2007. "Longitudinal Assessment of Mental Health Problems Among Active and Reserve Component Soldiers Returning from the Iraq War." *JAMA* 298, no. 18: 2141–48.

Monahan, Evelyn M., and Rosemary Neidel-Greenlee. 2003. *And If I Perish: Frontline U.S. Army Nurses in World War II*. New York: Alfred A. Knopf.

Monahan, Evelyn M., and Rosemary Neidel-Greenlee. 2010. *A Few Good Women: America's Military Women from World War I to the Wars in Iraq and Afghanistan*. New York: Anchor Books.

Montgomery, Adam. 2017. *The Invisible Injured: Psychological Trauma in the Canadian Military from the First World War to Afghanistan*. Montreal: McGill–Queen's University Press.

Moore, Frank, ed. 1862. *The Rebellion Record: A Diary of American Events, with Documents, Narratives, Illustrative Incidents, Poetry, Etc.* Vol. I. New York: G. P. Putnam.

Moore, French R. 1945. "The Doctor at Guadalcanal and Tarawa." In *Doctors at War*, edited by Morris Fishbein, 233–46. New York: E. P. Dutton.

Moyer, Melinda Wenner. 2021. "'A Poison in the System': The Epidemic of Military Sexual Assault." *New York Times Magazine*, August 3, 2021.

Mueller, John E. 1973. *War, Presidents and Public Opinion*. New York: John Wiley & Sons.

Murphy, Jarrett. 2003. "What's a War Cost These Days?" CBS News, February 28.

Myers, Charles S. 1915. "A Contribution to the Study of Shell Shock: Being an Account of Three Cases of Loss of Memory, Vision, Smell, and Taste, Admitted into the Duchess of Westminster War Hospital, Le Touquet." *Lancet* 185, no. 4772: 316–20.

Nash, William P., Teresa L. Marino Carper, Mary Alice Mills, Teresa Au, Abigail Goldsmith, and Brett T. Litz. 2013. "Psychometric Evaluation of the Moral Injury Events Scale." *Military Medicine* 178, no. 6: 646–52.

Neel, Spurgeon. 1973. *Medical Support of the U.S. Army in Vietnam*. Washington, DC: Department of the Army.

Neiberg, M. 2010. "World War I: An Unwinnable Conflict, 1914–1916." In *War Since 1900*, edited by Jeremy Black, 33–55. London: Thames and Hudson.

Neufeldt, Victoria, and David B. Guralnik, eds. 1988. *Webster's New World Dictionary of American English*. 3rd College ed. New York: Webster's New World.

O'Callaghan, Jerry A. 1954. "The War Veteran and the Public Lands." *Agricultural History* 28, no. 4: 163–68.

O'Connell, Mary Ellen. 2002. "The Myth of Preemptive Self-Defense." American Society of International Law Task Force Paper, Presidential Task Force on Terrorism.

O'Hanlon, Michael. 2003. "Estimating Casualties in a War to Overthrow Saddam." *Orbis*, Winter 2003, 21–40.

Oberly, James W. 1990. *Sixty Million Acres: American Veterans and the Public Lands Before the Civil War*. Kent, OH: Kent State University Press.

Office of Management and Budget. 1947. *The Budget of the United States Government for the Fiscal Year Ending June 30 1948*. Washington, DC: Government Printing Office.

Owens, Brett, John F. Kragh, Joseph C. Wenke, Joseph Macaitis, Charles Wade, and John B. Holcomb. 2008. "Combat Wounds in Operation Iraqi Freedom and Operation Enduring Freedom." *Journal of Trauma, Injury, Infection, and Critical Care* 64, no. 2: 295–99.

Page, Evelyn. 1989. *The Story of Air Evacuation*. Dallas, TX: Taylor.

Pai, Anushka, Alina M. Suris, and Carol S. North. 2017. "Posttraumatic Stress Disorder in the *DSM-5*: Controversy, Change, and Conceptual Considerations." *Behavioral Sciences* 7, no. 1: 7.

Parker, B. 2014. *The Physics of War: From Arrows to Atoms*. Amherst, NY: Prometheus Books.

Parker, P., S. Mossadegh, and C. McCrory. 2014. "A Comparison of the IED-Related Eye Injury Rate in ANSF and ISAF Forces at the UK R3 Hospital, Camp Bastion, 2013." *Journal of the Royal Army Medical Corps* 160: 73–74.

Paul, J. R. 1972. "Stanhope Bayne-Jones (1888–1970): Medical Dean, Microbiologist and Epidemiologist, and Medical Historian." *Yale Journal of Biology and Medicine* 45, no. 1: 22–32.

Peltier, Heidi. 2020. "The Cost of Debt-Financed War: Public Debt and Rising Interest for Post-9/11 War Spending." 20 Years of War: A Costs of War Research Series. Watson Institute for International and Public Affairs, Brown University.

Pennington, H. 2019. "The Impact of Infectious Disease in War Time: A Look Back at WWI." *Future Microbiology* 14, no. 3: 165–68.

Peoples, George E., Tad Gerlinger, Robert Craig, and Brian Burlingame. 2005. "The 274th Forward Surgical Team Experience During Operation Enduring Freedom." *Military Medicine* 170, no. 6: 451–59.

Perkins, Jeremy G., Laura R. Brosch, Alec C. Beekley, Kelly L. Warfield, Charles E. Wade, and John B. Holcomb. 2012. "Research and Analytics in Combat Trauma Care: Converting Data and Experience to Practical Guidelines." *Surgical Clinics of North America* 92: 1041–54.

Pew Research Center. 2017. "With Budget Debate Looming, Growing Share of Public Prefers Bigger Government." April 24, 2017. http://www.people-press.org/2017/04/24/with-budget-debate-looming-growing-share-of-public-prefers-bigger-government/attachment/32/.

Phibbs, Brendan. 1987. *The Other Side of Time: A Combat Surgeon in World War II*. Boston: Little, Brown.

Phillips, Michael M. 2020. "Last Person to Receive Civil War–Era Pension Dies." *Wall Street Journal*, June 2, 2020.

Pitman, Roger K., Mark W. Gilbertson, Tamara V. Gurvits, Flavia S. May, Natasha B. Lasko, Linda J. Metzger, Martha E. Shenton, Rachel Yehuda, and Scott P. Orr. 2006. "Clarifying the Origin of Biological Abnormalities in PTSD Through the Study of Identical Twins Discordant for Combat Exposure." *Annals of the New York Academy of Sciences* 1071: 242–54.

Plante, Trevor K. 2004. "The National Home for Disabled Volunteer Soldiers." *Prologue Magazine* 36, no. 1. https://www.archives.gov/publications/prologue/2004/spring/soldiers-home.html.

Pols, Hans. 1999. "The Repression of War Trauma in American Psychiatry After World War II." In *Medicine and Modern Warfare*, edited by Roger Cooter, Mark Harrison and Steve Sturdy, 251–76. Amsterdam: Rodopi Press.

Potter, B., and C. Scoville. 2006. "Amputation Is Not Isolated: An Overview of the US Army Amputee Patient Care Program and Associated Amputee Injuries." *Journal of the American Academy of Orthopaedic Surgeons* 14, no. 10: S188–90.

Price, Richard M. 1997. *The Chemical Weapons Taboo*. Ithaca, NY: Cornell University Press.

Priest, Dana, and Anne Hull. 2007. "Soldiers Face Neglect, Frustration at Army's Top Medical Facility." *Washington Post*, February 18, 2007.

Prince, Carolyn, and Maya E. Bruhns. 2017. "Evaluaton and Treatment of Mild Traumatic Brain Injury: The Role of Neuropsychology." *Brain Sciences* 7, no. 8: 105.

Radford, Alexandria Walton, Alexander Bentz, Remmert Dekker, Jonathan Paslov, and Sean A. Simone. 2016. "After the Post-9/11 GI Bill: A Profile of Military Service Members and Veterans Enrolled in Undergraduate and Graduate Education." Department of Education, Washington, DC.

"Rangel Introduces Bill to Reinstate Draft." 2003. CNN, January 8, 2003. https://www.cnn.com/2003/ALLPOLITICS/01/07/rangel.draft/.

Rankin, Fred W. 1945. "American Surgeons at War." In *Doctors at War*, edited by Morris Fishbein, 173–93. New York: E. P. Dutton.

Reger, Mark A., Derek J. Smolenski, Nancy A. Skopp, Melina J. Metzer-Abamukang, Han K. Kang, Tim A. Bullman, Sondra Perdue, and Gregory A. Gahm. 2015. "Risk of Suicide Among US Military Service Members Following Operation Enduring Freedom or Operation Iraqi Freedom Deployment and Separation from the US Military." *JAMA Psychiatry* 72, no. 6: 561–69.

Reid, Brian Holden, and John White. 1985. "'A Mob of Stragglers and Cowards': Desertion from the Union and Confederate Armies, 1861–65." *Journal of Strategic Studies* 8, no. 1: 64–77.

Reilly, Robert F. 2016. "Medical and Surgical Care During the American Civil War, 1861–1865." *Baylor University Medical Center Proceedings* 29, no. 2: 138–42.

Reister, F.A. 1975. *Medical Statistics in World War II, Medical Department United States Army in World War II*. Washington, DC: Office of the Surgeon General, Department of the Army.

Remick, Kyle N. 2016. "Leveraging Trauma Lessons from War to Win in a Complex Global Environment." *Army Medical Department Journal*, April–September 2016, 106–13.

Resnick, Brian. 2011. "Civil War Recruitment Posters." *The Atlantic*, October 28, 2011.

Richards, Steven C., Arthur H. Lundquist, and Todd E. Richards. 2016. "Water for Warfighters in Iraq and Afghanistan: A Summary of Lessons Learned." *United States Army Medical Department Journal*, April–September 2016, 182–87.

Ricks, Thomas E. 2006. *Fiasco: The American Military Adventure in Iraq*. New York: Penguin.

Robinson, John B., Michael P. Smith, Kirby R. Gross, Samual W. Sauer, James J. Geracci, Charlie D. Day, and Russell S. Kotwal. 2016. "Battlefield Documentation of Tactical Combat Casualty Care in Afghanistan." *United States Army Medical Department Journal*, April–September 2016, 87–94.

Robinson, Lori, and Michael E. O'Hanlon. 2020. "Women Warriors: The Ongoing Story of Integrating and Diversifying the American Armed Forces." Brookings Institution, May 2020. https://www.brookings.edu/essay/women-warriors-the-ongoing-story-of-integrating-and-diversifying-the-armed-forces/.

Rogers, Frederick B., and Katelyn Rittenhouse. 2014. "The Golden Hour in Trauma: Dogma or Medical Folklore?" *Journal of Lancaster General Hospital* 9, no. 1: 11–13.

Ross, Davis R. B. 1969. *Preparing for Ulysses: Politics and Veterans During World War II*. New York: Columbia University Press.

Rostker, B. D. 2013. "Providing for the Casualties of War: The American Experience Through World War II." RAND Corporation, Santa Monica, CA.

Rowlands, T. K., and J. C. Clasper. 2003. "The Thomas Splint—A Necessary Tool in the Management of Battlefield Injuries." *Journal of the Royal Army Medical Corps* 149, no. 4: 291–93.

Rubel, Robert C. 2011. "The Future of The Future of Aircraft Carriers." *Naval War College Review* 64, no. 4: 1–16.

Rush, Robert M., Neil R. Stockmaster, Harry K. Stinger, Edward D. Arrington, John G. Devine, Linda Atteberry, Benjamin W. Starnes, and Ronald J. Place. 2005. "Supporting the Global War on Terror: A Tale of Two Campaigns Featuring the 250th Forward Surgical Team (Airborne)." *American Journal of Surgery* 189: 564–70.

Russell, Dale W., Ronald J. Whalen, Lyndon A. Riviere, Kristina Clarke-Walper, Paul D. Bliese, Darc D. Keller, Susan I. Pangelian, and Jeffrey L. Thomas. 2014. "Embedded Behavioral Health Providers: An Assessment with the Army National Guard." *Psychological Services* 11, no. 3: 265–72.

Rutkow, Ira M. 2005. *Bleeding Blue and Gray: Civil War Surgery and the Evolution of American Medicine*. Mechanicsburg, PA: Stackpole Books.

Sadler, Anne G., Brenda M. Booth, Deanna Nielson, and Bradley N. Doebbeling. 2000. "Health-Related Consequences of Physical and Sexual Violence: Women in the Military." *Obstetrics and Gynecology* 96, no. 3: 473–80.

Salazar Torreon, Barbara, and Sofia Plagakis. 2022. "Instances of United States Armed Forces Abroad, 1798–2022." Congressional Research Service, Washington, DC.

Salmon, Thomas W. 1919. "War Neuroses and Their Lesson." *New York Medical Journal* 109 (January–June): 993–94.

Sarnecky, Mary T. 1999. *A History of the U.S. Army Nurse Corps*. Philadelphia, PA: University of Pennsylvania Press.

Sartin, Jeffrey S. 1993. "Infectious Disease During the Civil War: The Triumph of the 'Third Army.'" *Clinical Infectious Diseases* 16, no. 4: 580–84.

Sbordone, Robert J., and Jeffrey C. Liter. 1995. "Mild Traumatic Brain Injury Does Not Produce Post-Traumatic Stress Disorder." *Brain Injury* 9, no. 4: 405–12.

Schlesinger, Arthur, Jr. 1998. "National Turning Point." *American Heritage* 49, no. 3 (May/June).

Schmidt, James M., and Guy R. Hasegawa, eds. 2009. *Years of Change and Suffering: Modern Perspectives on Civil War Medicine*. Roseville, MN: Edinborough Press.

Schneidermann, Aaron I., Elisa R. Braver, and Han K. Kang. 2008. "Understanding Sequelae of Injury Mechanisms and Mild Traumatic Brin Injury Incurred During the Conflicts in Iraq and Afghanistan: Persistent Postconcussive Symptoms and Pottraumatic Stress Disorder." *American Journal of Epidemiology* 167, no. 2: 1446–52.

Schoenbaum, Michael, Ronald C. Kessler, Stephen E. Gilman, Lisa J. Cople, Steven G. Heeringa, Murray B. Stein, Robert J. Ursano, Kenneth L. Cox, and Army STARRS Collaborators. 2014. "Predictors of Suicide and Accident Death in the Army Study to Assess Risk and Resilience in Servicemembers (Army STARRS): Results from the

Army Study to Assess Risk and Resilience in Servicemembers (Army STARRS)." *JAMA Psychiatry* 71, no. 5: 493–503.

Schubert, Frank N. 1994. *Mobilization: The US Army in World War II*. Washington, DC: Department of the Army.

Schultz, Jane E. 2004. *Women at the Front: Hospital Workers in Civil War America*. Chapel Hill, NC: University of North Carolina Press.

Schuyler, Ashley C., Sara Kintzle, Carrie L. Lucas, Hadass Moore, and Carl A. Castro. 2017. "Military Sexual Assault (MSA) Among Veterans in Southern California: Associations with Physical Health, Psychological Health, and Risk Behaviors." *Traumatology* 23, no. 3: 223–34.

Scott, Christine. 2018. "Veterans Affairs: Historical Budget Authority, FY1940–FY2012." Congressional Research Service, Washington, DC.

Scott, Russel, and John M. Howard. 1955. "Hepatic Function Following Wounding and Resuscitation with Plasma Expanders." In *Battle Casualties in Korea: Studies of the Surgical Research Team*, edited by John M. Howard, 179–90. Washington, DC: Army Medical Service Graduate School, Walter Reed Army Medical Center.

Scott, Wilbur J. 1990. "PTSD in *DSM-III*: A Case in the Politics of Diagnosis and Disease." *Social Problems* 37, no. 3: 294–310.

Seck, Hope Hodge. 2019. "As Teens Born After 9/11 Reach Military Age, Recruiters Face New Challenges." Military.com, January 2, 2019.

Severo, Richard, and Lewis Milford. 1989. *The Wages of War: When America's Soldiers Came Home - From Valley Forge to Vietnam*. New York: Simon and Schuster.

Shackelford, Stacy A., Marcie Fowler, Keith Schultz, Angela Summers, Samuel M. Galvagno, Kirby R. Gross, Robert L. Mabry, Jeffrey A. Bailey, Russ S. Kotwal, and Frank K. Butler. 2015. "Prehospital Pain Medical Use by U.S. Forces in Afghanistan." *Military Medicine* 180, no. 3: 304–9.

Shane, Leo. 2022. "VA to Get $300B, Its Biggest Budget Ever, Under Federal Spending Deal." *Military Times*, December 20, 2022.

Shanker, Thom. 2009. "Gates Seeks to Improve Battlefield Trauma Care in Afghanistan." *New York Times*, January 27.

Shanks, G. Dennis. 2016. "Historical Review: Problematic Malaria Prophylaxis with Quinine." *American Journal of Tropical Medicine and Hygiene* 95, no. 2: 269–72.

Shay, Jonathan. 1991. "Learning About Combat Stress from Homer's *Iliad*." *Journal of Traumatic Stress* 4, no. 4: 561–79.

Shay, Jonathan. 2002. *Odysseus in America: Combat Trauma and the Trials of Homecoming*. New York: Scribner.

Shen, Yu-Chu, Jeremy Arkes, and John Pilgrim. 2009. "The Effects of Deployment Intensity on Post-Traumatic Stress Disorder: 2002–2006." *Military Medicine* 174, no. 3: 217–23.

Shephard, Ben. 2001. *A War of Nerves: Soldiers and Psychiatrists in the Twentieth Century*. Cambridge, MA: Harvard University Press.

Sherman, Nancy. 2015. *Afterwar: Healing the Moral Wounds of Our Soldiers*. New York: Oxford University Press.

Shinkman, Paul D. 2013. "6 Predictions Days Before the Iraq War." *US News and World Report*, March 19, 2013.

Shryock, Richard H. 1962. "A Medical Perspective on the Civil War." *American Quarterly* 14, no. 2: 161–73.

Simmons, James Stevens. 1945. "Preventive Medicine in the Army." In *Doctors at War*, edited by Morris Fishbein, 137–71. New York: E. P. Dutton.
Singer, J. David, Stuart Bremer, and John Stuckey. 1972. "Capability Distribution, Uncertainty, and Major Power War, 1820–1965." In *Peace, War, and Numbers*, edited by Bruce M. Russett, 19–48. Beverly Hills: Sage Publications.
Skocpol, Theda. 1992. *Protecting Soldiers and Mothers: The Political Origins of Social Policy in the United States*. Cambridge, MA: Harvard University Press.
Skocpol, Theda. 1993. "America's First Social Security System: The Expansion of Benefits for Civil War Veterans." *Political Science Quarterly* 108, no. 1: 85–116.
Smith, Clarence McKittrick. 1956. *The Medical Department: Hospital and Evacuation, Zone of Interior, United States Army in World War II, The Technical Services*. Washington, DC: Office of the Chief of Military History, Department of the Army.
Smith, Dale C. 1982a. "The Rise and Fall of Typhomalarial Fever: I. Origins." *Journal of the History of Medicine and Allied Sciences* 37, no. 2: 182–220.
Smith, Dale C. 1982b. "The Rise and Fall of Typhomalarial Fever: II. Decline and Fall." *Journal of the History of Medicine and Allied Sciences* 37, no. 3: 287–321.
Smith, Tyler, Margaret A. K. Ryan, Deborah L. Wingard, Donalt J. Slymen, James F. Sallis, and Donna Kritz-Silverstein. 2008. "New Onset and Persistent Symptoms of Post-Traumatic Stress Disorder Self Reported After Deployment and Combat Exposures: Prospective Population Based US Military Cohort Study." *British Medical Journal* 336, no. 7640: 336–71.
Smock, David. 2003. "Would an Invasion of Iraq Be a 'Just War?'" United States Institute of Peace, Washington, DC.
Soderdahl, Doug, Kevin Kniery, and Wayne Causey. 2021. "Dr. Stacy Shackelford: The Development of the Joint Trauma System and Improving Care from Point of Injury Through the Spectrum of Medical Evacuation." *WarDocs—The Military Medicine Podcast*, July 21.
Sonne, Paul. 2018. "Trump Rankles Veterans with Comments About PTSD and California Shooter." *Washington Post*, November 9, 2018.
Spinella, Philip C., Jeremy G. Perkins, Kurt W. Grathwohl, Alec C. Beekley, and John B. Holcomb. 2009. "Warm Fresh Whole Blood Is Independently Associated with Improved Survival for Patients with Combat-Related Traumatic Injuries." *Journal of Trauma, Injury, Infection, and Critical Care* 66, no. 4: S69–76.
Stagner, Anessa. 2014. "Healing the Soldier, Restoring the Nation: Representations of Shell Shock in the USA During and After the First World War." *Journal of Contemporary History* 49, no. 2: 255–74.
Stanton, M. D. 1976. "Drugs, Vietnam, and the Vietnam Veteran: An Overview." *American Journal of Drug and Alcohol Abuse* 3, no. 4: 557–70.
Stein, Murray B., and Thomas W. McAllister. 2009. "Exploring the Convergence of Posttraumatic Stress Disorder and Mild Traumatic Brain Injury." *American Journal of Psychiatry* 166, no. 7: 768–76.
Stevenson, Sarah Sand. 1976. *Lamp for a Soldier: The Caring Story of a Nurse In World War I*. Fargo, ND: North Dakota Nurses' Association.
Stiglitz, Joseph E., and Linda J. Bilmes. 2008. *The Three Trillion Dollar War: The True Cost of the Iraq Conflict*. New York: W. W. Norton.
Stillé, Charles J. 1868. *History of the United States Sanitary Commission: Being The General Report of Its Work During the War of the Rebellion*. New York: Hurd and Houghton.

Strobel, Warren P. 2022. "War Game Finds U.S., Taiwan Can Defend Against a Chinese Invasion." *Wall Street Journal*, August 9, 2022.

Stuhmiller, James H. 2008. *Blast Injury: Translating Research into Operational Medicine*. Edited by William R. Santee and Karl E. Friedl. Fort Sam Houston, TX: Borden Institute.

Stundal, Logan. 2022. "The Epidemiology of Civil War." Department of Political Science, University of Minnesota.

Summerfield, Derek. 2001. "The Invention of Post-Traumatic Stress Disorder and the Social Usefulness of a Psychiatric Category." *British Medical Journal* 322: 95–98.

Suris, Alina M., and Lisa Lind. 2008. "Military Sexual Trauma: A Review of Prevalence and Associated Health Consequences in Veterans." *Trauma, Violence, and Abuse* 9, no. 4: 250–69.

Sutch, Richard C. 2015. "Financing the Great War: A Class Tax for the Wealthy, Liberty Bonds for All." Berkeley Economic History Laboratory Working Paper No. 2015-09.

Sweeney, John. 1999. "Lest We Forget: The 306 'Cowards' We Executed in the First World War." *The Guardian*, November 13, 1999.

Tatu, L., and J. Bogousslavsky. 2014. "World War I Psychoneuroses: Hysteria Goes to War." *Frontiers in Neurology and Neuroscience* 35: 157–68.

Taubenberger, Jeffery K. and Morens, David M. 2006. "1918 Influenza: The Mother of All Pandemics." *Emerging Infectious Diseases* 12, no. 1: 15–22.

Thomas, Roger, John G. McManus, Anthony Johnson, Paul Mayer, Charles Wade, and John B. Holcomb. 2009. "Ocular Injury Reduction from Ocular Protection Use in Current Combat Operations." *Journal of Trauma, Injury, Infection, and Critical Care* 66, no. 4: S99–102.

Thompson, George. n.d. "Battlefield Medicine: Introduction to the System." Kansas University Medical Center web series on "Medicine in the First World War." https://www.kumc.edu/school-of-medicine/academics/departments/history-and-philosophy-of-medicine/archives/wwi/essays/military-medical-operations/introduction-to-the-system.html. Accessed December 10, 2023.

Torreon, Barbara Salazar, and Sofia Plagakis. 2019. "Instances of Use of United States Armed Forces Abroad, 1798–2019." Congressional Research Service, Washington, DC.

Tretheway, Thomas 2021. "The Politics of Veterans' Pensions in America's Gilded Age." Department of History, University of Minnesota.

Trynovsky, Stephen K. 2014. "Beyond the Iron Triangle: Implications for the Veterans Health Administration in an Uncertain Policy Environment." School of Advanced Military Studies, United States Army Command and General Staff College, Fort Leavenworth, KS.

Tucker, Patrick. 2019. "US Marines Try Using Drones to Bring Blood to Battle." *DefenseOne*, October 22, 2019.

Turchik, Jessica A., and Susan M. Wilson. 2010. "Sexual Assault in the U.S. Military: A Review of the Literature and Recommendations for the Future." *Aggression and Violent Behavior* 15, no. 4: 267–77.

Turner, Sarah F., and John Bound. 2002. "Closing the Gap or Widening the Divide: The Effects of the G.I. Bill and World War II on the Educational Outcomes of Black Americans." NBER Working Paper 9044, National Bureau of Economic Research, Cambridge, MA.

"Union of Concerned Scientists. 2009. "Pressure Not to Diagnose PTSD at the U.S. Army and Department of Veterans Affairs." September 23. https://www.ucsusa.org/resour

ces/attacks-on-science/pressure-not-diagnose-ptsd-us-army-and-department-veterans-affairs.

US Gun Control: What Is the NRA and Why Is It So Powerful?" 2023. BBC, April 13, 2023.

Veatch, Robert M. 1977. *Case Studies in Medical Ethics*. Cambridge, MA: Harvard University Press.

"Veterans Deserve Support. But One Benefit Program Deserves Scrutiny." 2023. Editorial. *Washington Post*, April 3, 2023.

Wagner, Margaret E., Gary W. Gallagher, and Paul Finkelman, eds. 2002. *Civil War Desk References*. New York: Simon & Schuster.

"War Department Operations Plan Rainbow No. 5. 1941." 1941. Department of War, Washington, DC.

Warden, Deborah L., Lawrence A. Labbate, Andres M. Salazar, Rachael Nelson, Enid Sheley, James Staudenmeier, and Elisabeth Martin. 1997. "Posttraumatic Stress Disorder in Patients with Traumatic Brain Injury and Amnesia for the Event?" *Journal of Neuropsychiatry and Clinical Neurosciences* 9: 18–22.

Warner, Christopher H., George N. Appenzeller, Keri Mullen, Carolynn M. Warner, and Thomas Grieger. 2008. "Soldier Attitudes Toward Mental Health Screening and Seeking Care upon Return from Combat." *Military Medicine* 173: 563–69.

Watson, Mark Skinner. 1991. *Chief of Staff: Prewar Plans and Operations*. Washington, DC: Center of Military History.

Watson Institute. 2021. "Economic Costs." Watson Institute Costs of War Project, Brown University. https://watson.brown.edu/costsofwar/costs/economic.

Weina, Peter J. 1998. "From Atabrine in World War II to Mefloquine in Somalia: The Role of Education in Preventive Medicine." *Military Medicine* 163, no. 9: 635–39.

Welling, David R., Patricia L. McKay, Todd E. Rasmussen, and Norman M. Rich. 2012. "A Brief History of the Tourniquet." *Journal of Vascular Surgery* 55: 286–90.

White, Christopher E., and Evan M. Renz. 2008. "Advances in Surgical Care: Management of Severe Burn Injury." *Critical Care Medicine* 36, no. 7: S318–24.

White, James C. 1944. "Pain After Amputation and Its Treatment." *JAMA* 124, no. 15: 1030–1035.

Whitman, Walt. 1954. *Leaves of Grass*. New York: Signet Classics.

Wilson, John P. 1994. "The Historical Evolution of PTSD Diagnostic Criteria: From Freud to DSM-IV." *Journal of Traumatic Stress* 7, no. 4: 681–97.

Wilson, Kristin, and Jessica Dean. 2022. "Jon Stewart and Democrats Rail Against Stalled Burn Pits Legislation: 'This Is Bullshit.'" CNN Politics, July 28, 2022.

Wilson, Mitchell. 1993. "*DSM-III* and the Transformation of American Psychiatry: A History." *American Journal of Psychiatry* 150, no. 3: 399–410.

Wiltse, Charles M. 1965. *Medical Service in the Mediterranean and Minor Theaters, United States Army in World War II, The Technical Services*. Washington, DC: Office of the Chief of Military History, Department of the Army.

Wintermute, Bobby A. 2011. *Public Health and the US Military: A History of the Army Medical Department, 1818–1917*. New York: Routledge.

WNYC. 2009. "The True Cost of War." *On the Media*, February 27.

Wohlforth, William C. 1991. "The Stability of a Unipolar World." *International Security* 24, no. 1: 5–41.

Wojcik, Barbara E., Rebecca J. Humphrey, Brandon J. Hosek, and Catherine R. Stein. 2016. "Data-Driven Casualty Estimation and Disease Nonbattle Injury/Injury Rates in

Recent Campaigns." *United States Army Medical Department Journal*, April–September 2016, 8–14.

Wong, Leonard, and Stephen J. Gerras. 2021. *Veteran Disability Compensation and the Army Profession: Good Intentions Gone Awry*. Carlisle Barracks, PA: US Army War College Press.

Wood, Elisabeth Jean, and Nathaniel Toppelberg. 2017. "The Persistence of Sexual Assault Within the US Military." *Journal of Peace Research* 54, no. 5: 600–633.

Woods, Michael E. 2012. "What Twenty-First-Century Historians Have Said About the Causes of Disunion: A Civil War Sequicentennial Review of the Recent Literature." *Journal of American History* 99, no. 2: 415–39.

Woodward, Bob. 2004. *Plan of Attack*. New York: Simon & Schuster.

Wright, Kathleen M., Ann H. Huffman, Amy B. Adler, and Carl A. Castro. 2002. "Psychological Screening Overview." *Military Medicine* 167: 853–61.

Young, Allan 1995. *The Harmony of Illusions: Inventing Post-Traumatic Stress Disorder*. Princeton, NJ: Princeton University Press.

Young, Ryan, Jake Carpenter, and Paul P. Murphy. 2020. "Photos Show Bodies Piled Up and Stored in Vacant Rooms in Detroit Hospital." CNN, April 14, 2020.

Yun, Heather C., and Clinton K. Murray. 2016. "Infection Prevention in the Deployed Environment." *United States Army Medical Department Journal*, April–September 2016, 114–18.

Zacher, Mark W. 2001. "The Territorial Integrity Norm: International Boundaries and the Use of Force." *International Organization* 55, no. 2: 215–50.

Zunes, Stephen. 2002. "Seven Reasons to Oppose a U.S. Invasion of Iraq." Foreign Policy in Focus, August 1, 2002. https://fpif.org/seven_reasons_to_oppose_a_us_invasion_of_iraq/.

Index

For the benefit of digital users, indexed terms that span two pages (e.g., 52–53) may, on occasion, appear on only one of those pages.

Tables and figures are indicated by *t* and *f* following the page number

Accorsi, Pedro, 167
Adams, George Washington, 28
addiction, 23, 44, 178n.137
Adler, Jessica, 80–81, 136–37
Afghanistan War (2001). *See also* Afghanistan War medicine; *specific battles*
   burn pits and, 104
   case fatality rate in, 102
   cost assessments, 5, 92–93, 94, 122–23, 168
   data collection on, 96–97, 100
   Dover effect and, 7–8
   PPE in, 97, 105–8, 189n.94
   PTSD and, 124–25, 148–49
   veterans' benefits and, 119–20, 191n.160
   weapons in, 91–92, 103, 105
   women in, 109
   wounded-to-killed ratio in, 8, 122
Afghanistan War medicine
   artillery wounds, 62*f*
   blast injuries, 105–9
   burn treatments, 115
   disease and, 103–5
   doctors and, 95
   evacuations, 2, 90, 91–92, 101–2
   golden hour and, 91–92, 102
   gunshot wounds, 2, 62*f*, 105, 108–9
   hemorrhage control, 99, 107
   IED injuries, 91–92, 105–9, 115
   logistics of, 95
   nurses and, 95
   pain management, 115
   TCCC and, 99
   tourniquets, 2, 99, 110–12, 165–66, 170

   transfusions, 113
   traumatic brain injury, 148
African Americans. *See also* racism; segregation
   blood donations by, 71
   in Civil War, 21, 36–37, 39–40
   as doctors, 78
   education of, 84
   healthcare for, 39–40, 71, 87
   mustard gas and, 71
   as nurses, 78
   Tuskegee syphilis study and, 60
   veterans' benefits for, 42, 82–83, 85–86
   in World War I, 78
Agent Orange, 116
AI (artificial intelligence), 158, 159, 161–62
AIDS/HIV, 104
aircraft pilots, medical issues for, 66–67
air evacuations
   Afghanistan War, 90, 91–92, 101–2
   Iraq War, 90, 91–92, 101–2
   Korean War, 90, 100–2, 188n.73
   medical personnel on, 101–2
   on-the-fly adjustments, 101
   in Russia-Ukraine conflict, 159–60
   Vietnam War, 90–91, 100–2
   World War I, 184n.159
   World War II, 75–76, 101–2
airway obstructions, 114–15, 190n.142
Alcott, Louisa May, 35, 176n.51, 177n.102
all-volunteer force (AVF), 5, 6–7, 109, 116, 118, 147
al Qaeda, 92–93, 157, 158
Altschuler, Glenn, 86–87

228 INDEX

ambulances
  AI-driven, 159
  in Civil War, 15, 31–32, 33, 44–45
  horse-drawn, 11, 31, 32, 74
  in Korean War, 100–1
  medical personnel on, 32
  motorized, 72–74, 75, 100–1, 134–35
  in World War I, 72–74
  in World War II, 74, 75
American Legion, 11–12, 43, 80, 84, 85–86, 88, 120–21, 164
American Psychiatric Association, 124–25, 144, 145–46
American Red Cross, 15, 70–71, 184n.145
American Revolution. *See* Revolutionary War
amputations
  in Civil War, 14, 24–25, 27–29
  mortality rates for, 29
  prostheses following, 2–3, 82–83, 85
  for trench foot, 57–58
  Walter Reed effect and, 7–8
  in World War I, 65, 68–69
  in World War II, 63, 68–69
analgesia. *See* pain management
anesthetics, 25, 27–28, 68–69, 71, 115
antibiotics. *See also* penicillin
  pre-antibiotic era, 18, 29, 54–55
  sulfonamides, 60, 69, 78
antiseptics, 18, 67–68, 71, 115
Ardennes, Battle of (1944–45), 57–58
Arrears Act of 1879, 42, 131
artificial intelligence (AI), 158, 159, 161–62
artificial limbs. *See* prostheses
artillery wounds
  Afghanistan War, 62*f*
  Civil War, 26, 61, 62*f*
  Iraq War, 62*f*
  Korean War, 62*f*
  Vietnam War, 62*f*
  World War I, 62, 62*f*
  World War II, 1–2, 61–63, 62*f*
Atabrine, 56, 57, 60–61
AVF. *See* all-volunteer force

Bagozzi, Benjamin, 20–21
bargaining theory of war, 17
Barnes, Joseph K., 14–15

Barton, Clara, 36, 38
battle fatigue. *See* combat exhaustion
battles. *See specific names of battles*
Bayne-Jones, Stanhope, 52–53, 72, 74, 179n.13, 180n.31
bayonets, 15, 25–26, 83
Bell, Andrew, 18, 21, 22–23
Bellamy, Ronald, 110
Bellows, Henry, 30, 35–36
Berry, Frank, 74
bias. *See also* racism
  in data collection, 38
  in prewar cost assessments, 17
  in selection for military service, 126
  sexism, 71–72, 77–78
  veterans' benefits and, 42
Bickerdyke, Mary Ann, 36
Bilmes, Linda, 5, 92, 118–20, 149, 191n.160
biological weapons, 158, 161
Blackford, W. W., 25, 27–28
Blackwell, Elizabeth, 36–37
Blake, Henry, 70–71
blast injuries, 2–3, 26, 105–9, 106*f*, 148
blood banks, 70–71, 113–14, 166
bloodletting, 22
blood transfusions. *See* whole blood transfusions
blood vessel banks, 68–69, 183n.130
blue mass and blue pill, 22, 23, 176n.52
Blumin, Stuart, 86–87
body armor, 26–27, 97, 107, 109
Bollet, Alfred J., 36, 37, 38–39
Boner, James and Sophia, 43
Bonus March (1932), 83, 88
Boston Marathon bombing (2013), 170
Bradley, Omar, 57–58
Browne, Edward, 48
Bulge, Battle of the (1944–45), 57–58
Bull Run, First Battle of (1861), 25
Bull Run, Second Battle of (1862), 31
Bureau of War Risk Insurance (BWRI), 80–81, 82, 136–37
burn pits, 104, 121, 164
burns, 64, 65–66, 71, 115, 160–61
Burton, Warren, 21–22
Burwell, Walter, 66
Bush, George W., 5, 6–8, 92–93, 171

calomel (mercurous chloride), 20*t*, 23

CAPE (Cost Assessment and Program Evaluation), 168
carbon monoxide poisoning, 66, 67
Carlton, P. K., Jr., 159–60
case fatality rate (CFR)
  Afghanistan War, 102
  Civil War, 37, 87
  defined, 37, 63, 187n.39
  reporting inconsistencies, 97
  World War I, 87
  World War II, 63, 87
casualties. *See also* case fatality rate; Tactical Combat Casualty Care; wounded-to-killed ratio
  Civil War, 13, 37, 40, 44
  data collection on, 10, 39–40, 71, 78–80, 96–97
  definitions of, 7, 173n.14, 173–74nn.16–17
  Iraq War, 94, 155
  projections, 17, 48–51, 94, 169–70
  World War II, 13
casualty aversion theory, 6–7, 173–74n.17
CATs. *See* Combat Application Tourniquets
Caverley, Jonathan, 163
CCATTs (Critical Care Air Transport Teams), 92, 101–2, 122–23
CFR. *See* case fatality rate
Chase, Salmon P., 21
chemical weapons, 64–65, 158, 161
Cheney, Dick, 93, 94
Chimborazo Hospital (Richmond), 33
China, potential for US war with, 158, 159–61, 162
chloroform, 27–28, 68
Churchill, Edward, 60, 68, 69, 70, 76, 114, 115, 166
Cincinnatus (Roman citizen-soldier), 40
Civil War (1861–65). *See also* Civil War medicine; Confederacy; Union Army; *specific battles*
  African Americans in, 21, 36–37, 39–40
  case fatality rate in, 37, 87
  casualties of, 13, 37, 40, 44
  cost assessments, 16–18, 44, 45–46, 49, 175n.14
  data collection on, 37–40, 79f
  desertions during, 14, 38–39, 130

percentage of US population in, 193n.9
  psychological trauma and, 124–25, 127–32, 193n.5
  veterans' benefits and, 40–44, 45, 131–32
  weapons in, 1, 25–27, 61
  wounded-to-killed ratio in, 18, 40, 45
Civil War medicine. *See also Medical and Surgical History of the War of the Rebellion*
  amputations, 14, 24–25, 27–29
  artillery wounds, 26, 61, 62f
  disease and, 14, 15, 18–25, 20t, 44–45, 103
  doctors and, 18, 19–20, 21–25, 34, 36–37
  evacuations, 30, 31–34, 50
  gunshot wounds, 1, 26–27, 28, 61, 62f
  hemorrhage control, 28–29
  hospitals and, 1, 15, 21–22, 29, 31, 33–35, 44–45
  logistics of, 30–37, 50
  nurses and, 15, 35, 36, 44–45
  pain management, 27–28
  stereotypes of, 24–25, 27–28
  supply issues, 22–23, 29
  surgeries, 25, 27–29, 68
Combat Application Tourniquets (CATs), 2, 99, 110–12, 111f, 122–23, 170
combat exhaustion, 124–25, 129–30, 138–43, 145, 152
compartment syndrome, 112–13, 166, 190n.133
concussions, 26, 107–8
Confederacy. *See also* Civil War
  casualties among, 40
  cost assessments for, 16–17, 44
  desertions from, 14, 130
  disease and, 22–23, 24
  medical supply issues, 29
  veterans' benefits for, 42
  wounded-to-killed ratio for, 18, 45
Congressional Budget Office, 94, 169
Congressional Research Service, 92–93, 169
conscription, 5, 6–7, 86–87, 88–89, 90, 116, 163
Cost Assessment and Program Evaluation (CAPE), 168
counterinsurgency wars. *See specific conflicts*

COVID-19 pandemic, 31, 54–55, 164, 166–67, 170
Cowdrey, Albert, 55, 57, 69–70
Cowley, R. Adams, 76, 102
Critical Care Air Transport Teams (CCATTs), 92, 101–2, 122–23
crystalloids, 112–13, 166, 170, 190n.131
Curie, Marie, 67

DaCosta, Jacob, 127–28
damage control surgery, 2, 101, 115, 159
data collection
  on Afghanistan War, 96–97, 100
  biases in, 38
  on casualties, 10, 39–40, 71, 78–80, 96–97
  challenges of, 96, 99–100
  on Civil War, 37–40, 79f
  on First Gulf War, 96–97
  on Iraq War, 96–97, 100
  on Korean War, 96–97
  on Mexican-American War, 38
  race and, 39–40, 71, 78–80
  TCCC cards for, 10, 97–98, 98f, 99–100, 178n.120
  on Vietnam War, 96–97
  on War of 1812, 38
  on World War I, 78–80, 79f
  on World War II, 78–80, 79f
Davis, Jefferson, 175n.14
DDT (dichloro-diphenyl-trichloroethane), 56, 57, 60–61
Dean, Eric T., 129, 193n.5
DeBakey, Michael, 68–69, 78–80, 183n.130
Defense Department (DoD)
  Annual Report on Sexual Assault in the Military, 109
  Cost Assessment and Program Evaluation, 168
  Emergency War Surgery handbook, 97–98, 99–100, 105, 108, 161
  Medical Planners Tool Kit, 169–70
  Trauma Registry, 10, 97–100, 178n.120
dengue fever, 20–21
Dependent Pension Act of 1890, 42–43, 131
De Rond, Mark, 142–43
Diagnostic and Statistical Manual of Mental Disorders (*DSM*), 124–25, 144–46, 149
diarrhea, 19–20, 20t, 21–22, 56, 131
diphtheria, 55, 60, 103–4
disability compensation
  Civil War and, 42–43, 131–32
  manipulation of system for, 120
  means-testing for, 121
  reliance of veterans on, 2–3
  War of 1812 and, 17
  World War I and, 80–81, 82, 83
discrimination. *See* bias
disease. *See also specific diseases*
  in Afghanistan War, 103–5
  antibiotics for (*see* antibiotics)
  in Civil War, 14, 15, 18–25, 20t, 44–45, 103
  as endemic to warfare, 19–21
  germ theory of (*see* germ theory of disease)
  heroic theory of, 22, 24
  immunizations against (*see* immunizations)
  in Iraq War, 103–5
  in Korean War, 103
  postoperative, 29, 67–68
  race and, 21, 39
  in Spanish-American War, 24, 47, 50
  STDs (*see* sexually transmitted diseases)
  in Vietnam War, 103
  in World War I, 20–21, 52–53, 54–55, 57–60, 103
  in World War II, 52, 54–61, 59f
Dix, Dorothea, 36
doctors
  in Afghanistan War, 95
  African American, 78
  in Civil War, 18, 19–20, 21–25, 34, 36–37
  hiring practices, 34
  in Iraq War, 95
  in Korean War, 90
  medical kits for, 23, 33
  medical training for, 34
  psychiatrists, 133–37, 139, 141–42, 145, 194n.38
  on race and disease, 21
  women as, 34, 36–37, 166–67
  in World War I, 54, 64, 67, 78
  in World War II, 63–64, 67–68, 102
DoD. *See* Defense Department
Donald, David, 16
Dover effect, 7–8, 155–56
Downs, Jim, 39–40

draft. *See* conscription
drones, 6, 13, 158, 159, 161–62, 198n.8
DSM. See Diagnostic and Statistical Manual of Mental Disorders
du Cille, Michael, 191n.153
Dunant, Henri, 32
dysentery, 1, 15, 19–20, 20*t*, 21–22

Eastridge, Brian, 98–99, 110
education
   of African Americans, 84
   on military trauma, 95
   on STDs, 58
   subsidies for, 83–84, 156–57
   for veterans, 83–85, 86–87, 92, 119
Eisenhauer, Ian F., 198n.13
evacuations. *See* medical evacuations

Fair Oaks, Battle of (1862), 33–34
fatalities. *See* casualties
The Fate of Our Wounded in the Next War (Frank), 50
Faust, Drew Gilpin, 44
Fear, Nicola T., 196n.113
Fearon, James, 17
Feaver, Peter D., 173–74n.17
females. *See* women
field hospitals
   in Afghanistan War, 102
   ambulance transport to, 32
   in Civil War, 31, 33, 50
   in World War I, 72, 134
   in World War II, 72, 96–97
Finkel, David, 151
Finley, Alexander, 30
First Gulf War (1990–91), 95, 96–97, 118–19
First World War. *See* World War I
flak jackets, 67, 106–7
floating hospitals, 33–34, 76
Forbes, Charles, 81
Fort Fisher, Second Battle of (1865), 1
fractures, 26, 68–69, 105–6, 128–29, 129*f*
Franks, Tommy, 94
frostbite, 47, 67

gangrene, 23–24, 29, 65
GAR (Grand Army of the Republic), 43, 120–21

gas weapons, 48, 51–52, 61, 64–65, 71, 158
Gates, Robert, 102
Gelpi, Christopher, 173–74n.17
gender norms, 35–36
Geneva Conventions, 76, 122
Geneva Protocol (1925), 64–65
germ theory of disease
   in early stages of development, 19–20
   lack of acceptance/understanding, 18, 24, 29, 44–45, 47, 129–30
   modern medicine and, 12
   sanitation practices and, 52–53, 60–61, 67–68, 87
   transformative effects of, 48
   wound closure and, 71
GI Bill (Serviceman's Readjustment Act of 1944)
   advocacy for, 84
   African Americans and, 85–86
   components of, 84–85, 86–87
   renewals and amendments, 92, 116, 119, 163
   social benefits of, 86–87, 88–89
   traumatized veterans and, 143
   women and, 85–86
Gifford, Sanford, 141–42
Gillet, Mary, 47
goggles, 107–8
golden hour, 76, 91–92, 102, 122–23, 159
gonorrhea, 55, 58–61
Gordon, Suzanne, 109, 191n.153
Grand Army of the Republic (GAR), 43, 120–21
Grant, David N. W., 66–67
Great War. *See* World War I
gross stress reaction, 144–45
Guadalcanal, Battle of (1942–43), 74
guerrilla warfare, 47, 91
Gulf War Syndrome, 11–12, 121, 146
Gunderson, Gerald, 16, 44
guns. *See specific types of guns*
gunshot wounds
   Afghanistan War, 2, 62*f*, 105, 108–9
   Civil War, 1, 26–27, 28, 61, 62*f*
   Iraq War, 2, 62*f*, 105, 108–9
   Korean War, 62*f*
   Vietnam War, 62*f*, 189n.89
   World War I, 1–2, 61, 62*f*
   World War II, 1–2, 62*f*

232 INDEX

Hammond, William A., 14–15, 30, 33, 174n.8
Handley-Cousins, Sarah, 174n.7
Hawks, Esther Hill, 36–37
Hawley, Paul, 57–58
healthcare
  for African Americans, 39–40, 71, 87
  for veterans, 50, 58–59, 81, 82, 84–85, 88, 119–20, 137, 156–57, 164
Hearst, William Randolph, 84
helmets, 8–9, 63–64, 106–8
hemorrhage control. *See also* tourniquets
  in Afghanistan War, 99, 107
  in Civil War, 28–29
  in Iraq War, 107
  in Korean War, 110
  TCCC guidelines on, 98–99, 110, 161
  in Vietnam War, 110
  in World War II, 71
hemorrhagic fever, 103
hepatitis A, 103–4
heroic theory of disease, 22, 24
HIV/AIDS, 104
Holcomb, John, 95, 100, 113, 114
Holmes, Oliver Wendell, Sr., 31
Homer: *The Iliad*, 124
Homestead Act of 1862, 131–32
homosexuality, medicalization of, 145–46, 196n.99
Horowitz, Michael, 6–7, 173n.14
hospitals. *See also* field hospitals; *specific hospitals*
  in Civil War, 1, 15, 21–22, 29, 31, 33–35, 44–45
  evacuation, 72, 74, 134
  floating, 33–34, 76
  in Korean War, 90
  Mobile Army Surgical Hospitals, 90, 91
  pavilion-style, 29, 34–35
  for psychological trauma, 130–31, 133, 134–35, 136
  rehabilitation, 49–50
  segregated wards in, 78
  staffing issues, 34, 35
  for veterans, 82–83, 85–86, 156–57
  in World War I, 72
  in World War II, 72, 96–97
Hull, Anne, 191n.153
Humphreys, Margaret, 17, 35, 39–40

Hussein, Saddam, 93–94, 108–9
hypothermia, 66
hypoxia, 66, 159, 190n.133

IAVA (Iraq and Afghanistan Veterans Association), 11–12, 120–21, 164
IEDs. *See* improvised explosive devices
illness. *See* disease; *specific illnesses*
immunizations
  COVID-19, 54–55
  diphtheria, 55, 103–4
  hepatitis A, 103–4
  influenza, 54–55
  measles, mumps, rubella, 103–4
  smallpox, 19, 52–53, 55
  tetanus, 55, 103–4
  transformative effects of, 51–52
  typhoid, 52–53, 55, 180n.23
  yellow fever, 55
improvised explosive devices (IEDs), 2, 91–92, 101, 103, 105–9, 115, 148
Indian wars, 30, 47
infection. *See* disease; *specific infections*
influenza pandemic (1918), 1–2, 51–52, 54–55, 87, 103
injuries. *See also* artillery wounds; gunshot wounds
  blast, 2–3, 26, 105–9, 106f, 148
  burns, 64, 65–66, 71, 115, 160–61
  fractures, 26, 68–69, 105–6, 128–29, 129f
  frostbite, 47, 67
  from gas weapons, 64
  from IEDs, 2, 91–92, 105–9, 115
  maxillofacial, 63
  moral, 124–25, 148, 151
  TBI, 2–3, 8–9, 107–8, 110, 148, 170
  trench foot, 55, 57–58, 85
Innes, E. J., 21–22
international humanitarian law, 76, 198n.8
Iraq and Afghanistan Veterans Association (IAVA), 11–12, 120–21, 164
Iraq War (2003). *See also* Iraq War medicine
  burn pits and, 104
  casualties of, 94, 155
  casualty aversion theory and, 6–7
  cost assessments, 5, 92, 93–94, 122–23, 155, 168

data collection on, 96–97, 100
Dover effect and, 7–8
intelligence failures in, 93–94, 171
PPE in, 97, 105–8, 189n.94
PTSD and, 124–25, 148–49
veterans' benefits and, 104–5, 119–20, 191n.160
weapons in, 91–92, 103, 105
women in, 109
wounded-to-killed ratio in, 94, 122
Iraq War medicine
artillery wounds, 62*f*
blast injuries, 105–9
burn treatments, 115
disease and, 103–5
doctors and, 95
evacuations, 2, 90, 91–92, 101–2
golden hour and, 91–92
gunshot wounds, 2, 62*f*, 105, 108–9
hemorrhage control, 107
IED injuries, 91–92, 105–9, 115
logistics of, 95
nurses and, 95
pain management, 115
TCCC and, 99
tourniquets, 2, 110–12, 165–66, 170
transfusions, 113
traumatic brain injury, 148
Islamic State, 157, 158

Joint Trauma System (JTS), 92, 95, 100, 101–2, 122–23
Jones, Bessie Z., 176n.51
Jones, Edgar, 193n.5
junctional tourniquets, 99, 111*f*, 112, 112*f*

Karol, David, 173–74n.17
Kinder, John, 4–5, 42, 49, 80–81, 83, 136
Kirk, Norman, 52
Klay, Phil, 163
Korean War (1950–53). *See also* Korean War medicine
casualty aversion theory and, 6
data collection on, 96–97
PPE in, 67
prisoners of war in, 116
veterans' benefits and, 116
Korean War medicine
artillery wounds, 62*f*

disease and, 103
doctors and, 90
evacuations, 32, 75, 90, 100–2, 188n.73
gunshot wounds, 62*f*
hemorrhage control, 110
hospitals and, 90
transfusions, 112–13
Kotwal, Russ, 99
Kreps, Sarah, 155–56
Kriner, Douglas L., 173n.14, 173–74n.17

land mines, 63, 107–8, 189n.89
Larrey, Dominique-Jean, 11, 32
Lawson, Thomas, 30
laxatives, 20*t*, 22
lead, in medical treatments, 22, 23
leishmaniasis, 103–4
Letterman, Jonathan, 15, 33, 72
Levendusky, Matthew, 6–7, 173n.14
Lincoln, Abraham, 3, 16–17, 18, 175n.14
Lindsay, Lawrence B., 94
Linker, Beth, 48, 49–50

Mabry, Robert, 108
MacArthur, Douglas, 83
malaria
in Civil War, 20*t*, 21–24, 103
control programs, 56–57, 60–61
transmission of, 21
treatments, 20*t*, 22–24, 56
in Vietnam War, 103
in World War I, 20–21, 71
in World War II, 55–57, 71
Marble, Sanders, 85
Mayhew, Emily, 74
Mayo, Charles, 195n.84
McAllister, Thomas, 148
McPherson, James, 16–17, 36
meals ready-to-eat (MREs), 104, 180n.35
measles, 19, 60, 103–4, 128–29, 129*f*
Medical and Surgical History of the War of the Rebellion (MSHWR)
on amputations, 27, 28
casualties reported by, 40
data quality issues, 10, 37, 38
on diseases, 19–20, 21–22, 24
precedent set by, 14–15
on race, 39–40
on wounds, 26, 38–39

234 INDEX

medical evacuations. *See also* air evacuations; ambulances
   Afghanistan War, 2, 90, 91–92, 101–2
   Civil War, 30, 31–34, 50
   Iraq War, 2, 90, 91–92, 101–2
   Korean War, 32, 75, 90, 100–2, 188n.73
   for psychological trauma, 134–35, 140–41
   by rail, 33–34, 100–1
   by sea, 33–34, 76, 161, 198n.13
   Vietnam War, 90–91, 100–2
   World War I, 72–74, 73f, 184n.159
   World War II, 1–2, 72, 74–76, 101–2
Medical Planners Tool Kit, 169–70
Medical Reform Bill of 1862, 34
medications. *See specific names and types of medications*
meningitis, 60
MEPS (Military Entrance Processing Station) examination, 146
mercury, in medical treatments, 20t, 22, 23–24, 176n.52
Mettler, Suzanne, 86–87, 88–89
Metz, Battle of (1792), 32
Mexican-American War (1846–48), 18, 25–26, 30, 38
Middleton, William H., 195n.84
Miguel, Edward, 173–74n.17
military. *See also* military medicine; warfare
   active-duty members, 5, 162
   as all-volunteer force, 5, 6–7, 109, 116, 118, 147
   conscription, 5, 6–7, 86–87, 88–89, 90, 116, 163
   food procurement for, 53–54, 104, 180n.32
   PPE for (*see* personal protective equipment)
   public trust in, 116–17, 150–51, 191n.154
   reconditioning program created by, 85
   screening practices, 138–39, 146–47, 148–49
   strategies for boosting recruitment, 163, 198n.19
Military Entrance Processing Station (MEPS) examination, 146

military medicine. *See also specific conflicts*
   civilian medicine in relation to, 166–67, 170
   consequences of improvements, 3–4, 5, 6, 11–12, 13
   disease and (*see* disease)
   doctors and (*see* doctors)
   evacuations and (*see* medical evacuations)
   evidence-based, 78, 96–99
   frontier conflicts and, 12, 30
   future of, 159–62
   global developments, 11
   hospitals and (*see* hospitals)
   injuries and (*see* injuries)
   integration of components, 92
   investment in, 170–71
   lessons learned, 165–67
   logistics of, 30–37, 50, 71–78, 95, 100–2
   loss of knowledge and skills in interwar periods, 165–67
   naval medicine, 66, 71, 160–61
   nurses and (*see* nurses)
   policy recommendations, 170–71
   preventive, 44–45, 52–53, 60–61, 67–68, 71–72, 103, 105
   prolonged field care, 159–60, 161
   specialization within, 69
   surgeries and (*see* surgeries)
   trauma and (*see* psychological trauma)
military sexual trauma (MST), 109–10
Miller, Jeff, 163
Minié, Claude-Etienne, 25–26
minié balls, 1, 25–26, 27, 129, 173n.3
Mobile Army Surgical Hospitals, 90, 91
Mogadishu, Battle of (1993), 114
Monahan, Evelyn, 63–64, 77–78
Montgomery, Adam, 142–43, 150–51
Moore, French, 63–64
moral injury, 124–25, 148, 151
morphine, 27–28, 68, 95–96, 115
MREs (meals ready-to-eat), 104, 180n.35
MSHWR. *See Medical and Surgical History of the War of the Rebellion*
MST (military sexual trauma), 109–10
Mueller, John, 6–7
mumps, 19, 60, 103–4
muskets, 25–26

mustard gas, 64, 71
Myers, Charles, 132–33

National Football League, 170
National Research Council, 67, 70
naval medicine, 66, 71, 160–61
Neidel-Greenlee, Rosemary, 63–64, 77–78
Nightingale, Florence, 32–33, 35
nostalgia, 127–29, 130, 131, 152
nuclear weapons, 93–94, 158, 161, 163
nurses
    in Afghanistan War, 95
    African American, 78
    in Civil War, 15, 35, 36, 44–45
    denial of entry to veterans'
        organizations, 85–86
    in Iraq War, 95
    psychiatric, 138
    sexism experienced by, 77–78
    in World War I, 54, 77, 78
    in World War II, 77–78, 101–2

O'Hanlon, Michael, 94
Olmsted, Frederick, 30, 177n.80
Operation Enduring Freedom (OEF).
    See Afghanistan War
Operation Iraqi Freedom (OIF). See
    Iraq War
opium, 20t, 23, 27, 44, 68, 178n.137
O'Reilly, Robert M., 50
Otis, George A., 14–15

PACT Act of 2022, 121, 164
pain management, 27–28, 68–69, 115
Parker, Paul, 159, 161–62
pavilion hospitals, 29, 34–35
Pearl Harbor attack (1941), 66
peer/near-peer conflicts, 158, 160–61, 162, 163
penicillin
    social benefits of, 88–89
    for STDs, 60–61, 69
    sulfonamides vs., 69, 78
    survival rates and, 1–2, 67–68, 70
    for trench foot, 57–58
pensions
    Civil War and, 40–44, 45–46
    economic arguments for, 40–41

for families of deceased soldiers, 41–43,
    45–46, 173n.4
moral arguments for, 40–41
Revolutionary War and, 40
Spanish-American War and, 83
War of 1812 and, 17
Pensions Bureau, 15, 38–40, 42–43, 82,
    131, 185n.199
Perkins, Jeremy G., 99
Pershing, John J., 58
personal protective equipment (PPE)
    in Afghanistan War, 97, 105–8, 189n.94
    body armor, 26–27, 97, 107, 109
    eye protection, 108
    flak jackets, 67, 106–7
    helmets, 8–9, 63–64, 106–8
    in Iraq War, 97, 105–8, 189n.94
    in Korean War, 67
    in Vietnam War, 67, 106–8
    in World War I, 63–64
    in World War II, 63–64, 106–8
Phibbs, Brendan, 63–64, 65
physicians. See doctors
PIE method of treatment, 134, 140–41
plasma transfusions, 1–2, 69–71, 87, 113
platinum fifteen minutes, 102, 159
political polarization, 3–4, 92, 116, 121, 164
Polling Report, 7, 174n.18
Pols, Hans, 142–43
post-traumatic stress disorder (PTSD)
    Afghanistan War and, 124–25, 148–49
    blast injuries and, 2–3, 148
    causes of, 146, 152
    counterinsurgency operations and,
        147–48, 151–52
    diagnosis of, 124–26, 146
    Iraq War and, 124–25, 148–49
    prevalence of, 145–46, 147
    screening for, 147, 148–49
    sexual assault and, 110
    skepticism regarding, 125, 149–50
    social acceptance of, 150–51, 152–53
    traumatic brain injury and, 148
    treatments for, 148–49, 150
    veterans' benefits and, 149, 150–51, 152–53
    Vietnam War and, 145–46, 147
    windage in relation to, 129

PPE. *See* personal protective equipment
preventive medicine, 44–45, 52–53, 60–61, 67–68, 71–72, 103, 105
Priest, Dana, 191n.153
prisoners of war (POWs), 116, 183n.143
prolonged field care, 159–60, 161
prostheses, 2–3, 82–83, 85
prostitution, 58, 59–60
psychological trauma. *See also* post-traumatic stress disorder
    combat exhaustion, 124–25, 129–30, 138–43, 145, 152
    costs of, 124, 125–26, 131, 132, 137, 143, 151–53
    counterinsurgency operations and, 147–48, 151–52
    evacuations for, 134–35, 140–41
    gross stress reaction, 144–45
    hospitals for, 130–31, 133, 134–35, 136
    as invisible injury, 44, 126, 127–28, 132
    moral injury, 124–25, 148, 151
    nostalgia, 127–29, 130, 131, 152
    PIE method of treatment for, 134, 140–41
    in pre-psychological times, 127–32
    return to duty following, 134–36, 140–41, 195n.81
    shell shock, 124–25, 126, 129, 132–38, 139–40, 142–43, 152, 194n.61
    soldier's heart, 124–25, 126, 127–28
    stigma associated with, 140, 143, 152–53
    veterans' benefits and, 136–37, 149, 150–51, 152–53
    vulnerable populations, 126
    windage, 129
PTSD. *See* post-traumatic stress disorder

Q fever (*Coxiella burnetti* infection), 103–4
quinine, 20*t*, 21–23, 56

race. *See also* African Americans
    blood donations and, 71, 184n.145
    data collection and, 39–40, 71, 78–80
    disease and, 21, 39
racism. *See also* segregation
    in healthcare, 39–40, 71, 87
    negative effects on military performance, 71–72

    in rehabilitation practices, 82–83
    systemic, 39–40, 78–80, 87
radiological weapons, 158, 161
rail evacuations, 33–34, 100–1
rape. *See* sexual assault
Reed, Walter, 24
rehabilitation movement, 49–50, 80, 82–83, 136, 156–57
Reifler, Jason, 173–74n.17
reverse triage protocol, 160
Revolutionary War, 12, 18, 25–26, 40–41, 124–25
rifles, 1, 25–26, 61, 129
Roosevelt, Franklin Delano, 83–84
Ross, Ronald, 21
Rostker, Bernard, 145
Rumsfeld, Donald, 92–93
Russia
    invasion of Ukraine (2022), 10, 158, 159–60
    potential for US war with, 158, 159–61, 162
    TCCC guidelines adopted by, 11
Rutkow, Ira, 30

St. Elizabeth's Hospital (Washington, DC), 130–31
Salmon, Thomas, 133, 136
Sargent, John Singer: *Gassed*, 64–65
Satterlee Hospital (Philadelphia), 33, 35
Schauer, Stephen, 190n.142
Schlesinger, Arthur, 84–85, 86–87
school. *See* education
Schultz, Jane, 35–36
scurvy, 33, 127
sea evacuations, 33–34, 76, 161, 198n.13
Second World War. *See* World War II
segregation
    of blood donations, 71, 184n.145
    of casualty data, 39–40, 71, 78–80
    of doctors and nurses, 78
    of hospital wards, 78
Serviceman's Readjustment Act of 1944. *See* GI Bill
sexism, 71–72, 77–78
sexual assault, 109–10, 122
sexually transmitted diseases (STDs)
    educational campaigns, 58

gonorrhea, 55, 58–61
HIV/AIDS, 104
penicillin for, 60–61, 69
prophylactic kit for, 59–60, 59f
sexual assault and, 110
syphilis, 55, 58–59, 60–61
troop loss due to, 58–59
Shackelford, Stacy, 95, 112–13
Shay, Jonathan, 124
shell shock, 124–25, 126, 129, 132–38, 139–40, 142–43, 152, 194n.61
Shen, Francis X., 173n.14, 173–74n.17
Shephard, Ben, 142, 147
Shinseki, Eric, 164–65
Shryock, Richard, 31
Siegel, Robert, 121
Skocpol, Theda, 42–43
smallpox, 19, 52–53, 55
Smart, Charles, 21–22, 24
soldier's heart, 124–25, 126, 127–28
Solomon, Harry, 133, 136
Spanish-American War (1898), 12, 24, 47, 50, 83
Spanish Civil War (1936–39), 50–51
Spaulding, James, 1–3, 13
Springfield rifles, 1, 25–26
Stanton, Edward, 17
STDs. *See* sexually transmitted diseases
Stearns, H. P., 27
Stein, Murray, 148
stereotypes of Civil War medicine, 24–25, 27–28
sterilization practices, 29, 67–68, 77
Stewart, Jon, 121
Stiglitz, Joseph, 5, 92
suicide rates, 151
sulfonamides, 60, 69, 78
surgeries. *See also* amputations
 anesthetics for, 25, 27–28, 68–69, 71, 115
 in Civil War, 25, 27–29, 68
 conservation and excision, 28
 damage control, 2, 101, 115, 159
 golden hour for, 76
 reconstructive, 63
 sterilization practices for, 29, 67–68
 in World War I, 67–68
 in World War II, 63, 67–69

Suwannee sinking (1944), 66
Swan, Henry, 62–63, 70–71, 72, 76, 87, 171, 183n.143, 199n.41
syphilis, 55, 58–59, 60–61

Tactical Combat Casualty Care (TCCC)
 adoption by Russia, 11
 cards for, 10, 97–98, 98f, 99–100, 178n.120
 development of, 98–99, 100
 effectiveness of, 99
 first aid guidelines, 101
 on hemorrhage control, 98–99, 110, 161
Taliban, 92–93, 108–9
tank warfare, 50–52, 61, 65–66
TBI. *See* traumatic brain injury
TCCC. *See* Tactical Combat Casualty Care
tension pneumothorax, 114–15, 161
terrorism, 6, 92–93, 157. *See also specific organizations*
tetanus, 29, 55, 103–4
Thomas splint, 28, 68–69
THOR (Trauma Hemostasis and Oxygenation Research) network, 110, 190n.140
Tolopotomy Creek, Battle of (1864), 43
Tora Bora, Battle of (2001), 99
tourniquets
 CATs, 2, 99, 110–12, 111f, 122–23, 170
 criticisms of, 110–12, 165–66
 documentation of application, 95–96
 fit and oxygenation sensors for, 159
 junctional, 99, 111f, 112f, 112
 TCCC guidelines on, 98–99
transfusions. *See also* whole blood transfusions
 blood components for, 99, 112–13, 166
 plasma, 1–2, 69–71, 87, 113
trauma. *See* psychological trauma
Trauma Hemostasis and Oxygenation Research (THOR) network, 110, 190n.140
traumatic brain injury (TBI), 2–3, 8–9, 107–8, 110, 148, 170
trench fever, 54
trench foot, 55, 57–58, 85
trench warfare, 57–58, 74, 135–36, 147
Triplett, Irene, 45–46

238　INDEX

Triplett, Mose, 14, 15, 45–46
Trump, Donald J., 149–50
tuberculosis, 52, 82, 85, 140
turpentine, 20*t*, 23–24
Tuskegee Medical Center
　creation of, 82–83
　syphilis study, 60
typhoid
　Alcott and, 177n.102
　in Civil War, 15, 20*t*, 21–22, 24, 175n.31
　immunization against, 52–53, 55, 180n.23
　in Spanish-American War, 47, 50
　treatments, 20*t*
typhus, 24, 47, 55, 56, 60, 132, 176n.61

Ukraine, Russian invasion of (2022), 10, 158, 159–60
Union Army. *See also* Civil War
　African Americans in, 21
　ambulances of, 31–32, 33
　casualties among, 37, 40
　cost assessments for, 16–17, 44
　desertions from, 130
　disease and, 19–20, 20*t*, 21, 22–23, 24
　Medical Department of, 15, 30
　medical supply issues, 23
　psychological trauma and, 127, 128–29
　veterans' benefits for, 42–43, 131–32
　wounded-to-killed ratio for, 18, 40, 45
United States Medical Department
　in Civil War, 15, 30, 34–35
　hospitals constructed by, 34–35
　underpreparedness of, 30, 50
United States Public Health Service (USPHS), 52–53, 80–81, 136–37, 138–39
United States Sanitary Commission (USSC)
　in Civil War, 15, 19–20, 23, 30, 33–34
　data collection efforts, 38
　veterans' homes organized by, 41
　women in creation of, 23, 35–36, 176n.51

vaccinations. *See* immunizations
venereal diseases. *See* sexually transmitted diseases
Vet Center system, 149

Veterans Administration (VA)
　challenges for, 85
　disability ratings, 119–20
　establishment of, 81, 136–37
　expenditures, 82, 85, 86, 116, 118–19, 185n.199
　exposés of failures in, 164–65, 191n.153
　medical centers, 82, 85–86
　National Center for PTSD, 146
　PTSD and, 149, 150
veterans' benefits. *See also* disability compensation; GI Bill; pensions
　Afghanistan War and, 119–20, 191n.160
　for African Americans, 42, 82–83, 85–86
　bureaucratic structure for, 10–11, 15
　Civil War and, 40–44, 45, 131–32
　education, 83–85, 86–87, 92, 119
　for family members, 2, 173n.4
　First Gulf War and, 118–19
　future of, 162–65
　healthcare, 50, 58–59, 81, 82, 84–85, 88, 119–20, 137, 156–57, 164
　history and trajectory of, 3–4, 11–12, 117–19, 117*f*, 118*f*, 156–57
　inequality in distribution of, 164, 198n.24
　Iraq War and, 104–5, 119–20, 191n.160
　Korean War and, 116
　lobbying for, 43, 80, 88, 116, 121
　psychological trauma and, 136–37, 149, 150–51, 152–53
　Revolutionary War and, 40–41
　Spanish-American War, 83
　Vietnam War and, 116
　War of 1812 and, 17
　for women, 82–83, 85–86
　World War I and, 58–59, 80–83, 88
　World War II and, 58–59, 80, 83–87, 88–89
Veterans Bureau. *See* Veterans Administration
veterans' homes, 41, 131–32, 156–57
veterans' hospital system, 82–83, 85–86, 156–57
Veterans of Foreign Wars (VFW), 11–12, 83, 88, 120–21, 164
Vietnam War. *See also* Vietnam War medicine
　casualty aversion theory and, 6

INDEX 239

data collection on, 96–97
guerrilla warfare in, 91
napalm use during, 13
PPE in, 67, 106–8
psychological trauma and, 124–25, 145–46, 147, 193n.5
veterans' benefits and, 116
women in, 109
Vietnam War medicine
artillery wounds, 62*f*
disease and, 103
evacuations, 90–91, 100–2
gunshot wounds, 62*f*, 189n.89
hemorrhage control, 110
transfusions, 112–13, 114, 190n.140

Walker, Mary Edwards, 36–37
Walker Dip, 165, 166–67
Walter Reed effect, 7–8, 155–56
Walter Reed Hospital (Bethesda, Maryland), 82, 164–65, 191n.153
warfare. *See also* casualties; psychological trauma; weapons; *specific conflicts*
bargaining theory of, 17
benefits associated with, 9–10, 88–89
casualty aversion theory of, 6–7, 173–74n.17
conventional, 47, 91–92
costs of, 3–8, 13, 154–56, 167–71, 173n.14
disease as endemic to, 19–21
guerrilla, 47, 91
mechanization of, 48, 50–51, 104–5
policy recommendations, 167–70
tank, 50–52, 61, 65–66
trench, 57–58, 74, 135–36, 147
War of 1812, 17, 18, 38
War of Independence. *See* Revolutionary War
Warrior Resilience Centers, 148–49
war risk insurance program, 49, 80–81, 82, 136–37
weapons. *See also specific types of weaponry*
in Afghanistan War, 91–92, 103, 105
biological, 158, 161
chemical, 64–65, 158, 161
in Civil War, 1, 25–27, 61
in Iraq War, 91–92, 103, 105
in Mexican-American War, 25–26
nuclear, 93–94, 158, 161, 163
radiological, 158, 161
in Revolutionary War, 25–26
in World War I, 61–62, 64–65, 87
in World War II, 1–2, 61–63, 65–66, 87
Wessely, Simon, 193n.5
Whitman, Walt, 14, 35
whole blood transfusions
low-titer type O donors, 114, 190n.140
for prisoners of war, 183n.143
racial issues and, 71, 184n.145
supply and storage issues, 70–71, 104, 112–13
transition to, 1–2, 87, 114, 166, 170
Wilson, Mitchell, 196n.99
windage, 129
Wohlforth, William, 157
Wolfowitz, Paul, 94
women. *See also* nurses
in Afghanistan War, 109
aid societies formed by, 35–36
as doctors, 34, 36–37, 166–67
gender norms and, 35–36
in Iraq War, 109
in prostitution, 58, 59–60
sexism and, 71–72, 77–78
sexual assault and, 109–10, 122
USSC created by, 23, 35–36, 176n.51
veterans' benefits for, 82–83, 85–86
in Vietnam War, 109
Woodward, J. J., 14–15, 21–22, 37, 39
World War I (1914–18). *See also* World War I medicine
African Americans in, 78
case fatality rate in, 87
cost assessments, 48–50, 51
data collection on, 78–80, 79*f*
demobilization following, 82
objections to US entrance into, 4–5, 80
PPE in, 63–64
safe-war theory on, 4–5, 49
shell shock in, 124–25, 126, 129, 132–38, 139–40, 142–43, 152, 194n.61
trench warfare in, 57–58, 74, 135–36, 147
veterans' benefits and, 58–59, 80–83, 88
war risk insurance program during, 49
weapons in, 61–62, 64–65, 87
wounded-to-killed ratio in, 87

World War I medicine
    amputations, 65, 68–69
    artillery wounds, 62, 62f
    disease and, 20–21, 52–53, 54–55, 57–60, 103
    doctors and, 54, 64, 67, 78
    evacuations, 72–74, 73f, 184n.159
    gunshot wounds, 1–2, 61, 62f
    hospitals and, 72
    logistics of, 71–74, 77, 78
    nurses and, 54, 77, 78
    rehabilitation movement and, 49–50, 80, 82–83, 136, 156–57
    supply issues, 68
    surgeries, 67–68
World War II (1939–45). *See also* World War II medicine; *specific battles*
    case fatality rate in, 63, 87
    casualties of, 13
    combat exhaustion in, 124–25, 129–30, 138–43, 145, 152
    cost assessments, 50–51, 88
    data collection on, 78–80, 79f
    demobilization following, 83
    food rations during, 53–54, 180n.35
    Pearl Harbor attack (1941), 66
    PPE in, 63–64, 106–8
    prisoners of war in, 183n.143
    Suwannee sinking (1944), 66
    tank warfare in, 61, 65–66
    veterans' benefits and, 58–59, 80, 83–87, 88–89
    weapons in, 1–2, 61–63, 65–66, 87
    wounded-to-killed ratio in, 87
World War II medicine
    aircraft pilots and, 66–67
    amputations, 63, 68–69
    antibiotics, 57–58, 60–61, 69, 70
    artillery wounds, 1–2, 61–63, 62f
    burn treatments, 65–66
    disease and, 52, 54–61, 59f
    doctors and, 63–64, 67–68, 102
    evacuations, 1–2, 72, 74–76, 101–2
    golden hour and, 76
    gunshot wounds, 1–2, 62f
    hemorrhage control, 71
    hospitals and, 72, 96–97
    logistics of, 71–72, 74–78
    nurses and, 77–78, 101–2
    pain management, 68–69
    surgeries, 63, 67–69
    transfusions, 69–71, 112–13, 166, 183n.143
wounded-to-killed ratio
    Afghanistan War, 8, 122
    Civil War, 18, 40, 45
    data collection challenges and, 10–11
    history and trajectory of, 8, 9f, 156
    Iraq War, 94, 122
    Mexican-American War, 18
    Revolutionary War, 18
    War of 1812, 18
    World War I, 87
    World War II, 87
Wounded Warrior Project, 164

X-ray technology, 44–45, 47, 67

yellow fever
    in Civil War, 20t, 22, 23–24, 103
    immunization against, 55
    transmission of, 24, 47
    treatments for, 20t, 22, 23–24
Young, Allan, 148, 193n.5
Young, Hugh, 58